"MOST IMMEDIATE . . . CRUISER FORCE WITHDRAW TO THE WESTWARD AT HIGH SPEED."

The time is July 4, 1942. Convoy PQ17 is heading northeast through icy waters in the perpetual daylight of the Arctic summer. Now word is flashed from London that the German battleship *Tirpitz,* the cruiser *Hipper,* and the pocket battleships *Lützow* and *Scheer* are proceeding with a dozen destroyers to the attack. U-boat "wolf packs" operating off North Cape are shadowing the convoy, while at advanced bases in Finland and Norway over 200 Heinkel 115's and Stuka dive bombers are ready to strike. The decision is made: The word goes out to the convoy to scatter. In the confusion some ships will be sunk—but some will escape. It is the hardest decision the commanding admiral can make, and it seals the fate of 23 ships and hundreds of men . . . for two-thirds of convoy PQ17 will not run the gauntlet, 23 of 35 ships will not get through. . . .

From the darkest days of 1941 to the end of the war, THE RUSSIAN CONVOYS tells a story of epic courage and seamanship—for in these ships were the supplies that kept Russia in the fight and helped win the final victory over Nazi Germany.

RELATED READING IN BALLANTINE WAR BOOKS

THE RUSSIAN CONVOYS

B. B. Schofield

BALLANTINE BOOKS  NEW YORK

This edition published by arrangement with Dufour Editions

First Printing: April, 1967

Printed in the United States of America

BALLANTINE BOOKS, INC.
101 Fifth Avenue, New York, New York 10003

Preface

Although much has been published concerning the convoys to and from Russia during the Second World War, the tendency has been either to concentrate on the naval aspect of the operations as a whole, or on one of the many stirring incidents which occurred during their passage. Excellent as are many of these accounts, the impact on events of political decisions as revealed by Sir Winston Churchill in *The Second World War* and by the record of the *Führer Naval Conferences,* together with other material now available, does not appear to have received sufficient attention. It seemed to the author that a more comprehensive narrative, amplifying that given by Captain S. W. Roskill, R.N., in *The War at Sea 1939–1945,* and backed by personal knowledge of what took place, would help to clear up such controversial issues as that caused by the scattering of convoy PQ17, why the Arctic route to Russia was preferred to the safer one by the Persian Gulf, and whether Russia really needed the supplies sent to her at such great cost.

I would like to take this opportunity of thanking all those who, in one way or another, have assisted me in the preparation of the manuscript of this book. In particular I acknowledge my indebtedness to the Director of the Historical Section of the former Admiralty, Lieutenant-Commander P. K. Kemp, F.R.Hist.S., R.N. (Retd), the Director of the Military Historical Research Bureau of the Federal German Navy, Captain Gerhard Bidlingmaier; the Right Honourable the Earl of Avon, K.G., P.C., M.C.; Admiral of the Fleet the Lord Fraser of North Cape, G.C.B., K.B.E.; Admiral Sir Henry Moore, G.C.B., C.V.O., D.S.O.; Admiral Sir Geoffrey Miles, K.C.B., K.C.S.I.; the late Admiral Sir Patrick Brind, G.B.E., K.C.B.; Admiral E. L. S. King, C.B., M.V.O.; Major-

General K. G. Exham, C.B., C.B.E.; Mr. Edward Crankshaw; and Dr. J. Rohwer.

I am also most grateful to Captain H. Hamilton, R.N. (Retd), for permission to consult the private papers of his brother, the late Admiral Sir Louis Hamilton, K.C.B., D.S.O., and to the Director of the National Maritime Museum, Greenwich, for making them available together with other material. Finally I would like to pay tribute to my wife who typed the manuscript and assisted me with much helpful advice.

B. B. SCHOFIELD

Newholme, Lower Shiplake
July 1964

Contents

The Illustrations

Photo insert appears between pages 120 and 121

FIGURE

Maps and Diagrams in the Text

Acknowledgment

The Author and Publishers wish to thank the following for permission to reproduce the illustrations which appear in this book:

The Imperial War Museum, for figs 1-6, 15-16, 17, 20-22, 24-26, 28, 31-32, and 34.

Suddeutscher Verlag Bilderdienst, Munich, for figs 7, 11-13, and 18. Ullstein Bilderdienst, Berlin, for figs 8-10, 14, 23, 27, 29-30, 33, and 35.

Acknowledgment is also due to the publishers for permission to quote from the following books: Cassell and Company Ltd, Sir Winston Churchill's *The Second World War*, and George Weidenfeld and Nicolson Limited, Admiral Dönitz' *Memoirs*.

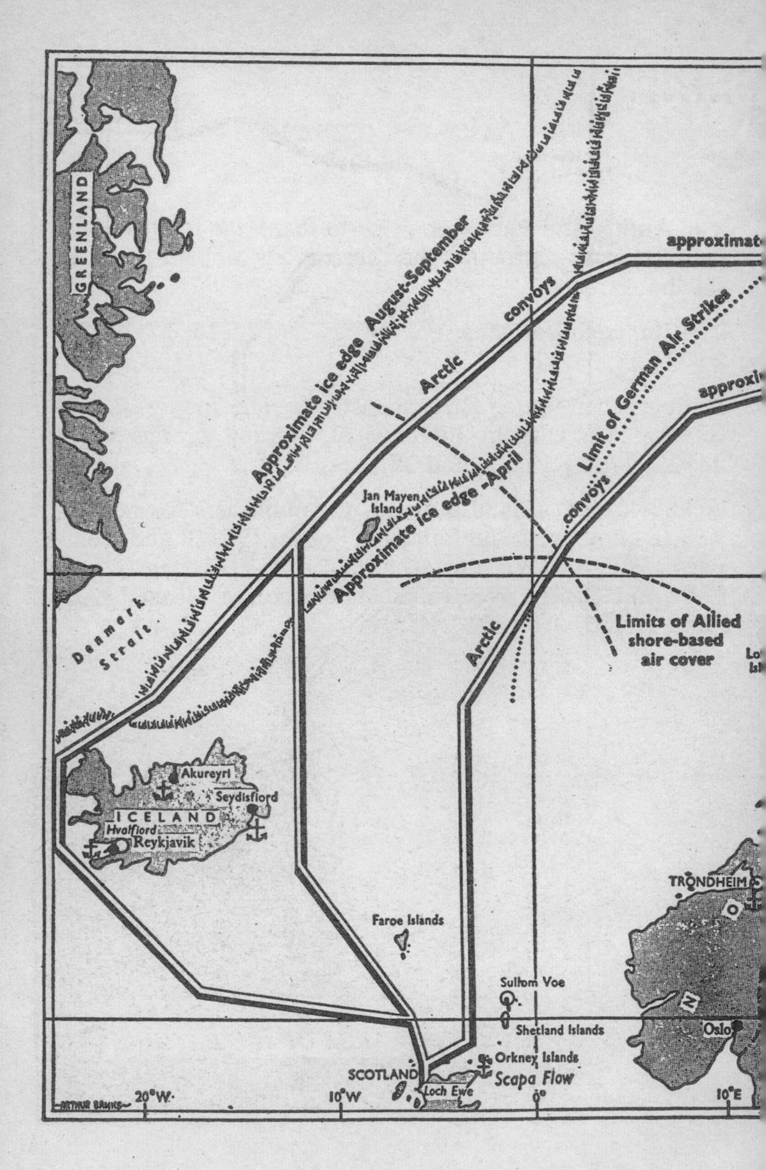

GREENLAND
Approximate ice edge August-September
Arctic
convoys
approximat
Limit of German Air Strikes
approxi
Jan Mayen Island
Approximate ice edge -April
Arctic
convoys
Denmark Strait
Limits of Allied shore-based air cover
Akureyri
Seydisfiord
ICELAND
Hvalfiord
Reykjavik
TRONDHEIM
Faroe Islands
Sullom Voe
Shetland Islands
Orkney Islands
Scapa Flow
SCOTLAND
Loch Ewe
Oslo
20°W
10°W
0°
10°E
ARTHUR BANKS

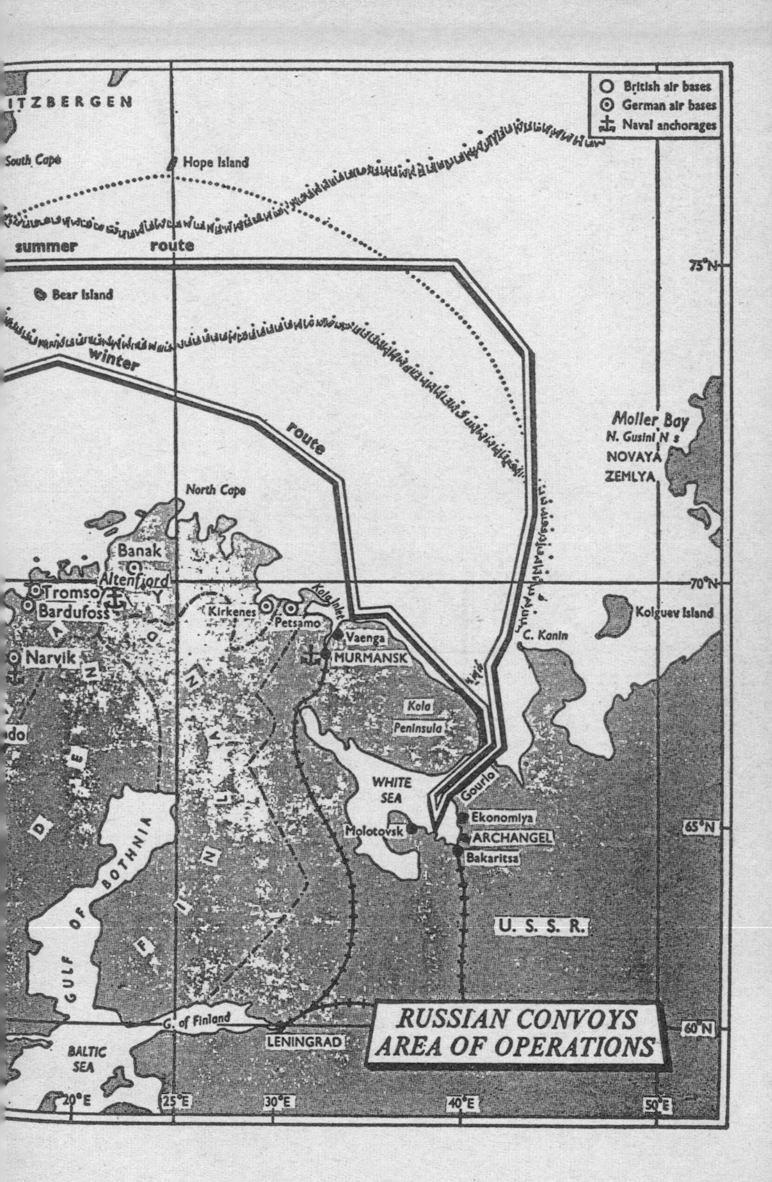
ITZBERGEN
British air bases
German air bases
Naval anchorages
South Cape
Hope Island
summer
route
Bear Island
winter
route
75°N
Moller Bay
N. Gusini N s
NOVAYA
ZEMLYA
North Cape
Banak
Altenfiord
Tromso
Bardufoss
Kirkenes
Petsamo
Kola Inlet
Vaenga
MURMANSK
Narvik
Kola
Peninsula
70°N
Kolguev Island
C. Kanin
WHITE
SEA
Gourlo
Ekonomiya
Molotovsk
ARCHANGEL
Bakaritsa
65°N
GULF OF BOTHNIA
FINLAND
U. S. S. R.
G. of Finland
LENINGRAD
BALTIC
SEA
60°N
20°E
25°E
30°E
40°E
50°E
RUSSIAN CONVOYS
AREA OF OPERATIONS

Introduction

Between the coasts of Greenland and Norway, a distance of some 900 miles, lies one of the most turbulent stretches of water in the world. Across it a never-ending succession of gales bearing rain, sleet, hail and snow, sweep north-eastward, lashing the sea with their fury, and causing it to mount up in protesting waves of tremendous height, which hurl themselves against the gnarled and rocky coast of Norway. Speeding round the North Cape, these storms enter the Barents Sea where, their destructive mission accomplished, the high barometric pressure over the Polar ice-cap forces them into the upper atmosphere.

The warm waters of the Gulf Stream, meandering lazily across the Atlantic, past the east coast of Iceland, flow on up the coast of Norway where they divide, one stream turning north past Bear Island and along the west coast of Spitzbergen, the other flowing along the Murman coast and into the Barents Sea. The effect produced by the mingling of these comparatively warm waters with the colder and less saline waters of the Polar region is not only to make the region noted for the frequency of fog, but also to give unusual variations in the thermal layers and the density of the sea, features which are a great handicap to the operator of underwater sound detection apparatus, searching for submarines which lie hidden in the depths. Further, the temperature of the sea in these latitudes rarely exceeds 40° so that a man unfortunate enough to find himself immersed in these icy waters has little chance of survival unless rescued within a very short time.

The drift ice which forms the northern boundary of this tempestuous area, advances and recedes with the seasons. In winter the southern edge sometimes approaches to within 80 miles of the North Cape, whereas in summer clear water may be found round the shores of Spitzbergen, especially on the west coast which, as already mentioned, is washed by an offshoot of the Gulf Stream.

An additional hazard of navigation in these latitudes arises from the freezing of the spray as it falls on a ship buffeting her way through the angry sea. If allowed to accumulate unchecked, the weight of ice thus formed can so add to the top weight that a small ship will become unstable and capsize. Finally, in time of war, when ships navigate without lights, the almost perpetual darkness which persists in latitude 77 North for instance, for 115 days in each year, makes station-keeping in convoy or formation at these times one long nightmare throughout the voyage. And while concealing darkness, for all its difficulties, makes it harder for enemy aircraft to locate the ships which they are searching to destroy, the long summer days when the sun never sinks out of sight for the whole 24 hours, enables them to attack 'all round the clock' until the defenders are well nigh worn out and ammunition is running low.

It is within this Poseidon's battle-ground that the epic struggle which is the subject of this story, took place. It tells how German attempts to interfere with the carrying of war material to Russia were thwarted, despite the position of strategic advantage the former had acquired by the occupation of Norway; of how officers and men of warships, aircraft and merchant ships showed a courage and a devotion to duty in the face of odds which no words can adequately convey; of how enemy forces failed to seize their opportunities because of the crippling restrictions under which they were obliged to operate. It is a story of a battle which lasted three years and seven months, a battle not just between two enemies locked in mortal combat, but one, too, against some of the worst natural conditions to be found anywhere in the world, which only human endurance coupled with discipline and seamanship of a high order were able to overcome.

1

Caught Napping

Seize today, and put as little trust as you can in the morrow
Horace

On 9 April 1940, under the pretext of protecting the peace-loving inhabitants from the threat of a British invasion, German forces began the occupation of Norway. Only a month earlier Grand Admiral Raeder, Commander-in-Chief of the German Navy, had warned Hitler: 'The operation in itself is contrary to all principles in the theory of naval warfare'; but he had added: 'In spite of this the C.-in-C. Navy believes that, provided surprise is complete, our troops can and will successfully be transported to Norway.'[1] The gamble came off because as we shall see, Allied counter-measures were feeble, hesitant and mistimed, and Admiral Raeder succeeded in gaining for his fleet a position of immense strategic advantage which, although not foreseen at the time by either of the contestants, was to have a profound effect on the conduct of the war at sea.

Grand Admiral Erich Raeder, who plays an important role in the first part of this story, was an able strategist who fully understood the significance of sea-power in the development of foreign policy. He was the type of man who wins respect because of his integrity, but not affection. He gave sound advice, but he had not the wit and nimbleness of mind to present it in such a way as to appeal to his volatile and unpredictable Führer who had bought his allegiance with promises of naval grandeur, unattained because of the premature outbreak of war. He foresaw the need for the creation of a strong naval air arm to offset Germany's inferiority in surface ships *vis-à-vis* Britain, and this brought him into conflict with

[1] Report of C.-in-C. Navy to the Führer, 9 March 1940.

the Commander-in-Chief of the Air Force, Reichsmarschall Hermann Göring. His failure to appoint an admiral with real authority to represent him at Hitler's headquarters, and his own infrequent visits there, left the field to his enemy who never failed to seize an opportunity to decry the navy's efforts. This antagonism between the two Commanders-in-Chief was to have far-reaching effects in the conduct of the war.

The country whose fate for the ensuing five years was so ruthlessly determined that April morning, is often referred to as 'the land of the midnight sun' since one-third of it lies within the Arctic circle, and is therefore subject to days of perpetual light in summer and almost total darkness in winter. It is famed for its snow-capped mountains, deep glassy fiords, and rugged, inhospitable coastline. The major part of the population lives by and from the sea, and if account were taken of all the indentations and fiords along the coast it would measure six times its nominal length of 2,100. Until later seized by the Germans, Norway was divided from Russia by a narrow strip of Finland which included the port of Petsamo, important for the nickel mines in its vicinity. Ninety miles south-west of the North Cape, the northern-most point of Europe, lies Altenfiord, an anchorage of strategic importance of which the Germans were to make good use. A hundred and fifty miles further south, at the head of the long Vestfiord, lies the port of Narvik from which in the winter months the Germans drew vital supplies of Swedish iron-ore. Three hundred and fifty miles south of Narvik lies Trondheim, the former capital and third largest city in the country, with a land-locked harbour which, together with the still larger port of Bergen further south, the Germans turned into U-boat and repair bases. From these ports they sailed to harry the convoys with which the Allies sought to supply Russia, after the latter had become the victim of Hitler's duplicity.

An important feature of the Norwegian coast is the Inner Leads, a channel between the coast proper and the outlying islands, which enables ships proceeding up and down the coast between Narvik and ports to the south to remain within territorial waters for the greater part of the voyage.

Besides its strategic value, Norway was of great economic importance to Germany. Four and a half million tons of iron-ore were shipped annually to her from the ports of Narvik and Kirkenes, and this, together with some six and a half million tons coming direct from Sweden through the Baltic, accounted for four-fifths of Germany's total iron-ore consumption. If, as a consequence of an allied occupation of Norway, Sweden had thrown in her lot with them, Germany's position would have been precarious in the extreme and she would not long have been able to continue the war. Mr Churchill was well aware of these facts, and in his capacity as First Lord of the Admiralty ever since September 1939 he had been pressing his colleagues in the Cabinet to agree to the project of mining Norwegian territorial waters in order to prevent the use of the Inner Leads by German ships. If these could be forced out into the open sea our superior naval forces would be able to destroy them. But as Mr Churchill sadly records, 'The Foreign Office arguments about neutrality were weighty, and I could not prevail.'[1] And while he continued to press his point 'by every means and on all occasions', Admiral Raeder was becoming more and more worried about the possibility of British intervention in Norway. On 10 October 1939 he pointed out to Hitler how it would assist the prosecution of submarine warfare to obtain bases on the Norwegian coast, especially Trondheim. He suggested that these might be obtained with the help of pressure by Russia. At that time Hitler's mind was focused on plans for the invasion of the Low Countries and France, so he did not pay too much attention to the Admiral's advice, but a fortnight later Norwegian action in refusing to allow an illegally seized American ship with a German prize crew on board to proceed through the Leads to Germany, caused him to reflect on what Raeder had said.

At the end of November 1939 Russia invaded Finland, and Mr Churchill 'welcomed this most favourable breeze'

[1] *The Second World War,* Vol. I, p. 424.

as a means of achieving the major strategic advantage of cutting off Germany's iron-ore supplies, by coming to Finland's help. He realised that such action might impel the Germans to invade Scandinavia, but, he asserted, 'We have more to gain than to lose by a German attack on Norway and Sweden.' In this he was quite correct, provided the prize went to the Allies and not to the Germans!

On 6 January 1940 the Foreign Secretary warned the Norwegian Ambassador in London of Allied intentions to put a stop to the use of Norwegian territorial waters by German blockade runners, as well as by the iron-ore ships, by the laying of mines in selected areas along that country's coast. Not unnaturally, reactions by both the Norwegian and Swedish Governments were unfavourable. It must, however, have been obvious that news of this *démarche* was certain to reach the Germans, and that they would initiate counter-measures, so that it was imperative to follow up words with deeds and not let the matter rest, as was in fact done.

On 3 April, following discussions between the new French Prime Minister, M. Paul Reynaud, and the British Government, it was decided that the mining of Norwegian waters should take place as planned on 5 April, together with the landing of troops at Narvik, Trondheim, Bergen and Stavanger, the principal ports on the Norwegian coast south of Tromsoe. By now reports of the German preparations, including the embarkation of troops, were beginning to reach London and Paris, but an argument between the governments of the two countries about the laying of floating mines in the Rhine, one of Mr Churchill's favourite projects, which the Prime Minister, Mr Chamberlain, had agreed should be carried out simultaneously with operations off Norway, caused a postponement of three days in the execution of the latter. It was the delay resulting from this unfortunate wrangle which enabled the Germans to anticipate the Allies in the seizure of what was to prove a strategic asset of incalculable value to Germany in the struggle which lay ahead. Even so, had the Allies properly evaluated the intelligence they received about German troop movements and seized the fleeting opportunity which occurred of attacking the German troop transports while they were at sea on passage to their destinations, the Germans would not have been able to seize the key points along the Norwegian coast from which they were able to establish their hold on the whole country. British submarines in the Skagerrak did well to sink seven ships and one tanker, and they lost three of their number in so doing, but they could not of themselves prevent the passage of the invading fleet. On 7 April Admiral Sir Charles Forbes, C.-in-C. of British Home Fleet based on Scapa Flow, had at his disposal two battleships, two battle-cruisers, seven cruisers and some 28 destroyers. His only carrier, the *Furious*, and another battleship were available, but anchored in the Clyde. Had these forces been sailed or even brought to short notice immediately news of the German movements was received, the story might have had a different ending, but not only was there delay in passing the intelligence reports to him, but the Admiralty indicated that they were of doubtful value. It was not until the evening of that day that he received definite information that the enemy's main forces were at sea. In the official *History of the War at Sea* the author, Captain Roskill, comments: 'There was thus a complete failure to realise the significance of available intelligence—let alone to translate it into vigorous and early counter-action.'[1] A belated attempt to drive the enemy out of Trondheim failed and although by the end of May and after some 25,000 allied troops had been landed there, the German garrison of 2,000 troops at Narvik was forced to surrender, the Allies were unable to hold on to their gain because of the success of Hitler's offensive against France and the Low Countries. During the subsequent evacuation Britain lost one of her three remaining large aircraft carriers, the *Glorious*, and her escort of two destroyers. On the German side success had not been obtained without loss, and the Navy in particular received a severe mauling. Both the battle-cruisers *Scharnhorst* and *Gneisenau* had been damaged, as also had the pocket battleship

[1] *The War at Sea,* Vol. I, p. 159.

Lützow and three destroyers; the cruisers *Blücher, Karlsruhe* and *Königsberg* and two others were severely damaged; ten destroyers had been sunk and one severely damaged, so that the effective strength of the German Navy in Home Waters was temporarily reduced to one pocket battleship, one heavy and three light cruisers, and seven destroyers. However, the important iron-ore supplies from Narvik were now assured, and several excellent harbours and airfields from which ships, submarines and aircraft could be despatched to attack Allied shipping had been acquired. German air supremacy proved the dominant factor during the operations against Norway, a fact which proved the correctness of Raeder's appreciation and served to emphasise our own deficiencies in this respect for which during the next three years a heavy price was to be paid in men and ships. On balance therefore, Mr Churchill's claim that 'we are greatly advantaged by . . . the strategic blunder into which our mortal enemy has been provoked'[1] seems even at that time to be wide of the mark—later it was to prove utterly false.

After the fall of France and Britain's rejection of his peace overtures, Hitler found himself without any clear idea of what his next step should be. As in the case of Norway he changed his mind several times, and so kept everyone guessing as to what were his real intentions. 'I am not able to say', Admiral Raeder has written in his memoirs, 'when Hitler first began to consider seriously the possibility of a campaign against Russia . . .',[2] but there seems little doubt that the project had been in his mind for some time. On 18 December 1940 he ordered the supreme commanders of the three services to make preparations 'to overthrow Soviet Russia in a rapid campaign'. In vain Admiral Raeder, with great strategic insight, pleaded for an intensification of the war in the Mediterranean as the best means of achieving a favourable outcome of the struggle against Britain. 'Once again I expressed my profound misgiving at the thought of any attack on Russia before we had beaten Britain', he says.

---

[1] *Hansard.*

[2] *Struggle for the Sea,* p. 193.

His arguments were supported by Baron Weizsacker, the Head of the German Foreign Office, and even by Göring, but it was all to no avail, and on 22 June 1941 Operation 'Barbarossa', as the plan for the invasion was styled, was launched.

The opening of the campaign against Russia had inevitable repercussions on British maritime strategy, for as Captain Roskill points out 'it gradually shifted the focus of the Home Fleet's responsibilities from the passages between Scotland and Greenland, to the north-east, and in particular to the waters between northern Norway and the varying limits imposed by the Arctic ice.'[1] The primary task of the British Home Fleet based on Scapa Flow up to this time had been to intercept any German surface ships attempting to break out into the Atlantic and interfere with Allied shipping. A glance at the map shows plainly that since Norway had fallen into German hands the task had become much more formidable. The distance between the north-western tip of Scotland and the south-east coast of Iceland is 330 miles, and the Denmark Strait between Iceland and Greenland although narrowed by ice at certain times of the year is 180 miles wide, whereas that between Norway and the Shetlands is only 160 miles. Although simultaneously with their seizure of Norway the Germans had occupied Denmark, fortunately they made no attempt to seize that country's two dependencies, Iceland and the Faroes.

The state of the German fleet at the beginning of July 1941 was as follows: the fast new battleship *Tirpitz* was almost complete and undergoing trials in the Baltic; the two battle-cruisers *Scharnhorst* and *Gneisenau* were in Brest and believed to be damaged; the cruiser *Prinz Eugen* had returned three weeks previously from an unrewarding cruise in the Atlantic; the pocket battleship *Lützow* was in dock at Kiel, having been torpedoed on 13 June when attempting to leave the Skagerrak for Trondheim prior to breaking out into the Atlantic; the cruiser *Hipper* and the light cruisers *Emden* and *Leipzig* together with

[1] *The War at Sea,* Vol. I, p. 485.

available destroyers were in the Baltic or approaches thereto.

On 2 December 1940 Admiral Sir Charles Forbes, on appointment as Commander-in-Chief, Plymouth, was relieved by Admiral Sir John Tovey, previously second-in-command to Admiral Sir Andrew Cunningham in the Mediterranean. Of Sir John's departure from his command, Admiral Cunningham wrote: 'He was a great loss to us in the Mediterranean, and to me personally. His advice, outspoken criticism, loyal support, cheerful optimism and imperturbability were a great help.'[2] But what was the Mediterranean fleet's loss was the Home Fleet's gain, and the new Commander-in-Chief was ideally suited to tackle the difficult problems with which his command was faced.

Although on paper disposing of considerable strength, the Home Fleet was constantly being called upon to provide ships to fulfil a number of duties in other areas but at the time in question had available two battleships, two carriers, four cruisers and about 20 destroyers. Mr Churchill foresaw the arrival of a British fleet in the Arctic which would be of 'enormous value' in its effect on the Russian navy and the general resistance of the Russian army. But a fleet needs a base from which to operate and, as we shall see, this was something which the Russians could not provide.

As a first step to implement the Government's decision to aid Russia, Admiral Tovey sent Rear-Admiral Vian to reconnoitre the Russian port of Murmansk which lies at the head of the Kola Inlet, a distance of 2,000 miles from Scapa Flow. Besides being the only ice-free port in north Russia, the importance of this harbour lay in its rail communication with Moscow and the south, a fact of which the Russians were fully conscious. At the seaward end of the inlet on its eastern shore is the bay of Vaenga about which more will be heard, and on the western side near the entrance lies the Russian naval base of Polyarnoe. Admiral Vian reported that the anti-aircraft defences were inadequate to permit the Kola Inlet to be used as a

---

[2] Viscount Cunningham of Hyndhope, *Sailor's Odyssey*.

base for our forces since it was only a few minutes' flying time from the German air bases at Kirkenes and Petsamo. In any case, as subsequent events were to show, the Russians were not over-anxious to share their meagre facilities with their allies.

At the end of July Admiral Vian was ordered to make a reconnaissance of the Norwegian islands of Spitzbergen which lie 450 miles north of the North Cape. Although in summer the bays, especially those on the west coast, are generally ice-free, this is not so in the winter, and apart from a camp for the men who work the coal mines, there are absolutely no facilities. It is doubtful if even the redoubtable American Sea-Bees could have made a base out of those mountainous and ice-covered islands. Hence it was decided to evacuate the Norwegian and Russian workers and destroy the coal-mining equipment. Yet these islands did serve on occasion as refuelling *rendezvous* and were to be the scene of several minor forays during the next few years. At one time they were being used simultaneously by both Allied and German meteorological parties.

It was not long before a request was received from the Russians for attacks to be made on German ships sailing between Kirkenes and Petsamo. A force comprising the carriers *Furious* and *Victorious*, the cruisers *Devonshire* and *Suffolk*, with six destroyers under Rear-Admiral W. F. Wake-Walker, accordingly sailed from Scapa on 23 July to comply with the Russian request, but the results achieved were small. While the operation was in progress the minelayer *Adventure* reached Archangel with a load of mines, a gift which the Russians greatly appreciated. Thus operations in the Arctic began with a comparatively minor action, like the overture which precedes the raising of the curtain at the start of grand opera. Meanwhile, an exchange of telegrams between Mr Churchill and Stalin had begun which revealed the latter's complete lack of understanding of maritime warfare. Yet Stalin never ceased to pour out 'niagaras of folly and mis-statement on the question of opening a second front in order to relieve the pressure on his hard-pressed armies. More practicable was aid in the form of war materials such as tanks, aircraft, guns, ammunition, trucks and stores which could be loaded into ships and transported to Russian ports.

There were three routes by which such supplies could be sent: across the Pacific from the United States to Vladivostok and thence by rail across Siberia; through the Persian Gulf to the ports of Hormuz and Basra, and thence overland; or direct from Britain, and later Iceland, to Murmansk. Of these the last was the shortest and most direct, but it was also the most dangerous, because the enemy could hardly fail to locate the convoys in which the loaded merchant ships were formed unless conditions were exceptionally unfavourable for air reconnaissance. The enemy established no less than six airfields in northern Norway, two of which, as already stated, were within a short distance of Murmansk itself, so that in addition to attacks en route the ships could be, and often were, attacked in harbour after arrival. With U-boat bases at Bergen and Trondheim, it was an easy matter for the enemy to establish submarine patrol lines across the probable route of the convoy. Finally, he could, if he so wished, employ his heavy ships to intercept the merchant ships particularly during the latter part of their journey when they passed east of a line drawn from the southern end of Spitzbergen through Bear Island to the North Cape in Norway—an area in which it was difficult for us to give them adequate protection. Supplies were in fact carried to Russia by all three routes during the war, but our concern in this book is with those which went by the Arctic route, across the top of the world.

2

Start of the Convoys

Bis dat qui cito dat
Attributed to Publius Syrus

THE GERMAN ARMIES DROVE deeper and deeper into the heart of Russia, and as they advanced capturing factories and workshops, Russia's ability to make good her losses in equipment was being steadily reduced. Stalin left Mr Churchill in no doubt about the 'mortal menace' confronting his people, and of their urgent need of weapons with which to repel the invaders. For his part, the British Prime Minister, true to his word to do everything that 'time, geography and our growing resources' would allow, had issued instructions to give effect to this promise.

The Russian Ambassador to Britain at the time was Mr Maisky, and an example of his approach to the problem of the Russian convoys is given by the following incident which occurred at a time when German resistance to their passage was at its height. The Assistant Chief of the Naval Staff responsible to the First Sea Lord for the Admiralty side of the convoys found himself sitting next to the Ambassador at an official lunch party and decided to seize the opportunity presented of explaining to him the difficulties to be overcome in carrying supplies to his country at that time. Mr Maisky appeared to be interested and waited politely until the Admiral had finished. The latter felt that he had presented his case reasonably well and without undue exaggeration, but Mr Maisky merely turned and looking him straight in the face said without a trace of emotion, 'Yes, yes, Admiral, but if you will only try you will find it is not so difficult.'[1]

---

[1] In 1943, Mr Maisky made amends when he referred publicly to the Russian Convoys as 'a Northern Saga of heroism, bravery and endurance'.

A factor which was to have an important bearing on the fate of the Russian convoys was the difference between the British and German systems of command, the salient points in each organisation being as follows. The British Prime Minister, Mr Churchill, was also the Minister of Defence and in addition to presiding over the Defence Committee of the Cabinet, he kept close and constant touch with the Chiefs of Staff of the three services, as the list (by no means exhaustive) of his personal minutes to them in his history of the Second World War plainly shows. No one better than he appreciated the vital importance of sea-power in the prosecution of the war, in contrast to the German Führer who, fortunately for his enemies, never learned this proven lesson of history.

In the First Sea Lord, Admiral of the Fleet Sir Dudley Pound, Mr Churchill had as his naval adviser a man of outstanding ability and experience. Although at the time he was 62 there was no question of his fitness for the job. He had something of Churchill's mental and physical toughness, which no doubt contributed to the strong bond of sympathy which grew up between them. They had their differences, but only when the Prime Minister considered that higher political considerations were paramount did he disregard his First Sea Lord's advice, and it may be remarked, on each occasion with unfortunate results.

Although, as we shall see, the most fateful decision Admiral Pound was ever called upon to make, gave rise to a storm of criticism, no one who had been privileged to serve on his staff could ever doubt that his action on that occasion and on all others of great moment was motivated solely by a desire to do what he believed to be in the best interests of the nation and of the Service to which he had devoted his life.

The First Sea Lord dealt directly with the Commanders-in-Chief and Flag Officers in command of detached squadrons. In the case of the Home Fleet, the flagship when in harbour at Scapa Flow was connected with the Admiralty by a direct telephone and teleprinter line so that it was possible for the Commander-in-Chief to discuss matters with the First Sea Lord in person, an advantage shared by no other sea-going Commander-in-Chief. As far as air co-operation was concerned, the Commander-in-Chief Home Fleet was well served. The Admiralty was closely linked with the Commander-in-Chief Coastal Command of the Royal Air Force with his headquarters at Northwood, and there was a Combined Area Headquarters at Pitreavie, near Rosyth, manned by a mixed naval and air force staff with whom the Commander-in-Chief dealt for his normal day-to-day reconnaissance and strike requirements. If extra aircraft were required, he had only to ask the Admiralty and they would pass his request on to C.-in-C. Coastal, who alone was in a position to consider the overall commitments of his command. The main trouble during the first years of the war was the shortage of aircraft—otherwise the liaison between the two services was as good as it could be. This was due largely to the personality of the Commander-in-Chief Coastal Command on the outbreak of war, Air Chief Marshal Sir Charles Bowhill, who started his career at sea and whose understanding of its particular problems never left him.

On the enemy's side the command situation reflected all the weaknesses which in two world wars have contributed to Germany's defeat. There was no Chiefs of Staff Committee, no Joint Planning and Intelligence staffs, and no means by which the country's military, economic and political policy could be integrated. As Supreme Commander of the Armed Forces of the Reich, Hitler expected, and got, frequent situation reports from the Commanders-in-Chief of the three services, but he alone made the decisions. Rarely was a conference held in which the general conduct of the war, as far as it affected all three services, was discussed. The Headquarters of the German Naval Staff was in Berlin. After the fall of France, two theatre commanders were appointed: Naval Group West with headquarters in Paris; and Naval Group North with headquarters in Kiel. The latter was responsible for all operations in the north, Norwegian and Arctic seas, and subordinate commands in the area were as follows:

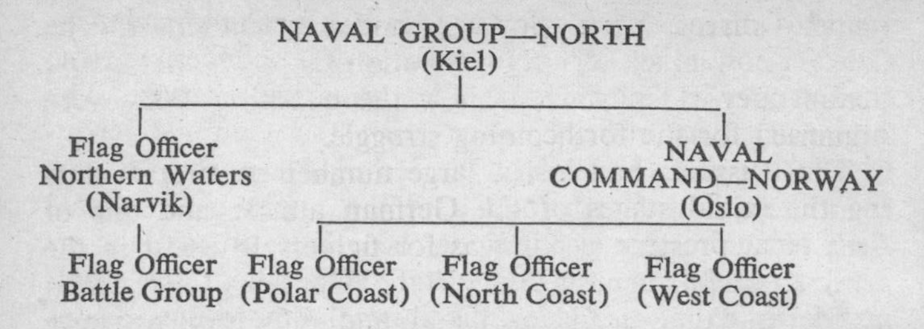

The Admiral Commanding Norway was responsible for all matters relating to Norway as a base for naval operations; he was not concerned with the direction of the fleet units stationed there, but coast defences, minelaying and minesweeping came within his purview. Under him were three Flag Officers for the three sections into which the coast was divided, Polar, North and West. The operational chain of command passed from the Naval Staff in Berlin through Group North, thence through the Flag Officer Northern Waters to the sea-going commander of the Battle Group. This rather cumbersome organisation remained in force until March 1943, when the Flag Officer Northern Waters was abolished, his duties being taken over by Naval Group North, who also assumed the title of Admiral Commanding the Fleet. In May 1944 Group North was abolished and Naval Command Norway became the operational authority. The Flag Officer Northern Waters was not only responsible for issuing operation orders to the Battle Group, but he also operated the U-boats allocated to the area and such air force formations as might be attached to the navy for tactical purposes. The Air Command in Norway, which was to play such an important part in the operations against the Arctic convoys, was known as '*Luftflotte* V', and this was subdivided into three Air Commands: North-east, North-west, and Lofoten, with headquarters at Kirkenes, Trondheim or Stavanger, and Bardufoss respectively. Thus, with the exception of Kirkenes where the Flag Officer Coast was based, the Navy and Air Commands were not contiguous. Such naval air forces as there were, consisting of a small number of He.115 seaplanes, came under the Air Commander, and all aircraft operating with the navy reported direct to the Air Commander concerned, and he decided how much of the information should be passed on to the navy. This, then, is how the opposing sides were organised for the forthcoming struggle.

The Russians had lost a large number of aircraft during the initial stages of the German attack, and one of their most pressing needs was for fighters to assist in the defence of Murmansk, which the Germans had determined to capture. The quickest and most efficient way of delivering such aircraft was to embark them in an aircraft carrier, escort her to within range of the airfield to which they were to be delivered, and fly them off. This had been done in the Mediterranean to reinforce Malta, using the veteran carrier *Argus*, originally designed as a merchant ship but converted to her present function towards the end of the First World War. Thus it came about that the first convoy to north Russia which the Commander-in-Chief Home Fleet was called upon to organise included the *Argus*, carrying 24 Hurricane fighters of No. 151 Wing of the Royal Air Force. The balance of 15 aircraft were crated and embarked in one of the six merchant ships included in the convoy and loaded with raw materials of which the Russians were particularly short, such as rubber, tin, wool, etc. The convoy sailed from Iceland on 21 August, escorted by six destroyers and covered by the carrier *Victorious* and two cruisers, all under the command of Rear-Admiral Wake-Walker. At the appropriate time the 24 fighters flew off the *Argus* and landed at Vaenga airfield, 17 miles outside Murmansk. German air activity in the vicinity of the Kola Inlet caused the ship containing the crated aircraft to be diverted to Archangel, where they were assembled with Russian assistance within nine days and rejoined the rest of the Wing at Vaenga on 12 September.

Early in August two British submarines, *Tigris* and *Trident*, had been sent to the Russian base at Polyarnoe on the Kola Inlet whence they operated with such success against German coastal shipping on the Murman coast as to encourage the Russian submarines stationed there to do likewise. At that time the German anti-submarine forces in the area were too weak to afford proper protection to this traffic on which their troops operating in the far north depended for their supplies. By September it had virtually ceased, and on 17th of that month Raeder was obliged to report to Hitler that 'At present troop transports are unable to proceed east of the North Cape; supply steamers can do so only at very great risk.' He also renewed his plea for the capture of Murmansk which he stated was 'an important prerequisite for the protection of our supplies,[1] but all Hitler would promise him was that the railway line would be cut.

The port and railhead of Murmansk which was to be the scene of so much activity during the next four years, lies at the head of the Kola Inlet 200 miles east of the North Cape of Norway. Being ice-free all year round it was of necessity the terminal port for the Arctic convoys. It was here that the majority of the cargoes brought by the convoys were unloaded. The facilities for this left much to be desired. There was no crane with a lift of more than 11 tons, that is, suitable for unloading tanks, so a crane ship had to be sent there to do the job. This ship proved a useful lever for exerting peaceful persuasion on the Russian port authorities when these became more than usually difficult. Observers have recorded that there was a general lack of organisation which had to be seen to be believed, coupled with an absence of anything approaching a spirit of team work, which could not fail to exasperate the Allied missions which had been sent to assist with the unloading of the ships. The city itself was built largely of wood and in consequence suffered severely from the incendiary raids to which it was subjected. The concrete buildings which survived the bombing stood grey and gaunt amid the ruins. Yet it had seen better days, and had once been a pleasant and reasonably prosperous town of tree-lined boulevards and attractive villas.

A few miles below Murmansk on the eastern shore of the inlet lies Vaenga Bay where the oiler from which the British ships refuelled was moored. It afforded a poor anchorage, the water being deep and the holding ground bad, the Russians being at that time unwilling to allow

[1] *Führer Naval Conference Report,* 19 September 1941.

Allied warships other than submarines the use of their naval base at Polyarnoe, it was here that the convoy escorts were obliged to anchor. At the head of the bay there was a pier, alongside which two destroyers could berth, and ashore a hutted camp had been constructed in which survivors from the torpedoed ships were accommodated. The merchant ships awaiting their turn to unload were anchored between Murmansk and Vaenga where they received frequent visits from enemy bombers.

The Russian naval base at Polyarnoe, much coveted by Admiral Raeder, was a narrow deep inlet affording excellent shelter to the ships berthed at its wooden jetties, but it was not until the convoys had been running for about two years that the British escort vessels were invited to share its scanty facilities.

Similarly not until 1944 did the Russians allow the establishment of a small auxiliary naval hospital at Vaenga to care for the sick and injured survivors and a naval sick bay at Polyarnoe. They were of the opinion that the facilities they were able to offer were adequate, but of course this was not so.

The terrain between Murmansk and the Finnish border was exceedingly difficult for military operations, being almost totally devoid of roads, and the Russians offered strong resistance to the German attempts to capture the town. However, the latter did succeed in cutting the railway, but the Russians soon made good this break in their line of communications by constructing a link to the line running between Archangel and Moscow, thereby restoring Murmansk to its position as a supply port for their northern armies, and by the following year they had so strengthened the defences round Murmansk that the city was never again seriously threatened.

Whenever possible a proportion of the ships in each convoy went to the port of Archangel, some 400 miles south-east of Murmansk, where the unloading facilities were superior to those at the last-named port. The Russians made strenuous efforts to keep both it and the neighbouring unloading berths at Molotovsk, Ekonomiya and Bakaritza open during the winter by the use of icebreakers, but their ability to do so depended to a certain extent on the weather and the condition of the ice in the Gourlo, the narrow stretch of water leading from the Barents to the White Sea. During the first winter of the convoys their expectations in this respect were not fulfilled. Conditions ashore at Archangel were somewhat better than at Murmansk, but for the inhabitants of the northern *oblasts* the food situation was grim. Being remote from the area where active fighting was in progress their ration, which was related to their alleged contribution to the war effort, was on the lowest scale.

The Admiralty's intention was to run convoys to north Russia on a 40-day cycle, and their protection was the responsibility of the Commander-in-Chief Home Fleet. As we have seen, the strategic advantages lay with the enemy. The route was open to U-boat attack throughout its entire length. The greater part of it was also subject to domination by the enemy's air forces, and in particular that extending to the eastward of the North Cape. British shore-based air support was limited to what could be provided from Iceland and the Shetlands. Navigational difficulties, especially during the winter months, were considerable, since it was rarely possible to take sights and there were no radio beacons by which a ship's position could be checked.

As regards surface attack, with the two battle-cruisers *Scharnhorst* and *Gneisenau* and the cruiser *Prinz Eugen* still in the French port of Brest, the only heavy ship to be considered was the new battleship *Tirpitz*, a sister ship of the *Bismarck*, now believed to be ready for sea. She was a fine ship both in appearance and in manner of her construction. Despite long years between the wars when warship building in Germany was restricted by the Treaty of Versailles, the German naval constructors had not lost their cunning, as the design of the pocket battleships had shown. As armament, the *Tirpitz* carried eight 15-inch guns firing a projectile weighing 1,960 lb, compared with the *King George V*'s ten 14-inch guns firing one weighing 1,590 lb. Thus the latter's broadside was some 200 lb heavier than that of the German ship. Although the *Tirpitz* was nearly three knots faster, one big advantage the *King George V* class had over their opponent was the radar equipment with which they were fitted both for search and gunnery purposes, which was greatly superior to anything the Germans had and outclassed the superb optical rangefinders with which they had equipped their ships.

Mr Churchill, harking back to the deficiencies in British naval gunnery during the First World War, was grieved that the new British battleships did not mount nine 16-inch guns, and in reply to a memorandum from the First Sea Lord dated 28 August 1941 in which he had stated 'As long as the *Tirpitz* is in being it is essential to have two ships of the *King George V* class available to work in company', he commented: 'The fact that the Admiralty consider three *K.G.V.*'s must be used to contain the *Tirpitz* is a serious reflection upon the design of our latest ships.' In referring to three ships Mr Churchill was, of course, making allowance for one ship to be away refitting and giving leave, but the Admiralty's reason for insisting on a two-to-one standard was dictated by the immense and serious problem which would arise should the *Tirpitz* succeed in breaking out into the Atlantic. She would not only paralyse the movement of shipping, but would make heavy demands on the limited resources available to locate her and bring her to action. Of the two pocket battleships, which with their 11-inch guns could do a great deal of damage to a convoy of merchant ships, only one, the *Scheer*, was believed to be ready for sea. There was also the heavy cruiser *Hipper*, armed with eight 8-inch guns, and four light cruisers armed with 6-inch guns, which were believed to be in the Baltic but which could, of course, be moved to one of the north Norwegian ports. Much would depend on the ability of Coastal Command of the Royal Air Force to maintain constant observation of the Skagerrak and of the harbours along the Norwegian coast, but the calls on the command already exceeded the availability of aircraft, and bad weather and poor visibility must inevitably reduce the efficiency of such reconnaissance patrols as were possible. At this time, besides his flagship *King George V*, Admiral Tovey had also the *Prince of Wales* of the same class under his command, but two months later he was to lose the latter when, contrary to Admiral Pound's advice, she was sent to the Far East.

But the most serious weakness of the Home Fleet, and one which was to affect profoundly the operation of the Arctic convoys, was the shortage of aircraft carriers armed with efficient and modern aircraft; without them it was impossible to challenge the enemy's domination of the Barents Sea area, which he was able to achieve by virtue of his airfields in north Norway.

The shortage of anti-submarine escorts was still acute, and all it was possible to allocate to the Russian convoys in the early stages of their existence were two destroyers, a minesweeper and two trawlers for those outward bound, and one destroyer and two minesweepers for those returning from Russia. One cruiser accompanied each convoy right through to Russia, while a second one remained in support, west of Bear Island. As the convoys approached the Murman coast the escort was reinforced by some of the five minesweepers based at Kola Inlet. The Russians also sent out a few destroyers to assist in escorting the convoys in. The only air support which could be provided, came from Nos. 330 and 269 squadrons of Coastal Command based in Iceland, and covered only the first 150 miles of the voyage. Thereafter it consisted only of long-range patrols searching for U-boats off the north Norway coast. Judged by any standard therefore, the escorts of these convoys could hardly have been weaker, and Admiral Tovey never ceased to represent this fact to the Admiralty. In addition to the close escort and cover for the convoys, it was necessary for a strong force to be at sea capable of dealing with the *Tirpitz* and the *Scheer* should they attempt to interfere with the convoy's passage. This force would also have to avoid being drawn too far to the north in case this was part of a German plan to enable a raiding force to break out into the Atlantic from the Skagerrak, nor could it afford to ignore the threat of air attack from the Norwegian airfields unless carrier-borne air support was available.

An event which was to be of great help to Admiral Tovey in preventing the unobserved break-out of German ships into the Atlantic, was the occupation of Iceland on

7 July 1941, by forces of the United States, and the assurances given by the President regarding the surveillance of the Denmark Strait. Although not known to the Admiralty at the time, after the loss of the *Bismarck* Hitler had decided against the despatch of any more surface warships on raiding missions in the Atlantic, but in default of this knowledge, this possibility was to remain one of the Commander-in-Chief's main anxieties.

On 28 September the first of the so-named PQ series of convoys left Iceland bound for Archangel. It consisted of ten ships escorted by the cruiser *Suffolk* and two destroyers. On the same day Lord Beaverbrook accompanied by President Roosevelt's special representative, Mr Averell Harriman, reached Moscow to draw up an agreement with the Russians regarding future supplies. Most unfortunately they accepted the Russian demand that these should be delivered by the Arctic route, although this was, as has been mentioned, the most dangerous and unreliable of the three. Convoy PQ1 had an uneventful passage and reached its destination on 11 October.

Under the influence of Beaverbrook's passionate conviction that aid to Russia must take precedence even over Britain's own requirements, on 6 October Churchill told Stalin of his intention to run 'a continuous cycle of convoys leaving every ten days', and further: 'In arranging this regular cycle of convoys we are counting on Archangel to handle the main bulk of the deliveries.'

This promise was made, as has been recorded, at a time when 'the Soviet Union was on the brink of collapse' with the Germans only 30 miles from Moscow, and the opinion is expressed that 'The British offer possibly prevented the catastrophe [of Russian defeat] even if in the long run the loss of life and ships on the Murmansk run exceeded the value of the goods thus carried.'[1] For their part the Admiralty loyally attempted to implement the government's decision. To Admiral Tovey the greatly shortened cycle meant that he would have great difficulty in providing a sufficiently strong escort for each convoy.

---

[1] J. Leasor and General Sir Leslie Hollis, *War at the Top*, p. 203.

With a convoy sailing every ten days a minimum of four cruisers and eight destroyers would be necessary, and allowing for defects and refits this meant that he would have only the bare number of the latter to act as a screen to the covering force. As an officer who had spent much of his service in destroyers, he well knew that with the onset of winter and the bad weather which was a feature of the area through which the convoys would have to pass, damage would mount up. Although in a normal year, as already mentioned, the White Sea might be expected to start freezing over in December, the Russians had stated that they expected to keep the port of Archangel open throughout the winter. In the event they managed to keep the Gourlo open until 12 December and five ships were berthed at Molotovsk on the 23rd, but on this occasion the icebreaker leading the convoy in became fast in the ice at the head of her charges, where she was obliged to remain until the following June when the White Sea was once again open to shipping.

In mid-November it became evident that Russian resistance was unlikely to collapse as Hitler had predicted it would, and that the German armies would be obliged to await the return of spring before renewing their attempts to capture Moscow. On 13 November Admiral Raeder reported to Hitler that it was important to bring up supplies and strengthen the coast defences in the Arctic area. He also remarked that enemy activity in the area had been less than expected, but that the long nights were favourable for the passage of convoys, though unfavourable for U-boat operations. 'Winter weather with blizzards, storms and fog has an adverse effect', he told the Führer, and once more he reminded him that air reconnaissance was lacking. He unsuccessfully attempted to obtain Hitler's permission to move the *Tirpitz* to Trondheim in December as soon as repairs and the arcticisation in progress had been completed. An Atlantic sortie by this ship, he pointed out, was not possible because of the shortage of oil fuel, estimated at that time to amount to 116,000 tons. On the other hand there was no shortage of diesel oil, so he suggested that the pocket battleship *Scheer* might be sent out instead. But with memories of the fate of the *Graf Spee* still in mind, Hitler vetoed the suggestion and said he would prefer to see her moved to Trondheim or Narvik. Soon after this conference Raeder moved five of his big destroyers to northern Norway and ordered the U-boat command to increase the number of submarines in the area so as always to have three instead of two on patrol. The destroyers were powerfully armed ships mounting five 5.9-inch guns and eight torpedo tubes, and Admiral Tovey would have liked to increase the strength of the through escort to meet this threat, but he was unable to do so, so long as he was obliged to run convoys at such short intervals, or unless more ships were allocated to his command. Fear of sharing the fate of the *Lützow* seems to have resulted in extreme caution regarding the movements of the *Scheer*, for she did not in fact reach northern Norway until the following February. By mid-December, because of the gales which were now an almost permanent feature in the northern latitudes and because of the long hours of darkness, Admiral Tovey concluded that once past Bear Island it was an acceptable risk to disperse the convoys and allow ships to proceed to their destination at their best speed. By so doing the escort vessels were enabled to fuel in the Kola Inlet instead of at Archangel, thereby saving four days on the round trip. This problem of fuelling was to remain a serious one throughout the long years of the Russian convoys. The length of the convoy route varied between 1,500 and 2,000 miles according to position of the ice edge, and although escorts steaming at an economical speed might just have made the voyage, the ever-present possibility of having to increase speed to attack a submarine or to lay smoke to protect the convoy from surface attack meant that there must always be a sufficient reserve of fuel in hand to meet such emergencies. In consequence it was the practice to sail a tanker in every convoy to allow of refuelling during the passage, if the weather permitted.

By the end of the year 53 loaded ships had been safely escorted to north Russia and 34 had returned; not one had been lost, but it had not been possible to keep to the ten-day cycle envisaged by the Prime Minister. The average interval between convoys worked out at 15 days and this was due partly to a report reaching the Admiralty at the end of October of a possible break-out into the Atlantic by the *Scheer* and perhaps the *Tirpitz*, which as we now know was vetoed by Hitler. This led to a postponement of nine days in the sailing of the third convoy. But it was also due to the physical impossibility of repairing the damage received by the escort ships as a result of the exceptionally severe weather encountered on passage.

So far the Russian navy had not given any assistance with the protection of the convoys, although the protocol of the agreement which Lord Beaverbrook and Mr Harriman had concluded in Moscow only committed Great Britain and the United States to 'give aid to the transportation of the materials to the Soviet Union'. The Russians had some 20 submarines, 12 destroyers, some torpedo and motor torpedo boats, minesweepers and patrol craft based on Archangel and Murmansk, some of which were suitable to augment the slender convoy escorts which we were able to provide. But from the start they adopted the attitude that the donor had a duty to deliver the goods, and although they did sally out to meet incoming convoys during the last leg of their voyage and provided welcome and effective anti-aircraft fire, they took no part in the protection of the convoys on the long haul between Iceland and Bear Island. The situation was neatly summed up by Sir Alan Herbert:

> We might have said 'Our shipping's on the stretch
> You shall have all the tanks that you can fetch'
> But that is not the way we fight this war
> We give them tanks and take them to the door.[1]

Japan's devastating attack on the United States fleet in Pearl Harbour on 7 December had repercussions in every theatre of the war. So far the supplies of weapons and raw materials sent to Russia by the Arctic route, although amounting to some 750 tanks, 800 fighter air-

---

[1] A. P. Herbert, *Less Nonsense* (Methuen, 1944).

craft, 1,400 vehicles and more than 100,000 tons of stores, could only be regarded as a trickle in comparison with the magnitude of the front along which fighting had been taking place. As the American economy turned over wholly to war production, these supplies increased apace, and the problem became one of transportation with which the Arctic route was quite unable to contend. But from the point of view of the Commander-in-Chief Home Fleet, the naval reinforcements which now became immediately available were an asset of incalculable value.

3

The 'Tirpitz' Makes a Sortie

'Tis not in mortals to command success

Addison

Quoted by Lord St. Vincent in a letter to Nelson after the failure to capture Santa Cruz, July 1797

AT A MEETING WITH Admiral Raeder on 29 December 1941 Hitler again considered the future of the *Tirpitz*'s movements, but his main preoccupation on this occasion was the fear of an Allied invasion of Norway. His anxiety on this account had undoubtedly been stimulated by a series of minor raids carried out by small parties of Commandos on the Norwegian coast during the past weeks, and the news which had just reached him of two raids carried out the previous day on a larger scale than any hitherto. These comprised a landing in the Vestfiord area by a small force under Rear-Admiral L. H. K. Hamilton, the scale of which was halved by reason of defects which developed in one of the two ships carrying the assault troops, and a highly successful raid on Vaagso island, 90 miles north of Bergen, by a small force under Rear-Admiral H. M. Burrough. In this latter raid five merchant ships, two trawlers and a tug had been sunk, and the coastal batteries destroyed.

It was hardly the time of year for a full-scale invasion,

but Hitler was so obsessed with the idea that Raeder had to wait until his meeting with the Führer on 12 January, before obtaining permission for the *Tirpitz* to be moved from the Baltic to Trondheim. Her mission Raeder said would be to attack the British convoys to north Russia and shipping in the Arctic Ocean, the bombardment of targets of military importance, and general interference with enemy operations. In view of the acute fuel shortage at the time, he well knew that there was no great likelihood of the battleship being able to carry out more than a fraction of this ambitious programme, but as a sound naval strategist, he was well aware that by her presence alone in northern Norway, she would tie down a sizeable proportion of the British fleet and prevent the reinforcement of other theatres of the war, especially the Mediterranean and the Indian Ocean.

The move of the *Tirpitz* was accomplished on the night of 14/15 January, but it was not until the 17th that Admiral Tovey was informed that she might be at sea. As a result of the uncertainty which existed regarding her movements, the sailing of the next convoy to Russia was postponed. However, on 23 January reconnaissance aircraft located her at anchor in Asafiord, 15 miles east of Trondheim. She was well camouflaged and protected by a zareba of anti-torpedo nets.

The previous day, at another of his periodic conferences with the head of his navy, Hitler reverted to the threat of an Allied attack on Norway, which he declared to be the decisive theatre of the war. He ordered reinforcements of surface ships and U-boats to be sent there 'unquestioningly and without regard to any other considerations'. However, the following day, on hearing of the heavy sinkings being achieved by the U-boats in the Atlantic, he countermanded his instructions to move all available submarines to Norway. Despite this, on 24 January Raeder instructed Dönitz as head of the U-boat command to increase the number of these vessels in northern Norway from four to eight, to keep two at instant readiness at both Trondheim and Bergen, and to maintain eight in the Iceland-Hebrides area. This tying down of 20 U-boats in northern waters, at a time when they were scoring great and easy successes in American waters, was particularly displeasing to Dönitz, who did not hesitate to acquaint his chief with his views. 'I myself', he wrote afterwards, 'was convinced that the Allies would not attempt a landing in Norway. I therefore asked Naval High Command to consider whether it would not be possible indirectly to protect Norway by using all available U-boats for the war on shipping.'[1]

To Mr Churchill the presence of the *Tirpitz* at Trondheim was a matter of deep concern. On 25 January, in a minute to the Chiefs of Staff Committee, he wrote: 'The destruction or even the crippling of this ship is the greatest event at sea at the present time. No other target is comparable to it. If she were even only crippled it would be difficult to take her back to Germany . . . The entire naval situation throughout the world would be altered, and the naval command in the Pacific would be regained . . . The whole strategy of the war turns at this period on this ship, which is holding four times the number of British capital ships paralysed, to say nothing of the two new American battleships retained in the Atlantic.'[2] Admiral Raeder could not have asked for better confirmation of his strategy.

Mr Churchill called for attacks to be made on the *Tirpitz* by both carrier-borne torpedo aircraft and by heavy bombers. Snugly tucked away in her fiord, the battleship, for all her size, was not an easy target. There was no room for torpedo aircraft to drop their torpedoes in the confined waters of the cliff-surrounded inlet, and she was over 500 miles from the nearest bomber airfield in northern Scotland, which meant that she was at the extreme range of the Halifax and Stirling bombers then in service. A small force of 16 of these was sent to attack her on the night of 29/30 January, but they did not score any hits.

The effort required to maintain a constant watch on this ship and to be ready to strike her if she put to sea, placed a heavy strain on Coastal Command and facilitated

---

[1] *Memoirs,* p. 208.

[2] *The Second World War,* Vol. IV, p. 98.

the next move in the execution of Hitler's order to concentrate the full strength of the fleet in Norwegian waters to counter the threat of invasion. This was the transfer of the battle-cruisers *Scharnhorst* and *Gneisenau* and the cruiser *Prinz Eugen* from the port of Brest to Germany. The operation took place on 11/12 February but was robbed of the success so nearly achieved as both the battle-cruisers were mined off the Dutch coast. The *Gneisenau* was subsequently hit by heavy bombers whilst in a floating dock undergoing repairs, and as a result she was put out of action for the rest of the war, her big guns being used for coast defence in Norway and Holland.

The day after the break-through from Brest, Raeder was well received by Hitler and the Norwegian situation was discussed. As a result it was decided to move the pocket battleship *Scheer* and the cruiser *Prinz Eugen*, together with all available torpedo-boats and destroyers, to Trondheim and Narvik, and to extend the coastal minefields. The move of the warships took place during the period 21-23 February and was observed by reconnaissance aircraft of Coastal Command. Admiral Tovey received the information in time to despatch the carrier *Victorious* to a position from which her aircraft could attack them, but bad weather prevented the former from achieving success. On the morning of the 23rd however, the submarine *Trident* managed to torpedo the *Prinz Eugen* as she approached the entrance to the Trondheim leads, causing damage which put her out of action for eight months.

Meanwhile the convoys to and from Russia had been fighting their way through the gales and blizzards of an Arctic winter. It is difficult for anyone who has never experienced the intense cold of the polar regions to comprehend fully what superhuman endurance was called for from the ships' companies of both the warships and merchantmen so engaged. The escort vessels patrolling ceaselessly round the convoys shook and shivered as they climbed to the crest of each foaming, mountainous wave, hesitated, then plunged to wallow for a moment in the trough, the process being repeated with exhausting monotony. Guns, ammunition, torpedoes and depth-charges became coated with frozen spray, so that it was one long struggle to keep them free of ice and ready for use in an all too likely emergency. To touch bare metal without a glove was to invite painful ice burns. The weight of clothing it was necessary to wear in what was generally an unsuccessful attempt to keep out the cold, became a burden almost too heavy to bear, as the long hours of watch dragged on. The faces of officers and lookouts peering over the edges of exposed bridges were whipped by driving snow and sleet until icicles formed on eyebrows, noses and beards.

In the merchant ships the strain of keeping station in such weather caused breakdowns in machinery, and the green seas breaking over them cast loose the deck cargo and injured the crew as they tried to resecure it. So far, only two of these ships had fallen victims to the patrolling U-boats and one of these was successfully towed in to Kola Inlet. While escorting her, the *Tribal*-class destroyer *Matabele* was torpedoed and sank in two minutes with heavy loss of life. The crew of the convoy rescue ship which arrived on the scene a few minutes afterwards, found the ocean dotted with men in life-jackets who stared at them with unseeing eyes and who moved to the rhythmic motion of the waves in a kind of macabre dance of death, an unpleasant reminder of the fact that survival in Arctic waters is a matter of minutes. Out of a ship's company of 200, only two were found to be alive.

Admiral Tovey considered that the Russian naval authorities should be able to prevent the U-boats operating so close to the entrance to the Kola Inlet, where the two merchant ships had been torpedoed, so he sent Rear-Admiral H. M. Burrough in his flagship, the cruiser *Nigeria*, to Murmansk to provide escort for the convoys between that port and Bear Island and to take the opportunity of encouraging our allies to greater efforts in this respect. He particularly hoped that they would provide fighter protection to the convoys during their approach to the port. After discussions lasting almost a month, Admiral Burrough returned with very little more than vague promises of help.

For his part, Admiral Tovey was fully expecting action

by the enemy's surface ships to interfere with the movement of the Russian convoys, and on 26 February he signalled to the Admiralty his proposals for dealing with such a situation. He considered that the protection of these convoys, while a major commitment of the Home Fleet, afforded an opportunity of bringing the enemy surface ships to action, and he thought that an area roughly between Jan Mayen Island and a point about 150 miles west of Bear Island was the one in which the risk of surface attack was greatest. He suggested that in order to enable him to cover both the outward- and inward-bound convoys with his heavy forces while the former were passing through this danger area, these should sail simultaneously at minimum intervals of 14 days. He pointed out that such a programme meant that his heavy ships would spend about five days in every 14 in northern waters, and that to carry it out he would need another four destroyers.

Admiral Tovey did not propose to take the whole of his fleet to sea in support of each convoy because he thought to do so would lead to a steady decline in its efficiency, but the Admiralty thought otherwise. In particular they were anxious that the heavy ships should have the benefit of fighter protection from the only carrier in his command, the *Victorious*. The *Tirpitz* was a very formidable opponent and with memories of the *Bismarck* action and the loss of the *Hood* fresh in mind, they wanted to make sure she would be met by a superior concentration of force.

So it came about that on 1 March convoys PQ12 of 16 ships and QP8, as the return convoys were called, of 15 ships sailed from Reykjavik and Kola Inlet respectively, and two days later Vice-Admiral Curteis with the *Renown, Duke of York,* the cruiser *Kenya* and six destroyers sailed from Hvalfiord to rendezvous with the Commander-in-Chief in the *King George V*, with the *Victorious*, the cruiser *Berwick* and six destroyers, which left Scapa on the 4th. The junction was effected at 10:30 a.m. on the 6th, and the cruiser *Kenya* was then detached to join the close escort of the convoy. Owing to engine defects the cruised *Berwick* was only capable of a speed of 27 knots and was to have been relieved by the cruiser *Sheffield*, but the latter was mined while on her way to join the fleet and had to return to Seidisfiord escorted by two of Admiral Curteis' destroyers. Another destroyer stopped to pick up a man who had fallen overboard, and these three destroyers did not rejoin the Commander-in-Chief until 9 March.

At noon on 5 March the outward-bound convoy PQ12 was sighted by a long-range Focke-Wulf reconnaissance aircraft, and on receipt of its report Hitler's permission was at once sought for the *Tirpitz*, wearing the flag of Vice-Admiral Otto Ciliax, who had commanded the battle-cruiser force during its dash up channel in February, to proceed to sea to intercept it. At the same time four U-boats on patrol west of Bear Island were redisposed on a line at right angles to the convoy's estimated lines of advance. It was 11 a.m. on the 6th before ap-

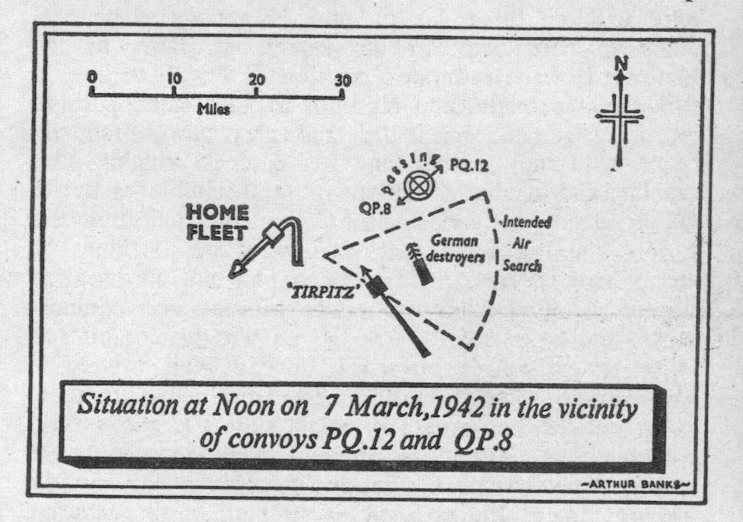

Situation at Noon on 7 March,1942 in the vicinity of convoys PQ.12 and QP.8

proval was given for the battleship to sail with an escort of three destroyers. The *Scheer*, who really formed part of the battle-group, remained behind because of her inferior speed compared with that of the *Tirpitz*. The sailing was not observed by Coastal Command's air patrols, which had been temporarily withdrawn because of a shortage of aircraft. Fortunately however, at about 6 o'clock that evening, as she was steering northwards at high speed, the *Tirpitz* was sighted and reported by the submarine *Seawolf* on patrol to the north of Trondheim, as 'a battleship or 8-inch cruiser'. The report reached Admiral Tovey soon after midnight on the 6th/7th. He was at that time about 200 miles south of the outward-bound convoy PQ12, which had run into loose pack ice and been obliged to alter course to the south-eastward to regain clearwater. During the night the destroyer *Oribi* was considerably damaged as a result of an encounter with ice, a reminder of the serious natural hazard which it afforded.

Realising that the *Tirpitz*, if it were indeed she, would be making straight for the convoys, unless she were attempting to break out—always a possibility to be kept in mind—the Commander-in-Chief turned to the northward to close them. He ordered *Victorious* to be prepared to carry out an air search at dawn to the southward of the estimated position of PQ12, to keep a striking force ready, and all ships to have steam for full speed by 8 a.m. When the cold grey dawn gradually broke, with snow squalls and fog patches bringing poor visibility and making conditions quite unsuitable for flying, the air search was cancelled. At about the same time the *Tirpitz* and her three destroyers were approaching the area where they expected to encounter the north-bound convoy. Admiral Ciliax, too, was without air reconnaissance, and he had nothing to go on but the one aircraft report of the convoy on which he had been ordered to sea. Aircraft reports, as he knew, were liable to be in error and the bad weather which kept *Victorious* from launching her aircraft, also prevented him from using the seaplanes with which his flagship was equipped. Thus he had no idea of the position or strength of the covering force under Admiral Tovey's command; in fact it appears that the High Command was not expecting such a powerful force to be in the vicinity, since on all previous occasions only a cruiser covering force had been observed. At about 10 a.m., having sighted nothing, Admiral Ciliax detached his three destroyers to spread and search north-westward across the expected course of the convoy, while he went on alone in the *Tirpitz* on a more westerly course. The convoy for which he was searching was at that time about 75 miles to the north of his position and had resumed its north-easterly course, so that his search took him well astern of it, and that of his destroyers rather less so.

The two convoys passed each other at noon and Admiral Tovey, who had approached to within some 75 miles of them, turned to the south-westward, little knowing that at that moment his opponent was only 60 miles away to the south-eastward and steering towards him at high speed. At 4.30 p.m. when the *Tirpitz* had crossed to the northward of the tracks of both convoys, having passed some 60 miles astern of PQ12 and 50 miles ahead of QP8, one of the German destroyers, the *Friedrich Ihn*, encountered the *Ijora*, a Russian straggler from the homeward convoy, which she sank at about 5.15 p.m. but not before her victim had managed to get off a distress message which was picked up by the *King George V*. Unfortunately, the position as received was incomplete, but soon afterwards radio bearings of a German ship which might possibly have been the *Tirpitz* were picked up by the flagship, so at 5.50 p.m. Admiral Tovey altered the course of his force to the eastward, the direction from which the bearing had come. Soon afterwards, he hauled round to the north-east and he was about to detach six of his destroyers to spread and sweep south-eastward, to intercept the *Tirpitz* if, as he thought possible, she might be returning to base, when the Admiralty informed him that it seemed possible that the *Tirpitz* intended to operate in the area east of Bear Island for some time and that it appeared that Admiral Ciliax was not aware of the presence of the Home Fleet in his vicinity. Admiral Tovey therefore, decided to carry on towards the convoys and keep his destroyers. At 7.40 p.m. another bearing was obtained of the same ship as previously, which showed that whoever she was, she was moving south at high speed, so soon after 8 p.m. he detached the six destroyers with orders to proceed to a position 150 miles to the south-eastward and then spread two miles apart and sweep northwards until 6 o'clock the following morning. If nothing had been sighted by then they were to proceed to Seidisfiord to refuel. At the same time he detached two other destroyers whose fuel was running low, to return to Iceland; he was thus left with only one destroyer in company.

Meanwhile, Admiral Ciliax, after regaining touch with his destroyers, one of which he detached to refuel at Tromsoe, set course to the eastward with the intention of recommencing the search for his quarry the following day. The Russia-bound convoy continued on its course to the north-east in the direction of Bear Island, so the result of the enemy's move was to take him once again to the south of the convoy. At 4 a.m. on the 8th Ciliax was obliged to detach his other two destroyers to refuel at Tromsoe, and three hours later he turned to the northward across the expected line of advance of the convoy, but at 10.45 a.m. having sighted nothing he turned west.

At midnight on the 7th/8th Admiral Tovey, having heard nothing further since the second intercepted, unidentified signal four hours previously, was confirmed in his opinion that by now the *Tirpitz* must be returning to base, so he turned south and steered for a position which by dawn would bring the *Victorious*'s aircraft within range of the Lofoten Islands, close to which the *Tirpitz* was expected to pass. The weather was still unsuitable for flying, so when by 4 a.m. nothing had been sighted, he presumed that the German ship had eluded him, and turned to the west and steered towards Iceland 'to collect some destroyers'. His four capital ships were now without an anti-submarine screen in waters in which he knew U-boats were operating, and he was therefore obliged to rely on zigzagging at high speed to minimise this threat.

Meanwhile, the Admiralty had ordered convoy PQ12 to pass north of Bear Island if ice permitted, but at noon on the 8th it again ran into ice and was forced to turn to the east and south-east to get away from it. Little did those on board the heavily laden merchant ships know that at the time the first turn was being made, the *Tirpitz* was only 80 miles away to the southward, and that Admiral Tovey with the covering force was 500 miles south-west of them.

At 11:20 a.m. on the 8th, Group North informed Admiral Ciliax that the convoy might be found further to the west, so throughout the afternoon he continued on a westerly course and ordered his three destroyers to rejoin him at 7 o'clock the next morning. However, at 6.15 p.m. Group North told him that it was possible that the convoy had turned back after being sighted by aircraft on the 5th and from this the Admiral inferred he had discretion to return to base. He accordingly amended the rendezvous for his destroyers to a position west of the entrance to Vestfiord and told his flag-captain to set course for Trondheim.

At 5.30 p.m. a message from the Admiralty informed Admiral Tovey that there was good reason to believe that the *Tirpitz* was still seeking the convoy in an area to the south of Bear Island, so at 6.20 p.m. the Commander-in-Chief altered round to the north-eastward. At about this time he decided that it was essential to break radio silence in order to inform the Admiralty of his intentions and of the fact that he was without an anti-submarine screen of destroyers. Radio communication in the area at the time was very bad and so he also asked the Admiralty to operate the cruisers and destroyers which he was expecting to join him. Although it is generally undesirable for ships at sea in wartime to send radio messages, there are exceptions to every rule and this was one of them. Admiral Tovey hoped that if the Germans intercepted his signal and thereby deduced that the battle fleet was out after the *Tirpitz*, they might well recall her, and this might be the means of saving the threatened convoy. Later that night the Admiralty told Admiral Tovey that radio intelligence showed that the *Tirpitz* was steering south, so at 2.40 a.m. he altered course to the south-east to cut her off and ordered the *Victorious* to be prepared to fly off a search and striking force at dawn. As the force approached the land the weather and visibility improved, and at 6.40 a.m. the carrier launched a searching force of six Albacore aircraft, followed at 7.30 a.m. by 12 more armed with torpedoes. Just before they took off,

Admiral Tovey sent them an encouraging signal: 'A wonderful chance, which may achieve most valuable results. God be with you.' Little did anyone know what a unique opportunity it was to prove.

At 8 a.m. one of the searching aircraft sighted and reported the *Tirpitz*, which at that time was some 60 miles due west of the entrance to Vestfiord steering towards Trondheim at high speed, with one destroyer in company. It appears that the sighting aircraft's report was heard by the *Tirpitz*'s radio-intelligence watch, for she hurriedly flew off her aircraft as fighter protection and then turned and made for the coast. At 8.42 a.m. she was sighted by the striking force about 20 miles away in the direction of the sun. The squadron commander intended to climb into the cloud in order to get ahead of his target, but half an hour later when the force was just about to pass over her, a sudden break in the clouds exposed the leading aircraft to the enemy's view, so the former knew that any hope of achieving surprise had been lost, and decided to attack at once. He was encouraged in his decision by the *Tirpitz*'s delay in opening fire and by her inaccuracy when she did. The aircraft attacked in subflights from both sides, but the conditions could not have been more difficult since with the wind ahead they had only an advantage of about 30 knots over their target. The full weight of the *Tirpitz*'s formidable anti-aircraft battery soon opened up, filling the sky with bursting shell, but with great courage and determination the aircraft pressed home their attacks. It was remarkable that only two of their number were shot down and even more astonishing that the great ship, twisting and turning to comb the tracks of the torpedoes streaking towards her from every direction, escaped unharmed. Commenting on this attack in his book *The Tirpitz*, Herr Brennecke remarks that Admiral Ciliax remains convinced that his flagship was hit by one or possibly two torpedoes which failed to detonate. 'I have never doubted', the Admiral says, 'that given her length and manoeuvrability, *Tirpitz* could avoid all torpedoes fired at point blank range.'[1]

---

[1] *The Tirpitz*, p. 52.

Thus in a matter of minutes an opportunity to achieve a success which would have profoundly affected naval operations all over the world, eluded the grasp of the Royal Navy; it was never to recur.

To Admiral Tovey the failure of the attack was a bitter disappointment. That the clinch which followed the long bout of shadow-boxing in which the weather had obliged him to indulge with his redoubtable opponent, should have had such an unsatisfactory result, was galling indeed. Although there is no evidence to substantiate Admiral Ciliax's opinion quoted above, it should not be entirely discounted, since torpedoes dropped at close range may not have had time to take up their proper depth setting and passed under the ship.

Oblivious of the narrow escape from destruction which they had had, the two convoys reached their appointed destinations without incident. PQ12, once clear of the ice, was shrouded in exceptionally thick and persistent sea-smoke rising many feet into the air, and this, coupled with a shrewd alteration of course, threw off a suspected enemy shadower, and enabled the convoy to reach Kola Inlet intact on 12 March. QP8 reached Iceland two days earlier.

Admiral Raeder was not at all pleased with the outcome of the sortie. 'The operation reveals', he told Hitler, 'the weakness of our naval forces in the northern area. The enemy responds to every German sortie by sending strong task forces, particularly aircraft carriers, which are the greatest menace to our heavy ships. The extreme weakness of our defences is evidenced by the fact that the enemy dares to advance in the coastal waters of the northern area without being smashed by the German air force.'[1] Considering that for five days a strong British force had been operating within 250 miles of the Norwegian coast and that the only response by the Luftwaffe had been an unsuccessful and belated attack by three aircraft on the last day, the Grand Admiral had just cause for complaint. Moreover, lack of air reconnaissance had prevented the *Tirpitz* from locating both the convoy and the

---

[1] *Führer Naval Conferences* 1942.

covering force and might have led to her loss. It is not surprising, therefore, that Admiral Raeder ended his report with a strongly worded request for much greater support from his air-force colleague Göring. He demanded that the British carriers should be made the primary target and he proposed that work on the German carrier *Graf Zeppelin* should be accelerated. Hitler approved this last request, and also the formation of a battle group composed of the *Tirpitz, Scharnhorst*, a carrier, two heavy cruisers and 12-14 destroyers. He undertook to consult Göring about strengthening the air force in Norway.

On the British side, too, there were lessons to be learned. The failure of the air strike to obtain a hit on the *Tirpitz* pointed to the need for a much higher degree of training among Fleet Air Arm crews to offset the rapid expansion and consequent dilution of this branch which the commissioning of new carriers had imposed. This was the first time that battleships had been used to give cover to these convoys, and following the precedent set with the Malta convoys, for which the support of heavy ships had been found necessary to counter the threat offered by the Italian battle fleet, the Admiralty had instructed Admiral Tovey to consider the protection of the convoy as his primary object. In his report on the operation the Commander-in-Chief criticised this instruction, contending that the destruction of the enemy's principal forces had traditionally always been the object of the British fleet. In his opinion the sinking of the *Tirpitz* must always take precedence over the safety of any convoy, and he pointed out that the dispositions required for the former would seldom, if ever, be the same for the latter. He would have preferred to divide his forces as he had originally proposed. Yet it is a matter for surmise whether a covering force of two ships like the *Renown* and *Duke of York* would really have been strong enough to drive off the *Tirpitz*, since the battle-cruiser was never designed to engage a heavy ship. Also, while the destruction of the *Tirpitz* must surely be the fleet's primary object, it might well be brought about by giving close support to the convoy with heavy ships. Admiral Tovey further contested the Admiralty's instruction that he was to provide fighter protection for all capital ships when they were within range of shore-based aircraft, as this obliged him to operate his two battleships, the battle-cruiser and the carrier together, in submarine-infested waters and, as we have seen, for a considerable period without an anti-submarine screen. Nevertheless, had the Luftwaffe cooperated in the way that Admiral Raeder wished, he might have been extremely glad of such protection.

The Commander-in-Chief was also severely critical of the way in which the Admiralty had signalled 'detailed instructions for the handling of his forces'. He was referring mainly to the instructions sent to the convoy to pass north of Bear Island, which in the event was not possible on account of the ice. Although shortly after the outbreak of the war Admiral Pound had promised Flag Officers in command of fleets and squadrons that the Admiralty would only interfere with the conduct of operations in certain circumstances, it is an unfortunate fact that this pledge was more honoured in the breach than in the observance. It was inevitable that the Admiralty should be the focal point for intelligence of enemy intentions and movements and that occasions would arise when they were better informed than a Flag Officer at sea, but rather than issue instructions to him based on such information there was a natural feeling he should be given the information and then left to take the appropriate action, having regard to the local conditions prevailing, of which it was impossible for the Admiralty to be aware. On the other hand, there was the problem of communications, which were particularly bad at times in northern waters, and the undesirability of breaking radio silence, which a Flag Officer would be obliged to do if he wished to issue instructions to detached forces. These factors, as will be seen, were to have an important bearing on future operations in Arctic waters. As far as the *Tirpitz*'s sortie is concerned, the Admiralty's appreciation of her movements, as we have seen, was more correct than that of the Commander-in-Chief, who had not the same facilities at his disposal.

On 19 March, in accordance with the plan approved by Hitler, the 8-inch-gun cruiser *Hipper* left Germany to join the other ships in Norwegian waters. Although the Admiralty received warning of the impending movement, Coastal Command reconnaissance and strike aircraft failed to locate her, and she joined the *Tirpitz* and *Scheer* at Trondheim. The build-up of German naval strength in northern Norway was thus carried one step further in the struggle which had begun in earnest for control of the Arctic route to Russia.

4

A Spirited Defence

> *Sir Richard utterly refused to turn from the enemy, alleging that he would rather choose to die, than dishonour himself, his country, and Her Majestie's shippe*
>
> Sir Walter Raleigh
> Hakluyt's 'The English Voyages' xxii

THE NEXT TWO CONVOYS to and from Russia, PQ13 and QP9, each consisting of 19 ships, left Iceland and Murmansk on 20 and 21 March respectively, and once again Admiral Tovey disposed his forces to deal with the enemy's expected reactions. On this occasion heavy ship cover was provided by the battle-cruiser *Renown*, flagship of Vice-Admiral A. T. B. Curteis, with the battleship *Duke of York* and the carrier *Victorious* in company.

The homeward convoy had an uneventful passage, but its escort was able to record the sinking of *U655* by the minesweeper *Sharpshooter*. The outward convoy, however, was less fortunate. When it was four days out it was struck by a savage storm which scattered the ships to the four winds in an orgy of violence. It took four days to blow itself out, and when on 27 March the senior officer of the escort force began to try and collect his charges, he scanned the horizon in vain for the sight of one of them. They were spread over a distance of some 150 miles; the Commodore's ship, the tanker *River Afton*, unable to steer within five points of the wind, had drifted towards the Lofoten Islands; the most easterly ship was the *Empire Ranger*, all alone and only about 80 miles north of the North Cape; 40 miles astern of her was a group of six merchant ships with an armed whaler in company; 35 miles further west was the S.S. *Harpalion* escorted by the destroyer *Fury*; while a further 65 miles astern was another group of six ships escorted by the destroyer *Eclipse*, the whaler *Sumba*, and the trawler *Paynter*. The cruisers *Trinidad* and *Nigeria* were searching for stragglers in an area 100 miles to the south-west of Bear Island. The following day was clear and sunny with occasional snow flurries, but the convoy was still dispersed when, just after 10 a.m., the cruiser *Trinidad*, which had swept to the eastward during the night, sighted a German reconnaissance aircraft. The enemy lost no time in taking action, and within an hour dive-bombing attacks commenced and continued throughout the day, but only two ships were sunk, the *Empire Ranger*, romping ahead of the convoy, and the *Raceland*, a straggler from the easternmost group of six ships.

Meantime, Admiral Schmundt (Admiral, North Norway) had sailed the destroyers *Z26, Z25*, and *Z24* from Kirkenes to locate and attack the convoy. They were to sweep west along its estimated track, spread three miles apart. At 10.45 p.m. one of them came across the boats of the *Empire Ranger* and rescued the survivors, and then just after midnight the *Z26* encountered a straggler, the S.S. *Bateau*, which she sank by gunfire after having taken off the crew, from whom she obtained information about the state of the convoy and its escort. The destroyers remained in this position for about an hour, then concluding that they were too far to the north-westward, they turned and swept to the southeast at 25 knots, a course which took them well to the south of the area in which the convoy then was. At 5.30 a.m. they turned and steamed due north for three hours, before recommencing their westward sweep. The weather now started to deteriorate, the visibility shortening as heavy snow squalls driven by a bitter wind swept down. It was under these conditions that half an hour later the cruiser *Trinidad*, with the destroyer *Fury* in company, steaming to the eastward at 20 knots to the support of four detached merchant ships, encountered the three German destroyers almost head on. Fire was opened immediately on the leading enemy ship, *Z26*, which was soon seen to be on fire, but not long after the *Trinidad* was obliged to make a large alteration of course to avoid torpedoes and the action was temporarily broken off. However, some 20 minutes later the damaged enemy, who had lost touch with her two consorts, was again sighted and received further severe punishment. Hoping to give her a *coup de grâce* the *Trinidad* fired a torpedo, which by an unusual mischance, subsequently attributed to the intense cold, ran erratically and, reversing its course, returned and hit the cruiser on the port side, causing severe damage and reducing her speed to eight knots. The destroyer *Eclipse*, in company with a group of eight merchant ships from the convoy, and two Russian destroyers, which had come out from Kola to join the escort, together with the *Fury* now became involved in a *mêlée* with the damaged *Z26*, and fighting ensued in the most appalling conditions with spray sweeping over the ships and freezing solid as it settled on gun-mountings, decks and bridges. The luckless enemy ship received further damage which finally brought her to a standstill in a sinking condition, and the *Eclipse* was just about to torpedo her when the other two enemy ships hove in sight and she was obliged to retire, but not before she had received two hits from the German's 5.9-inch guns, which holed her above the waterline and shot away her main aerials. Short of fuel and with nine seriously wounded men in need of urgent medical attention, she shaped course for Kola, which she reached the next morning with only 40 tons of fuel left. The two German destroyers, having rescued the survivors of the *Z26*, then returned to base, and the damaged *Trinidad* escorted by the *Fury* managed to struggle into Kola under her own steam at 9.20 a.m. the following day.

The convoy, still in two groups of eight and four ships, plus four ships still unaccounted for, steamed on towards its destination, unaware that a group of U-boats was lying in wait for it off the entrance. These succeeded in torpedoing two ships, but paid for their achievement by the loss of one of their number, *U585*, to the *Fury*. Of the missing ships, one, the *Induna*, towing the armed whaler *Silja* which had run short of fuel, had been trapped in heavy ice during the night of 28/29 March, from which she did not get clear until 3 o'clock the next afternoon, when she set course for the Kola Inlet. Five hours later the tow parted and the *Silja* disappeared in a snow squall. Unable to find her the *Induna* proceeded on her way alone, only to be torpedoed and sunk by a U-boat the following morning. Her survivors, several of whom died

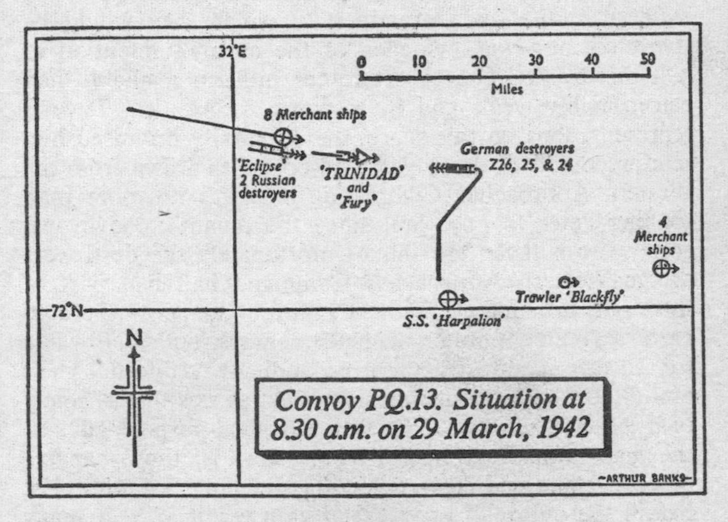

Convoy PQ.13. Situation at 8.30 a.m. on 29 March, 1942

of exposure in the open boats, were rescued three days later by a Russian minesweeper. The *Silja* was subsequently found by the destroyer *Oribi* and completed her voyage in tow of the minesweeper *Harrier*. It was thus 1 April before the last of the 15 surviving ships of the battered convoy berthed at Murmansk.

On the whole the German High Command was satisfied with the result of the attacks on the convoy, but the Naval Staff saw in the loss of the *Z26* a need for greater caution in the use of surface ships against the convoys. This view was not shared by Admiral Schmundt, who considered that the proper solution was to employ capital ship cover for the destroyers.

While convoy PQ13 was completing the last leg of its stormy voyage, 33 Halifax bombers set out on another but unsuccessful attempt to put the *Tirpitz* out of action.

The change from the winter months of almost perpetual darkness to those of perpetual daylight necessitated a review of the conditions under which the convoys were being sailed. Every day it was becoming easier for the German reconnaissance aircraft to locate them, and this fact, coupled with the build-up of enemy surface, submarine and air forces in northern Norway, pointed to an increase in the scale of attack to which they would be subjected, and was evidence of the enemy's intention to halt this traffic. The escort forces hitherto available had been pitiably weak and in response to Admiral Tovey's representations on this score, the Admiralty promised him reinforcements of destroyers and corvettes drawn from the Western Approaches Command. This was no more than robbing Peter to pay Paul since the Atlantic convoy escorts were still far too thin. Unfortunately the destroyers of the Western Approaches Command had had part of their gun armament removed in order to allow them to carry a greater number of depth charges, and their value for surface action was correspondingly reduced. Their anti-aircraft armament was also weak, as was that of many of the fleet destroyers. The fitting of dual-purpose guns as the main armament in destroyers, that is, those capable of both high- and low-angle fire, did not start until just before the outbreak of war and as a result a great many of these ships were of little use in providing long-range defence against air attack.

Admiral Pound was well aware of the difficulties to be overcome in attempting to run convoys to north Russia in face of mounting German opposition and the lengthening hours of daylight. He made his views known to the Defence Committee early in April and warned that losses on this route might become such as to make their running uneconomical.

The next two convoys, PQ14 eastwards and QP10 westwards, sailed on 8 and 10 April respectively, the former comprising 24 ships and the latter 16. Included in the escort of PQ14 was the cruiser *Edinburgh*, flying the flag of Rear-Admiral S. S. Bonham-Carter, and on board she carried sheets of steel plating with which to repair the damaged *Trinidad*, the Russians having been unable to provide the necessary material. The convoy's route had been selected on the assumption that by now the ice would have begun to recede, whereas in fact it was further south than usual. It was encountered south-west of Jan Mayen Island and as a result 16 ships and two of the escorting minesweepers were obliged to return to Iceland for repairs. The eight ships which continued the voyage were bombed intermittently but unsuccessfully from the 15th to the 17th, but on the 16th the Commodore's ship, the *Empire Howard*, blew up after being hit by two torpedoes from a U-boat, east of Bear Island. The Commodore, E. Rees, R.N.R., was not among the survivors. The seven remaining ships reached Kola Inlet on the 19th, bad weather with poor visibility obliging the German destroyers to abandon two attempts at a sortie against them. The homeward-bound convoy QP10 was heavily attacked by both aircraft and U-boats during the first three days of its passage, and as a result four ships were lost.

During the passage of these two convoys Hitler reviewed the naval situation with Admiral Raeder. He announced that there was an obvious need for torpedo-carrying aircraft. In fact, after a long delay due to the unwillingness of the navy to let the air force have torpedoes which the former considered an essentially naval weapon, Göring had at last got his way. The first 12 crews to be trained in this form of attack had just been sent to Bardufoss Airfield in north Norway, to operate the He.111 and Ju.88 aircraft which had been modified to take torpedoes, and they were soon followed by others. Hitler also directed that efforts must be concentrated on preventing Anglo-American aid reaching Russia. The convoys must be made the navy's principal target and plans must be worked out for a combined sea and air offensive to take place in June, to be followed by the despatch of the pocket battleship *Scheer* on a raiding mission. For his part, Raeder was obliged to report a deterioration in the oil fuel situation. Reserve stocks were down to 150,000 tons and Roumanian deliveries had declined.

The return of so many loaded ships to Iceland from convoy PQ14 aggravated still further the accumulation of supplies awaiting shipment to Russia by the Arctic route, and there was strong political pressure for the number of ships in the next outward-bound convoy to be increased. This was in direct opposition to Admiral Tovey's recommendation 'that these convoys, if they could not be postponed until the ice moved north should be limited in size'. The Commander-in-Chief's concern was occasioned more by the weather than by the threat of enemy action since, as we have seen, in the great gale encountered by the previous convoy the ships became so scattered that the escort was unable to afford them any protection, particularly against air attack, where cohesion is the essence of successful defence. But in the Admiralty, where a scientific analysis had been made of the losses in the Atlantic convoys, it had been shown that the number of ships sunk in any one attack of a given intensity remained more or less constant, so that the larger the convoy, the smaller the percentage loss. This argument, backed by political pressure and supported by the fact that from now on some improvement in the weather might reasonably be expected, led to Admiral Tovey's recommendation being over-ruled, the Admiralty deciding that the next outward convoy PQ15 should consist of 25 ships and sail on 26 April. The corresponding homeward convoy QP11 consisting of 17 ships was to sail two days later. The escort forces allocated to these convoys had been strengthened, that of PQ15 comprising four destroyers, four trawlers and for the first time an anti-aircraft ship, the *Ulster Queen* (a converted Irish Mail ship) and the Catapult Aircraft Merchant (CAM) ship *Empire Morn*. This last was an ordinary cargo ship, on board which a catapult had been fitted and from which a Hurricane fighter could be launched. They had been introduced in an attempt to provide a means of shooting down the German shadowing aircraft which invariably kept out of gun range while reporting the convoy's position, course and speed, thus facilitating its interception by patrolling

U-boats. The pilot of the Hurricane, his mission accomplished, had to ditch alongside a destroyer and pray for a speedy rescue from the icy water. It was an improvisation born of the lack of aircraft carriers for convoy protection, a need which had not been foreseen. Affording close cover to the convoy were the cruisers *Nigeria* (flying the flag of Rear-Admiral H. M. Burrough) and *London*, with two destroyers.

The escort of the west-bound convoy QP11 consisted of six destroyers, four corvettes and a trawler, close cover being provided by the cruiser *Edinburgh*, flagship of Rear-Admiral Bonham-Carter. Ships of the First Minesweeping Flotilla, based on Kola Inlet, and two Russian destroyers were to reinforce the escort during the first 24 hours of its passage.

As the strength of the Home Fleet had been seriously reduced by the withdrawal of ships for the capture of Madagascar, a detachment of the United States fleet comprising the new battleship *Washington*, flying the flag of Rear-Admiral Giffen, the carrier *Wasp*, the cruisers *Wichita* and *Tuscaloosa* and a squadron of six destroyers had been sent to reinforce it. These ships, with the exception of the *Wasp*, sailed with Admiral Tovey in the *King George V*, accompanied by the carrier *Victorious*, the cruiser *Kenya* and ten destroyers, four of which were American, to provide distant cover for the two convoys. As an additional precaution, four submarines were disposed off the Norwegian coast, with instructions to move north-eastwards in step with the outward convoy so as to be in a position to intercept the German ships based on Trondheim should they put to sea. They were to be joined later by a fifth submarine which accompanied the convoy as far as longitude 5° E. An unfortunate incident occurred on 2 May when one of these submarines, the Polish-manned *P551*, was sunk by the escorts of PQ15, because of her being 100 miles out of position.

The homeward convoy QP11, which had sailed as planned on 28 April, was sighted and reported by both aircraft and U-boats the following day. The next afternoon as the flagship *Edinburgh* was zig-zagging ahead of the convoy, she was struck by two torpedoes fired by

U456, one of which hit her amidships and the other right aft, blowing off her stern and with it her rudder. The destroyers *Foresight* and *Forester* and the two Russian destroyers in company, stood by the damaged ship, which, without much success, attempted to return to Kola Inlet some 250 miles away. Captain H. W. Faulkner, R.N., her captain, tried steering by main engines but with the wind and sea on the quarter the ship yawed heavily and little progress was made in the required direction. Admiral Bonham-Carter then ordered the *Forester* to take her in tow, but the tow soon parted, so the experiment was tried of the *Edinburgh* towing the *Foresight*, the latter acting as a steadying drogue. This proved more successful and for the next 16 hours the damaged ship and her escort continued in this fashion, unaware that all the while *U456* was shadowing them. By now the Russian destroyers were running short of fuel and had to return to base, so the *Edinburgh* slipped her tow to allow the *Foresight* to join her consort in providing anti-submarine protection, which was just as well, for there is no doubt that it was the presence of the destroyers which prevented the U-boat from attempting to finish off her victim. During the next 23 hours, by skilful use of her main engines —no less than 64 separate orders were passed from the bridge to the engine-room in one watch—the *Edinburgh* made slow progress eastward. On the evening of 1 May she was joined by the minesweepers *Harrier, Niger, Gossamer* and *Hussar*, together with a Russian torpedo boat and a tug, which had sailed from Kola Inlet to her assistance. The tug, unfortunately, was not powerful enough to tow the cruiser, but she proved useful in helping her to steer.

Convoy QP11 meanwhile proceeded on its homeward journey with its depleted escort. At 5.40 a.m. on 1 May, when it was about 150 miles to the eastward of Bear Island, it was unsuccessfully attacked by four torpedo aircraft, the first of such attacks which from now on were to prove such a menace to the Arctic convoys. Four U-boats were believed to be shadowing and endeavours were made to shake them off by large alterations of course. There was much ice about and the frequent snow squalls caused the visibility to vary between two and ten miles. Suddenly the destroyer *Beverley* on the convoy's port bow reported, 'Enemy in sight'. The Germans, fully aware of the way in which events had moved in their favour, had despatched the destroyers *Herman Schoemann, Z24* and *Z25* to find and attack what they believed was a weakly defended convoy. The German ships, mounting between them ten 5.9-inch and five 5-inch guns, were far more heavily armed than the four remaining British destroyers, which between them mustered only six 4.7-inch and three 4-inch guns. On receipt of the *Beverley*'s report the Senior Officer of the escort, Commander M. Richmond, in the aptly named destroyer *Bulldog*, immediately concentrated his ships and, despite the inferiority of his force, reacted with such boldness and aggressiveness to every attempt by the enemy to close the convoy, as finally to cause him to desist. Five times the German destroyers sought to drive off the defenders so as to get at the convoy, to be met each time by a defiance worthy of Sir Richard Grenville. Thanks to what a brother officer described as a superb display of poker playing on the part of Commander Richmond, the convoy proceeded on its way unharmed, and the German destroyers, having been ordered to attack the damaged *Edinburgh*, withdrew.

Before recounting the further exploits of the three enemy ships we must return briefly to PQ15. When two days out, in a position some 250 miles south-west of Bear Island, it was sighted and reported by enemy aircraft, but no attack developed for three days, when it was unsuccessfully dive-bombed by six Ju.88 aircraft, one of which was shot down. At 1.30 a.m. on 3 May, after passing the west-bound convoy QP11, it was again attacked, this time by six torpedo aircraft which, taking advantage of the haze and the half light, came in low and undetected by radar until they were within 6,000 yards of the convoy. They succeeded in sinking three ships including that of the Commodore, who happily was rescued, together with 137 other survivors. The enemy lost three aircraft. Although continuously shadowed by U-boats, these made no attempt to attack, then at 10.30 p.m. another bombing attack took place, one Ju.88 being shot down without loss or damage to the convoy. On the evening of the next day (4th) a south-easterly gale sprang up bringing heavy snow storms, and under this protective blanket the convoy reached Kola Inlet at 9 p.m. the following day.

At 6.30 a.m. on 2 May the three enemy destroyers came upon the *Edinburgh* making about three knots under her own steam and steering with the aid of the tug on her port bow and the minesweeper *Gossamer* secured astern. First to sight the enemy was the minesweeper *Hussar*, who boldly opened fire with her one 4-inch gun. In accordance with Admiral Bonham-Carter's previously issued instructions, Captain Faulkner immediately slipped both tows and engaged the enemy, while his ship, unable to steer, circled slowly round at her maximum speed of about eight knots. For all her serious damage, the cruiser still had plenty of fight in her, and it was not long before she registered hits on the leading German ship, the *Herman Schoemann*, and brought her to a standstill in a sinking condition. By now the destroyers *Forester* and *Foresight* had joined in the battle, which became one of hide and seek in and out of the snow squalls and the smoke screen laid by the destroyers to cover the *Edinburgh*. At 6.50 a.m., just as she had fired three torpedoes at the enemy, the *Forester* received three hits, which killed her captain, Lieutenant-Commander G. P. Huddart, R.N., and obliged her to stop. The *Z24* had also fired torpedoes which passed under the *Forester* and sped on towards the unmanoeuvrable *Edinburgh*; one of these, almost at the end of its run, struck the cruiser on the side opposite to that against which the U-boat's torpedo had exploded, thus almost cutting the ship in half. Nevertheless she continued to engage the enemy, but it was now plain to both the Admiral and his Flag-Captain that there was no longer any hope of saving her. A moment later, Commander Salter in the *Foresight*, who had interposed his ship between the enemy and the damaged *Forester*, drew on himself the concentrated fire of the enemy ships at a range of about 4,000 yards. He went on to full speed and sought to retire under the cover of smoke, but four hits, one of them in a boiler room, brought his ship to a halt. One of the four minesweepers had been sent to Kola to guide two Russian destroyers to the scene and the three remaining, behaving as the Admiral afterwards said 'like three young terriers', with the utmost gallantry, endeavoured to carry on the battle, but to everyone's surprise and relief, the two enemy destroyers, having rescued some 200 of the *Herman Schoemann's* ships company and scuttled her, withdrew at high speed. It appears that in the poor visibility they had mistaken the minesweepers for destroyers, though this should not have deterred them from achieving a substantial victory and destroying the entire British force.

After a time the badly damaged *Forester* and *Foresight*, taking it in turns to screen each other while repairs were effected, managed to get under way again, but for the *Edinburgh* the end was obviously near and the Admiral ordered the minesweepers to take off her crew, among whom casualties fortunately had been light. Down in her sick bay were a number of injured merchant seamen taking passage, and these were with difficulty carried to the upper deck and transferred to the minesweepers in which, with the rest of the *Edinburgh*'s ship's company, they returned to Vaenga. When everyone had been taken off the Admiral ordered the *Foresight* to sink her with her one remaining torpedo. The total casualties in the British ships amounted to four officers and 74 men killed and 43 wounded.

In the previous chapter a brief account was given of conditions ashore at Vaenga, so it is not surprising to find frequent references in stories of the Russian convoys to the sub-human conditions under which survivors from allied warships and merchant ships were obliged to live. The plain fact however, is that the Russians had nothing better to offer. Food in the northern *oblasts* was desperately short and the bulk of the population was on a diet which elsewhere would have been considered insufficient to keep body and soul together. Thus it was that although the survivors of the *Edinburgh* when they landed had not had a hot meal for 48 hours and the weather was bitterly cold, all the authorities were able to offer them was a bowl of thin watery soup and a crust of hard rye bread, and on this diet, supplemented by anything the visiting ships could spare, they existed until repatriated. On arrival in camp each man was issued with one blanket and a piece of synthetic soap. Captain Faulkner was deeply concerned about the conditions under which his men were obliged to live, but there was little that he or anyone else could do about it.

While these events were taking place, Bomber Command, on 28 and 29 April, renewed its attacks on the *Tirpitz*, once again without success.

But there were still greater set-backs in store. On 1 May the battleship *King George V*, while at sea with the covering force, in dense fog rammed and sank the *Tribal*-class destroyer *Punjabi*, and the latter's depth charges exploding as she went down so damaged the battleship that she had to be docked for repairs. The battleship *Duke of York*, to which Vice-Admiral Curteis had transferred his flag, took her place in the covering force.

On the evening of 13 May the cruiser *Trinidad*, which with the aid of the plating brought by the unlucky *Edinburgh* had been made sufficiently sea-worthy to enable her to steam at 18 knots, set sail for the United States, flying the flag of Rear-Admiral Bonham-Carter and accompanied by the destroyers *Somali, Matchless, Foresight* and *Forester*, the last two having also had their action damage repaired. Rear-Admiral Burrough, flying his flag in the *Nigeria*, with the cruisers *Kent, Norfolk* and *Liverpool*, was patrolling west of Bear Island to cover her passage, and distant cover for the movement was provided by the Home Fleet which sailed from Scapa on 15 May. A long-range fighter escort for the first 200 miles of the passage had been promised by the Russians, but in the event only three aircraft arrived, and having covered the ships for three-quarters of an hour they returned to base. German reconnaissance aircraft sighted the cruiser and her escort on 14 May, when they were but 100 miles out, and the same evening shortly before 10 o'clock they were unsuccessfully attacked by 25 Ju.88's. At 10.37 p.m. a force of ten torpedo aircraft came in and dropped their torpedoes. Eight minutes later a lone Ju.88 dived on the cruiser from the cover of low cloud and released a stick of bombs, one of which hit her abreast the bridge on the starboard side and burst on the lower deck, starting a fire between decks under the bridge. A second bomb, which either hit or burst close alongside, blew off a temporary patch on her side, flooding a magazine and other compartments and producing a list. The fires from the explosion of the first bomb spread rapidly, but the ship was still capable of steaming and succeeded in avoiding the torpedoes which had been aimed at her just before the bomb had fallen. She also avoided another lot of torpedoes fired at her a quarter of an hour later. But by midnight the fires were out of control and in the position she then was, with U-boats in the vicinity and the certainty that air attacks would be renewed, there was virtually no hope of salving her, and the Admiral concurred in the Captain's proposal to abandon ship. The destroyers were ordered to take off the crew, and when this had been done the Admiral directed the destroyer *Matchless* to sink her. One officer and 60 naval ratings had been killed, and by a cruel twist of fate the 20 injured merchant seamen who had survived the loss of the *Edinburgh* were also killed by the explosion of the bombs.

The loss of two valuable cruisers in this manner was a matter of deep concern to Admiral Tovey, and after he had discussed the situation with Rear-Admiral Bonham-Carter, he fully supported the latter's recommendation that until the aerodromes in north Norway were neutralised, the convoys should be suspended until such time as darkness afforded some protection. 'If they must continue for political reasons,' he told the Admiralty, 'very serious and heavy losses must be expected.' The First Sea Lord had reached a similar conclusion; the considered naval opinion, therefore, was against the sailing of further convoys to Russia until the autumn.

But in the political field a very different climate of opinion was building up. Under the first protocol governing the supplies to be made to Russia which Beaverbrook and Harriman, as already mentioned, had signed in Moscow on 1 October 1941, it had been stipulated that exact quantities of the goods specified would be delivered by 30 June 1942, and the Russians were most insistent that this bargain should be fulfilled to the letter. After a slow start, the Americans had now made available all the goods and the ships necessary to meet their share of the promised deliveries, and as the President informed the Prime Minister on 30 April, there were no less than 107 ships 'now loaded or being loaded in the United Kingdom and the United States prior to June 1st'. The fact was that totally unwarranted assumptions regarding the capacity of the Arctic convoys had been made on a high level in both countries and the expert advice tendered had been ignored. In September 1941 British and American sea-transport experts had favoured the development of an alternative supply route through the Persian Gulf, but it was not until the Germans had clearly demonstrated their ability to make the Arctic route prohibitively costly that action was taken to implement this suggestion.[1]

Mr Churchill was, therefore, obliged to explain to the President the impossibility of meeting his request to speed up the convoys in order to dispose of the accumulation of shipping. He explained that it was not just a question of transferring escort vessels from the Atlantic to the Arctic convoys, which might well have had disastrous consequences, since the escorts of the former were already too weak, but there was the ever-present threat of attack by the enemy's heavy ships and destroyers. After an earnest plea to the President 'not to press us beyond our judgment in this operation which we have studied most intently and of which we have not yet been able to measure the full strain', Mr Churchill concluded: 'Three convoys every two months, with either 35 or 25 ships in each convoy, according to experience, represent the extreme limit of what we can handle'[2]; but as we have seen, even this was contrary to the First Sea Lord's advice.

A few days later, a report having reached him that 90 loaded ships were awaiting convoy, Stalin proferred a request to the Prime Minister 'to take all possible measures to ensure the arrival of the above-mentioned materials in the U.S.S.R. in the course of May, as this is extremely important for our front'. At the time the German armies

[1] See *Command Decisions (U.S. Military History)*, Chap. 9.
[2] *The Second World War*, Vol. IV, p. 232.

were once again on the move, driving towards the Caucasian oil fields, and this no doubt lent urgency to the Russian request. In his reply, the Prime Minister promised that we would 'fight our way through to you with the maximum amount of war materials',[1] and he asked Stalin to increase the assistance being given by his naval and air forces to get the convoys through. The Russians had no naval air arm, and the Soviet Army Air Force, like the Luftwaffe, was not fully trained in naval cooperation, but they could well have done more to keep the U-boats from patrolling outside the entrance to the Kola Inlet. Mr Churchill summed up the problem for the Chiefs of Staffs Committee as follows: 'Not only Premier Stalin but President Roosevelt will object very much to our desisting from running the convoys now. The Russians are in heavy action and will expect us to run the risk, and pay the price entailed by our contribution. The United States ships are queueing up. My own feeling, mingled with much anxiety, is that the convoy [PQ16] ought to sail on the 18th. The operation is justified if a half gets through. Failure on our part to make the attempt would weaken our influence with our major Allies. There are always uncertainties of weather and luck which may aid us. I share your misgivings, but I feel it is a matter of duty.'[2] For the officers and men of the warships and merchant ships of the succeeding convoys, 'the way to glory' was to prove as perilous as the Admiralty expected it to be.

5

Aerial Menace

And in the air Death moans and sings

Julian Grenfell

ONE RESULT OF THE actions described in the previous chapter was the temporary elimination of the threat of

---

[1] *Ibid.*, Vol. IV, p. 233.
[2] *Ibid.*, Vol. IV, p. 233-4.

attack on the convoys by the German destroyers stationed in north Norway, since it was estimated that those not sunk had all been damaged sufficiently to be in need of repairs. There was, of course, still the threat offered by the pocket battleship *Scheer* based on Narvik and shortly to be joined by her sister ship *Lützow*. But in spite of this, Admiral Tovey considered that the loss of the two cruisers *Edinburgh* and *Trinidad* was a clear indication that the threat of U-boat and air attack in the area east of Bear Island was such that it was most undesirable to risk the heavy ships and cruisers in it.[1] He therefore decided to alter the dispositions for protecting the next two convoys, PQ16 and QP12, which were due to sail on 21 May from Hvalfiord in Iceland and the Kola Inlet respectively. The former, consisting of 35 ships under Commodore H. N. Gale, R.D., R.N.R., in the S.S. *Ocean Voice*, was the largest yet assembled and was the result of the political pressure referred to in the last chapter.

The close escort detailed to accompany PQ16 consisted of the minesweeper *Hazard*, and four ocean-going trawlers, *Northern Wave, Lady Madeleine, Retriever*, and *St Elstan*, to be reinforced when the convoy reached a point north-east of Iceland by five destroyers and five corvettes, all under the Escort Commander, Commander Onslow, in the *Tribal*-class destroyer *Ashanti*. Rear-Admiral Burrough, flying his flag in the cruiser, *Nigeria*, with the cruisers *Norfolk, Kent* and *Liverpool* in company, together with three destroyers, was to provide close cover west of Bear Island against a possible sortie by the *Scheer*, while the battle fleet was to cruise in an area north-east of Iceland ready to intercept the *Tirpitz*, should she put to sea. In addition, two submarines were detailed to accompany PQ16 in order to discourage the German surface ships from attacking it, and five British and three Russian submarines were to maintain patrols off the north-west and north coasts of Norway. After the move of the *Lützow* to join the *Scheer* was detected, and which took place after the convoys had sailed, the Russians were asked to instruct their submarines to make radio signals

[1] *London Gazette*, 13 October 1950, para. 21.

giving the impression that a larger number of submarines were on patrol than in fact was the case. Air patrols were arranged covering the area through which the convoys would pass as far north as a point 100 miles north-west of the North Cape, and four flying boats operating from Iceland were to give additional anti-submarine protection to within about 200 miles of Bear Island. In a further attempt to discourage attacks on ships of the convoy by the German dive-bombers, the merchant ships of the outward-bound convoy were fitted with kite-balloons.

The weak point of the plan was of course, the absence of fighter protection for the convoys, for the lack of which, as we had already discovered during operations in the Mediterranean, no amount of gunfire could compensate, but the great shortage of carriers, coupled with the many other commitments in which the Royal Navy was engaged in the Mediterranean and the Indian Ocean, left none to spare for the Russian convoys. On this occasion the Russians had promised to assist the passage of these convoys by mounting a large-scale air offensive on the German airfields in northern Norway, but in the event it turned out to be a minor affair, and took place after the Germans had completed their air attacks on the convoys.

PQ16 and QP12 sailed as planned, and for the former the first three days after leaving Iceland proved uneventful. On the morning of 23 May the trawler *Retriever* had to return to Iceland to make good a defect, and Commander Onslow, who with his destroyers and corvettes was due to join the convoy on that day, had some difficulty in finding it, as it had run into a bank of fog and the two columns in which it had been formed had lost touch with one another. It was early on 25 May before the two sections rejoined, and the Escort Commander was able to reform the convoy on a broad front of eight columns, so as to make it a more difficult target for the dive-bombers. These usually came in from astern and this formation allowed ships to develop their maximum anti-aircraft fire. At 6 o'clock that morning, when the convoy was some 20 miles south-east of Jan Mayen Island, Rear-Admiral Burrough with his four cruisers hove in sight, and closing the columns of merchant ships steaming in orderly array, he ordered his ships to take station between them, and his three destroyers to reinforce the anti-submarine screen around them. The stage was now set for the expected air attacks. An hour later the first German shadowing aircraft appeared and began to circle monotonously around, taking good care to keep outside effective gun range, while sending out regular reports of the convoy's position, course and speed. There was one CAM ship in the convoy, the *Empire Lawrence*, and the question arose whether or not to launch the Hurricane fighter which she carried and shoot down the snooper, or to keep it for the more serious trouble which was certain to arrive before long, for the prevailing good weather in which the convoy was now sailing was all to the enemy's advantage. It was wisely decided to keep the one and only fighter, for the time being.

During the afternoon of the 25th the homeward-bound convoy QP12 comprising 15 ships passed hull-down to the westward. This convoy was not sighted by the enemy until the morning of that day. Its CAM ship's fighter shot down the reporting aircraft, and although it was shadowed during the afternoon by other aircraft, no attacks developed, the convoy reaching Iceland four days later.

But for PQ16 trouble was just beginning.

Just after 8.30 p.m. that day a squadron of 12 Ju.88 dive-bombers was sighted approaching from the east. Following their usual tactics, they closed from astern, peeling off to attack at a height of between 15 and 20 thousand feet, and diving on their targets with a fearsome whine. They were greeted with a barrage of gun-fire, which filled the blue sky with the black and yellow plumes of bursting shell and this, interspersed with the crump of bursting bombs, helped to drown the spine-chilling noise of the attackers. After half an hour the enemy withdrew minus two of their number and their only success, a near-miss which damaged the S.S. *Carlton* sufficiently to necessitate her return to Iceland in tow of the trawler *Northern Spray*: a long and difficult voyage with small hope of support against air attack. Coordinated with the dive-bombing attack was one by seven Heinkel torpedo-carrying aircraft, and this threat was considered worthy of being dealt with by the *Empire Lawrence*'s one-shot Hurricane fighter. A tongue of flame on the ship's forecastle announced the aircraft's departure, and roaring into the attack, the pilot, Flight Lieutenant Hay, shot one down and seriously damaged another, and generally so broke up the attack that not one of the torpedoes found its mark. Unfortunately, the gunners in the convoy mistook the returning Hurricane for an enemy, and shot it down just as the pilot was preparing to 'ditch', severely wounding him. Prompt action by the destroyer *Volunteer* caused him to be rescued quickly and he lived to tell the tale, but not so his parent ship, as we shall see later.

With the sun shining throughout the whole 24 hours of an Arctic summer's day, words such as morning, noon and night no longer had their customary significance, and for the next ten hours the Germans carried out a series of tip and run raids which kept the gun crews on the *qui vive* and prevented them from getting any rest. It was this endurance factor which played such an important part in the defence of these convoys: in winter the cold and appalling weather, and in summer the possibility of air attack all round the clock.

In the early hours of the morning of the 26th the U-boats which had been skulking round the convoy ever since the previous day, waiting for a chance to attack but kept at a safe distance by a strong and alert anti-submarine screen, decided to take advantage of the poor sonar conditions prevailing. Just after 3 a.m. one of them managed to approach undetected and torpedo the S.S. *Syros*, which soon afterwards went down, 28 out of 37 of her crew being rescued by the minesweeper *Hazard* and the trawler *Lady Madeleine*.

By now the convoy was about 250 miles to the west-south-west of Bear Island, and the time had come for Rear-Admiral Burrough to act in accordance with his instructions and withdraw the cruiser force, so that he could patrol between the convoy and the Norwegian coast and thus be in a position to intercept the pocket battleships if they were sent to attack it. His departure meant that the anti-aircraft fire power of the convoy and its escort was seriously reduced but, as we have seen, Admiral Tovey decided that this had to be accepted.

The only air attack on the 26th took place after the withdrawal of the cruisers and was made by a mixed force of dive- and torpedo bombers. It would seem that the enemy, unaware of the weakening in the convoy's defences and remembering their previous reception, were reluctant to press home their attacks, with the result that they failed to score a single hit. Meanwhile, the escorts were kept busy driving off the U-boats which, growing bolder as a result of their one success, sought hard to repeat it. But Commander Onslow was not deceived by the lull in the air battle. He still had nearly four days' steaming and the most dangerous part of the voyage ahead of him, and he knew that once the Germans realised that the cruisers had gone they would press home their attacks with greater resolution. The only ships now remaining in the escort force with the ability to engage the Ju.88's before the latter dived to the attack were the A/A ship *Alynbank*, and the new destroyer *Martin*, whose 4.7-inch guns had the elevation necessary to enable them to be used in an A/A as well as the normal low-angle role. For the rest they had to depend on a variety of close-range weapons such as 2-pounder pom-pom, 40-mm Bofors, Oerlikon, and machine guns, which could not prevent an aircraft from releasing its bombs although they might hope to damage or even destroy it afterwards.

At 3.20 a.m. on the 27th the convoy was obliged to alter course to the south-east for two hours to avoid heavy pack ice, and soon afterwards the trawler *Lady Madeleine*, stationed on its port side, sighted a squadron of Heinkel torpedo aircraft hovering above the horizon waiting to pounce. However, they failed to press home their attack, but eight hours later the Germans renewed the assault with real determination and all the variety at their command. The sky had now clouded over, the ceiling being about 3,000 feet, which enabled the enemy to take up position unseen. High-level, dive- and torpedo bombers delivered their attacks from all sides simultaneously on merchant ships and escort vessels alike. The calm sea, so unusual in these stormy latitudes, was soon a forest of white plumes thrown up by the bursting bombs. The weight of the attack almost overwhelmed the defences, but warships and merchantmen fought back grimly against this savage onslaught which continued for nearly three hours. The first ship to succumb was the S.S. *Alamar*, followed soon afterwards by the American ship *Mormacsul*, near-missed by two bombs which split open her seams and she at once started to settle. At 2 p.m. six aircraft singled out the 12,000-ton CAM ship *Empire Lawrence* and dived on her from astern. Minutes later, when the smoke of the bursting bombs had cleared away all that remained of the ship and her cargo was a wrecked lifeboat in a pool of oil, together with a few bodies. The trawler *Lady Madeleine* succeeded in rescuing 16 of the ship's crew, some of them so badly wounded that they succumbed to their injuries soon afterwards.

Other disasters soon followed. Near misses damaged the American ship *City of Joliet* and the British *Empire Baffin*. The Polish destroyer *Garland*, near-missed by a bomb which on exploding detonated three more in the air above her, was swept by a hail of splinters which put both her forward guns out of action and covered her decks with killed and wounded men. With smoke billowing from her forecastle she continued to fight back with her remaining guns until ordered by the Escort Commander to proceed at her best speed to Murmansk and land her 43 casualties. The Russian tanker *Stari Bolshevik* had been hit and was on fire. Her crew, which included a number of women, fought the flames with superb courage and refused to abandon their ship. With the assistance of the French corvette *Roselys* they succeeded in getting the fire under control and in bringing their ship safely to port.

By about 2.30 in the afternoon the attacks eased up and the convoy, now reduced to 31 ships, steamed steadily eastward, with the *Stari Bolshevik* bringing up the rear under a towering pillar of smoke. Away to the north the blue-green edge of the ice was faintly discernible, and Commander Onslow decided that it was a suitable moment to alter the course of the convoy towards it so as to increase his distance from the enemy shore and to take advantage of the thicker weather which there appeared to be in that direction. The strain of the ordeal was beginning to tell on the gun crews of both warships and merchantmen, and although there was yet another three days to go, ammunition in several ships was beginning to run low.

Apart from an ineffective attack by eight Ju.88's at 5.20 p.m., there was a lull in the action until 7.45 p.m. when the enemy returned with dive-bombing and torpedo attacks. The ammunition ship *Empire Purcell* was hit by two bombs and blew up with a deafening roar in a flash of orange flame, seconds after her crew had abandoned her. A torpedo found its mark on the *Lowther Castle* which quickly filled and sank, then the Commodore's ship S.S. *Ocean Voice*, was hit and set on fire, a huge hole being torn in her side above the water line, but she managed to keep her station in the convoy and put out the fire. With every attack the Escort Commander's anxiety about the ammunition situation grew and he signalled all ships to exercise strict economy in its use. During the pseudo-night the corvette *Hyderabad* managed to transfer ammunition to some of the American ships which had expended their outfits. As Admiral Morison, U.S.N., has recorded, 'The United States was still unable to provide adequate armament or gun crews for all American cargo vessels',[1] and some had nothing larger than .30 machine-guns. Early next morning the *City of Joliet* sank as a result of her damage.

Help now came to the hard-pressed convoy in the form of low cloud and mist which enveloped and hid it from the prying eyes of the enemy aircraft which could still be heard circling overhead. At the same time the temperature fell rapidly, ice formed on masts, rigging and decks, but at long last the exhausted gun crews were able to snatch some sleep. During the forenoon of 28 May three Russian destroyers loomed up out of the mist and joined the escort, a welcome sign that the end of the voyage was approaching. Four Ju.88's made a faint-hearted attack

---

[1] *U.S. Naval Operations,* Vol. I, p. 171.

during the day, but the unfavourable weather discouraged further attempts. However, the following day when the convoy was obliged to alter course to the south to steer for the Kola Inlet, the weather cleared and the enemy returned. But the gun crews, refreshed by sleep and reinforced by the fire of the Russian destroyers, which seemed to be particularly effective, prevented the enemy from inflicting any further damage. However, that evening, after the Archangel section of the convoy, comprising six ships escorted by the A/A ship *Alynbank*, the destroyer *Martin*, and the two minesweepers, had parted company from the main body, which was then left without any long-range radar, the Germans mounted another heavy assault, 15 aircraft attacking the former and 18 the Murmansk section, but miraculously both groups escaped damage. On the final day, 30 May, three further attacks were made on the Murmansk section, during which two enemy aircraft were shot down, again without damage to the convoy. Then at long last Russian fighter aircraft appeared and covered the convoy, as one by one the gallant ships filed through the narrow entrance to the Kola Inlet, in the words of Commander Onslow, 'reduced in numbers, battered and tired, but still keeping perfect station'. Seven ships had been lost, five by bombing, one torpedoed by aircraft and one by U-boat. Considering the severity and duration of the attacks, this was a remarkable achievement, which Admiral Tovey attributed to the gallantry, efficiency and tireless zeal of the officers and men of the escorts, and to the remarkable courage and determination of those of the merchant ships, whose steadiness, good gunfire and excellent station-keeping was deserving of the highest praise.[1]

The exaggerated claims made by the pilots of the Luftwaffe gave the German High Command a completely false picture of the results of their assault on the convoy, and at the same time the U-boats' lack of success confirmed Dönitz in his belief that 'U-boat operations in northern waters are gravely prejudiced by the shortness

[1] *London Gazette*, 13 October 1950, p. 5144.

of the summer nights'.[1] As a result it was decided to make the former primarily responsible for the interdiction of the north Russian convoys. Although, naturally, the enemy's views were unknown to the Admiralty, the increasing danger from air attack was the obvious conclusion to be drawn from the story of PQ16 described above. It is now known that the enemy had some 260 aircraft deployed on airfields in the vicinity of the North Cape at this time, but despite Commander Onslow's plea, fully supported by Admiral Tovey, that the anti-aircraft defences of succeeding convoys should be strengthened by the inclusion of a carrier, more CAM ships, and more A/A ships, the Admiralty did not command the means to comply with it, without weakening our forces in other areas, which in light of the general strategy of the war were considered to be of greater importance.

The Admiralty's inability to provide the convoys with adequate air support and our Russian ally's lack of suitable aircraft as well as of air crews trained in naval co-operation, led both the Commander-in-Chief Home Fleet and the Commander-in-Chief Coastal Command, Air Marshal Sir Philip Joubert, to suggest that an advanced flying boat base should be established at Spitzbergen, or alternatively that flying boats should be based at Murmansk. At the same time they suggested reconnaissance and long-range fighter aircraft should be stationed in north Russia and that a squadron of torpedo bombers should be sent to Vaenga on the Kola Inlet as a threat to operations by the German heavy ships, should these try and operate in the area east of Bear Island. The Senior British Naval Officer North Russia, Rear-Admiral R. H. L. Bevan, who had been instructed to discuss the last-named proposal with the Russians, reported that they would welcome such a move, as also did Admiral Sir Geoffrey Miles, Head of the British Military Mission in Moscow. But the Admiralty finally decided against it, since at that time Coastal Command had only two squadrons of fully trained torpedo aircraft and there was always the possibility to be guarded against that the German heavy ships

[1] *Memoirs*, p. 209.

might attempt to break out again into the Atlantic, when such aircraft might prove invaluable.

Knowing as we now do what was in the mind of the German High Command and in the light of subsequent events, the Admiralty's descision was unfortunate, but our resources in comparison with the tasks they had to perform were so limited that every move had to be considered with the greatest care. It was, however, agreed that during the passage of the next convoy eight Catalina aircraft of Nos. 210 and 240 squadrons should operate from Lake Lakhta near Archangel and from Grasnaya on the Kola Inlet.

In accordance with Mr Churchill's promise to President Roosevelt the convoys to north Russia were to sail at intervals of about three weeks, so the next one, PQ17, was due to sail on 11 June. But the need to mount an operation to relieve the island of Malta had made such a heavy demand on the strength of the Home Fleet that the sailing of the Russian convoy had to be postponed until 27 June. Had it sailed on its original date it is just possible that it might have escaped the fate which befell it, but even if it had not been selected as the target for a trial of strength between the opposing forces, the evil day would have been merely postponed.

6

A Fateful Decision

We do that in our zeal
Our calmer moments are afraid to answer
Sir Walter Scott

IN THE ADMIRALTY THE problem of the Arctic convoys was under continuous study. Hitherto the losses, although serious, could be regarded as acceptable, having regard to the difficulties to be overcome, but the greater the amount of study given to the running of these convoys during the summer months, the larger grew the misgivings of the Naval Staff. If the enemy decided to mount a combined offensive using his aircraft and U-boats to the west and his surface ships to the east of Bear Island, heavy losses appeared inevitable.

Early in June information was received from Intelligence sources which indicated that this was precisely what the enemy was contemplating. The question the Admiralty had to decide therefore, was whether to collect a force sufficiently strong to drive off the *Tirpitz* and any other ships supporting her, and at the same time provide fighter protection for both the convoy, the covering and escort forces, as well as anti-submarine forces to deal with the U-boat threat to be expected, throughout the whole length of the convoy's voyage. It was certainly possible to mount such an operation, but to do so would have entailed withdrawing ships from theatres where they were needed for other equally important operations which in turn would have been seriously affected if any of the carriers or capital ships had been lost or badly damaged.

It meant, as Mr Churchill says, 'engaging a force vital to us out of proportion to the actual military importance of the Arctic Convoys'.[1] The military importance to which he refers will be discussed later, but it is well to consider briefly what might have happened had the Admiralty pursued this course of action. In the light of what we now know about the German intentions, it is clear that they would not have risked a surface action against superior forces, so the threat offered by the *Tirpitz* would have remained, but there would certainly have been a furious air battle. The Fleet Air Arm was still very poorly equipped as regards fighters and those it had were greatly inferior to those in the Luftwaffe, which were shore-based. As a result, some of our sorely needed carriers, which would have been the Luftwaffe's primary targets, would probably have been put out of action, if not sunk. As already mentioned, thermal conditions in these waters were in favour of the U-boats, and damaged ships, as experience had shown, were therefore an easy prey for them. On the whole it may be said that the Admiralty was

[1] *The Second World War,* Vol. IV, p. 239.

right to resist the temptation of a trial of strength with the Germans in circumstances so favourable to the latter. As Admiral Tovey has recorded, 'The strategical situation thus produced was wholly favourable to the enemy. His heavy ships would be operating close to their own coast, with the support of powerful shore-based air reconnaissance and striking forces, and protected if he so desired, by a screen of U-boats in the channels between Spitzbergen and Norway. Our covering forces on the other hand, if they entered these waters, would be without shore-based air support, one thousand miles from their base and with their destroyers too short of fuel to escort a damaged ship to harbour.'[1]

The endurance of the destroyers was, as we have seen, a dominant factor in all these operations. It could only be met by fuelling at sea, and although this was done whenever possible, there was always the uncertainty of accomplishment provided by enemy action and the weather conditions in the area.

Admiral Tovey's solution to defeat the enemy's plan was to reverse the course of the convoy for 12 or maybe 18 hours when it was halfway between Jan Mayen and Bear Islands, in order to lure the enemy into the western half of the area where our heavy ships could attack him. This might also provide our submarines with better targets. It was his intention that the plan would only be put into operation if there was evidence to show that the enemy had put to sea, and if the weather was suitable for air reconnaissance. There was no point in delaying the convoy's progress if the enemy were unaware of its position. The Admiralty, however, did not agree with the Commander-in-Chief's plan, although they were prepared to concede that circumstances might arise in which they (and not the Commander-in-Chief) would consider it desirable to order such a movement. It is by no means certain that Admiral Tovey's plan would have worked, because the enemy could afford to choose his moment for attack and was under no obligation to accept a position of disadvantage.

---

[1] *London Gazette*, 18 October 1950, p. 5144.

When Admiral Tovey learned that PQ17, like the previous convoy, was to consist of 35 ships, he suggested to the First Sea Lord that it should be run in two sections, as he still adhered to his opinion that large convoys were undesirable. It was during an unrecorded telephone conversation between them on this point that Admiral Tovey first learned that Admiral Pound had it in mind to order the convoy to scatter should it be assailed in the Barents Sea by a powerful German surface force which included the *Tirpitz*. The order to a convoy to scatter is an accepted naval principle in ocean warfare where a group of merchant ships is attacked by an enemy surface force greatly superior to that escorting it. It had been used successfully when a 37-ship convoy escorted only by the armed merchant cruiser *Jervis Bay* was attacked by the pocket battleship *Scheer* in mid-Atlantic, but the circumstances were entirely different in the Barents Sea, where lack of sea-room caused by the pack ice to the north prevented ships from escaping out of range of German shore-based aircraft. Moreover, experience had shown that mutual support was essential in the face of both air and U-boat attack, so that from every point of view Admiral Pound's suggestion came as a profound shock to Admiral Tovey.

It was not until the day the convoy was due to sail that the Admiralty issued instructions regarding the conduct of the forces engaged in the operation. These stated *inter alia* that the safety of the convoy against surface attack to the west of Bear Island must be met by our surface forces and to the east of that island must depend on our submarines; that the cruiser covering force was not intended to go east of Bear Island unless the convoy was threatened by the presence of a surface force which the cruisers could fight (that is, which did not include the *Tirpitz*); and in any case they were not to go beyond the longitude of the North Cape (25°E.). It will be noted that the Admiralty accepted the fact that if the *Tirpitz* were used to attack the convoy to the east of Bear Island, only the slender chance that she might be torpedoed by a submarine stood between the convoy and annihilation. It can be asked whether it was sound policy to send merchant ships into these waters with the scales weighted so heavily against them. As one Flag Officer had pointed out, the navy was paid to run such risks and warships with their high speed had some hope of avoiding the bombs and torpedoes aimed at them, but a slow, plodding merchantman had not that advantage. The answer is that the decision to continue running the convoys was made at the highest political level in the face of contrary naval advice, and the Admiralty having done its duty by remonstrance, had no option but to carry out the Government's instruction.

In general, the dispositions made for the protection of convoys PQ17 and QP13 and finally agreed with the Admiralty were similar to those employed for the previous convoys. The close escort under Commander J. E. Broome, R.N., in the *Keppel* consisted of six destroyers, four corvettes, three minesweepers and four A/S trawlers. Two A/A ships, *Palomares* and *Pozarika,* were included as well as one CAM ship, the *Empire Tide,* together with two submarines. An oiler sailed with the convoy and another one with a destroyer as escort, was to sail separately, and after fuelling the convoy escorts would transfer to the homeward-bound convoy, which was to sail simultaneously with PQ17. Close cover was to be provided by the British, cruisers *London* and *Norfolk* and the U.S. cruisers *Tuscaloosa* and *Witchita,* all under the command of Rear-Admiral L. K. H. Hamilton flying his flag in the *London*, with three destroyers in company. Heavy cover would be given by a force consisting of the battleship *Duke of York* flying the flag of the Commander-in-Chief Home Fleet, the U.S. battleship *Washington* flying the flag of Rear-Admiral Giffen, the carrier *Victorious* flying the flag of Vice-Admiral Sir Bruce Fraser, the cruiser *Nigeria* flying the flag of Vice-Admiral H. M. Burrough, the cruiser *Cumberland*, and 14 destroyers.

In an attempt to deceive the enemy, a dummy convoy consisting of five minelayers and four colliers, escorted by the cruisers *Sirius* and *Curaçao*, five destroyers and a few trawlers, was to simulate a raiding force bound for southern Norway, which it was hoped would draw the enemy's forces away from the other two convoys, especially as the movements of the battle fleet would be adjusted to give the impression of covering this supposed raiding force. In the event, the ruse failed, as the Germans did not sight the dummy convoy on either of the two attempts made to attract their attention to it, nor do they appear to have noticed it when it was ostentatiously anchored in Scapa Flow.

As recorded in the last chapter, Catalina aircraft of Coastal Command had been transferred to Grasnoya on the Kola Inlet, and these were to maintain patrols over the area east of Bear Island through which the convoy would pass.

Eight British, one French and two Russian submarines were established on patrol in areas off the North Cape, the Russians occupying the two inshore ones. These zones were to be moved east as the convoy passed north of them.

As a final, and almost clairvoyant touch, three rescue ships were included in the convoy—*Zaafaran, Rathlin* and *Zamelek*. These were small passenger ships of about 1,200 tons which had been specially fitted out for rescuing the crews of torpedoed merchant ships. They carried a small medical staff and equipment for the treatment of casualties, and proved invaluable as a means of saving life.

While the Admiralty and the Commander-in-Chief Home Fleet had been agreeing the measures to be taken for the protection of the next pair of convoys to and from north Russia, the German Naval command had been working on a plan to which they gave the name of *Roesselsprung* or 'Knight's Move'. It provided for an attack in force on the next convoy located sailing to Murmansk. The name seems to have had no particular significance, but it has a Wagnerian overtone. Up to now attacks on the convoys had been made by air, surface or submarine forces acting independently and in small groups, but this was to be a carefully coordinated attack in overwhelming strength.

The surface forces were organised in two groups: (a) the Trondheim group, comprising the battleship *Tirpitz* flying the flag of Admiral Schniewind, and the cruiser *Hipper*, together with six destroyers, and (b) the Narvik group, comprising the pocket battleships *Lützow* and *Scheer*, with six destroyers.

Three U-boats were to be in station on patrol north-east of Iceland by 10 June, to locate and report the movements of the convoy, and up to five more would be sent to patrol off Bear Island.

As regards the air, it was emphasised that extensive reconnaissance was essential to carry out the following tasks: (a) to maintain touch with the convoy and report the composition and strength of the Escort Force, and (b) to locate the heavy enemy forces. To do this, it would be necessary to cover the area enclosed by the Shetlands, Faroes, Iceland and Jan Mayen Islands, as well as the anchorages at Scapa, the Firth of Forth, Moray Firth and Reykjavik. Continuous contact to be maintained with any force located. If no heavy force were sighted, then an area 250 miles round the convoy must be carefully searched and patrolled. To prevent unfortunate incidents occurring, aircraft were to be instructed to attack only aircraft carriers and merchant ships unless the identity of the target was unmistakable. Operational command was entrusted to Group North (Admiral Carls) at Kiel, while tactical command would be exercised by the Fleet Commander in the *Tirpitz*. Group North also had control of the U-boats through the Flag Officer at Narvik (Admiral Schmundt). The object was the rapid destruction of the merchant ships and if this did not prove feasible, as many as possible were to be crippled and left to the U-boats and the Luftwaffe to finish off. If necessary, the *Tirpitz* and the *Hipper* would deal with the escort forces while the *Lützow* and *Scheer* concentrated on the merchant ships. Engagement with superior enemy forces was to be avoided, and every endeavour made to complete the operation before the enemy battleship covering force could intervene. Finally, both Group North and the Fleet Commander were given authority to cancel the operation at their discretion.

Admiral Raeder presented the plan to Hitler on 15 June and carefully explained the details with the aid of a chart. He emphasised all the favourable factors, such as the weather, and how the position of the ice edge, would oblige the convoy to remain within 200 to 250 miles of the Norwegian airfields for the latter part of its voyage. In particular, he pointed out the way in which the Luftwaffe dominated the Barents Sea, into which no enemy heavy ship had so far dared to sail. Further, he assured the Führer that the operation would only take place if the risk of meeting superior enemy forces was negligible and provided the Luftwaffe could ensure adequate air cover.

As always, Hitler's main concern was to avoid damage to his heavy ships, to which he considered aircraft were a great threat. He insisted that the enemy carriers must be located and put out of action by the Luftwaffe prior to any attack taking place. This restriction virtually vetoed the operation, since there could be no certainty that the carriers would be located or that they would be put out of action if they were. But Raeder knew better than to argue the point, and in an effort to circumvent this restriction he arranged for the operation to be carried out in two stages. As soon as the convoys were located, the Trondheim group would proceed up the coast to the Vestfiord, and the Narvik group to Altenfiord in the vicinity of the North Cape, where they would refuel. On receipt of a code word which would be sent when Hitler's sanction to the operation had been obtained, the two squadrons would proceed to rendezvous in a position 100 miles north of the North Cape, from which they would attack the convoy to the eastwards of Bear Island between longitude 20° and 30° E.

The two convoys sailed as planned on 27 June, and we will begin by following the progress of PQ17 under Commodore J. C. K. Dowding, R.N.R., all the ships of which had been routed to Archangel, Murmansk having been put temporarily out of action by bombing. One merchant ship grounded on leaving Reykjavik and another was damaged by drift ice in the Denmark Strait and had to return, so the convoy was reduced to 33 ships and the tanker *Gray Ranger*. The last-mentioned also received ice damage and so later changed places with the escorted tanker *Aldersdale*, which accompanied the convoy for the rest of its journey.

At noon on 1 July the convoy was located by enemy shadowing aircraft which, except for some brief intervals when it ran into fog, kept it under observation for the remainder of the voyage. The weather was fine and calm and the opportunity was taken to top up all the escort vessels with fuel. U-boats were sighted on the surface at some distance from the convoy and were put down by the escorts, although one approached close enough to fire torpedoes from which the convoy had to turn away. In the afternoon the homeward-bound QP13 passed. At about 6 p.m. nine torpedo-carrying aircraft made an unsuccessful attack on the convoy which had meanwhile been overtaken by Rear-Admiral Hamilton with his four cruisers. He decided to remain some 40 miles to the north out of sight of shadowing aircraft, so as to conceal his whereabouts from the enemy, and he hoped a favourable situation might develop which would enable him to engage the pocket battleships without the *Tirpitz*, but he was, of course, on the wrong side of the convoy to prevent the German ships from attacking it. On the evening of 2 July the convoy ran into fog, which lasted until the forenoon of the next day and enabled it to alter course to the east towards Bear Island without being observed by the enemy. Although the shadowing aircraft were temporarily thrown off the scent by this move several U-boats still remained in contact. During the afternoon Rear-Admiral Hamilton, having decided that the time had now come to disclose his presence to the enemy, closed to within 20 miles of the convoy, and believing he had been seen by a shadowing aircraft, he opened out again to his former distance, but in fact the enemy had not sighted his force. Soon afterwards he received a signal from the Admiralty informing him that the edge of the pack ice was further north than had been supposed, so he ordered his flagship to fly off her aircraft with a message to the senior officer of the escort, instructing him to pass 70 miles north of Bear Island and try to keep outside a range of 400 miles from Banak airfield, where it was believed the enemy had a heavy concentration of aircraft. Commander Broome, whose main consideration, as his instructions laid down, was to make as much easting as possible while the going was good, did not alter the course of the convoy as much to the north as his Admiral intended. At about 10.15 p.m. the cruiser force again closed the convoy, and this time it was sighted and reported by shadowing aircraft, which was just what Rear-Admiral Hamilton wished, for shortly before he had received information of the movements of the enemy surface ships. The presence of the two U.S. cruisers appears at first to have deceived the German pilots who reported them as aircraft carriers and the *London* as a battleship.

For several days previously, it had not been possible to obtain air reconnaissance of the German ships' anchorages, but on 3 July an aircraft was able to report that the *Tirpitz* and the *Hipper* were not in their accustomed berths at Trondheim. An attempted reconnaissance of Narvik was again unsuccessful. In fact, stage 1 of Operation *Roesselsprung* had been implemented on the afternoon of the previous day, 2 July, when the *Scheer* and *Lützow* accompanied by six destroyers sailed for Altenfiord, and the *Tirpitz* and *Hipper* with four destroyers for the Lofoten Islands off the entrance to the Vestfiord. The *Lützow* grounded while leaving her anchorage and took no further part in the operation but the other three ships moved to their appointed stations. Three destroyers of the *Tirpitz* group also ran ashore, and this left it with only one.

Early on the morning of 4 July a lone Heinkel torpedo bomber dived through a hole in the fog covering the convoy and torpedoed the American ship *Christopher Newport* which, after her crew had been taken off by a rescue ship, had to be sunk. The sea at the time was described as smooth as glass and the ceiling as between only 300 and 500 feet.

The Admiralty now knew that something was afoot with regard to the German ships, but their information was largely negative since they had no idea whether the former had gone to sea, or whether they were biding their time in one of the many fiords with which the north coast of Norway abounds. As a precautionary measure it was decided to give Rear-Admiral Hamilton discretion to proceed eastward of the limit previously laid down (the longitude of the North Cape) if the situation was thought to demand it, and unless otherwise ordered by Admiral Tovey. The Commander in Chief, however, did not consider that the information so far available regarding the enemy warranted 'a reversal of the policy agreed between the Admiralty and myself', which the reader will recall established that the safety of the convoy eastwards of the meridian of Bear Island must depend on our submarines. He accordingly ordered the cruisers to withdraw as soon as the convoy passed east of the North Cape, or earlier at the cruiser Admiral's discretion, unless the Admiralty could assure him that they were unlikely to encounter the *Tirpitz*. Rear-Admiral Hamilton, who had intended remaining in the vicinity of the convoy pending a clarification of the situation, but in any case not later than 2 p.m. on 5 July (by which time he would have been well into the Barents Sea) replied to Admiral Tovey's message to the effect that he intended withdrawing to the westward on completion of the refuelling of his destroyers, which he expected would be finished by 10 p.m. But at 7.30 p.m. the Admiralty told him to remain with the convoy pending the receipt of further instructions and of information which it was expected would shortly be available. He was at the time zig-zagging between 10 and 20 miles ahead of the convoy, which since 4.45 p.m. had been steering to the north-eastward to open the distance from Banak airfield. Two air attacks now took place; the first one at 7.30 p.m. was a somewhat half-hearted and unsuccessful affair by a number of dive-bomber and torpedo aircraft, but an hour later 25 torpedo aircraft made a more determined attack. Coming in fast and low, the leader succeeded in hitting the S.S. *Navarino* with two torpedoes before crashing in flames at the head of the convoy. The rest of the wing were not so bold, but they succeeded in torpedoing two more ships, the *William Hooper* and the Russian tanker *Azerbaijan*, but only the former together with the *Navarino* were lost, the tanker eventually reaching port safely. Once again the rescue ships proved their worth by the speedy rescue of the crews of the stricken ships.

Despite the losses recorded above, there was a quiet

feeling of confidence among the escort vessels and the ships of the convoy that providing that ammunition held out they could give a good account of themselves in any further action which the Luftwaffe decided to take. But while these attacks had been in progress, 2,000 miles away in Whitehall a conference was being held on the result of which the fate of these 30 well-found, heavily laden merchantmen and their crews was to depend.

In a room at the Admiralty the First Sea Lord with the Vice-Chief of the Naval Staff and some half dozen senior officers concerned with operational convoys sat discussing a situation which all had foreseen but to which, as has been stated, there was no satisfactory answer. In front of them lay a chart on which the latest information regarding both British and German ships was plotted and included circles showing the farthest positions which the latter could reach at various times as well as the estimated course and positions of Admiral Tovey's fleet and the convoy at corresponding hours. All that was known of the German ships was that they had left their anchorages and might therefore, even at that moment, be steering towards the ill-fated convoy which it was calculated they could reach by 2 a.m. the next day. This last, with Rear-Admiral Hamilton's cruiser force, was now 130 miles north-east of Bear Island, and Admiral Tovey with the Home Fleet was cruising in an area 350 miles to the west of it. One possibility was to reverse the course of the convoy and for the battle fleet to steer towards it at high speed until the two were within air-striking range of one another, which could have been about 2 a.m., i.e. the same time as the German ships might arrive. While such action would doubtless have kept them from attacking, it would have meant challenging the whole strength of the Luftwaffe in north Norway with one carrier, whose aircraft were not a match for those of the enemy. It also meant delaying the eastward progress of the convoy to no purpose, unless the fleet could continue to cover it until it was beyond the likely range of attack. This, as we have seen, the Admiralty were not prepared to sanction.

Another course was to withdraw the cruisers, which were no match for the *Tirpitz*, and leave the convoy to continue its course with its destroyer escort in the hope that by the use of smoke and the threat of torpedo attack some ships might be preserved from destruction. This had the merit of keeping the ships concentrated for mutual support against air and U-boat attack and there was always the possibility of fog descending to assist them.

Finally, there was the possibility of ordering the convoy to scatter in the hope that the German surface forces would not be willing to remain long enough in the area to round up individual ships, and although some would be sunk, a reasonable proportion might escape. The disadvantage of this plan was that once the convoy had scattered it would be impossible to reassemble it, and all cohesion in defence against both air and U-boat attack would be irretrievably lost.

It is evident that the threat of attack by the *Tirpitz* was uppermost in the mind of the First Sea Lord. He considered it to be the most serious of the three. Bad weather might save the convoy from air attack, the perpetual daylight was a hindrance to the U-boats, but only fog could prevent an attack by the surface ships. As already mentioned, he had turned the situation over in his mind long before it actually happened, and reached the conclusion that scattering the convoy was, in the circumstances, the right solution. Although the general feeling of the conference over which he was now presiding was against such action, the arguments advanced were not such as to cause him to change his opinion. When everyone present had had his say, he closed his eyes for a moment while he made up his mind, then turning to the Director of the Signal Division he said: 'Tell the cruisers to withdraw to the west at high speed, and the convoy to disperse.' In the whole of his long and distinguished career Admiral Pound could never have been called upon to make a more fateful decision.

7

The Ill-starred Convoys

The moist star upon whose influence Neptune's empire stands
Was sick almost to doomsday with eclipse

Hamlet

WHEN AT ABOUT 10 P.M. on 4 July Rear-Admiral Hamilton received the Admiralty's signal prefixed 'Most Immediate'—'Cruiser force withdraw to the westward at high speed', he assumed that the further information he had been promised was of so portentous a nature as to require drastic action. A few minutes later he received the further instruction, this time prefixed only 'Immediate'—'Owing to threat from surface ships the convoy is to disperse and proceed to Russian ports', but this was followed by another 'Most Immediate' message referring to the previous one, 'Convoy is to scatter'. The difference in meaning between 'disperse' and 'scatter' is important. Ships in convoy ordered to disperse would merely cease to keep formation, and each ship would proceed at her best speed to her destination. Since in the present instance all ships were bound for the same port, Archangel, they would obviously remain in fairly close company with each other for some hours. On the other hand, ships ordered to scatter immediately 'star', that is they proceed in accordance with a plan laid down on courses which will separate them from each other as quickly as possible. If there had been any doubt in Hamilton's mind about the imminence of surface action with the German fleet, it was completely dispelled by both the prefix and the wording of the last of the three messages, and the same interpretation was made by Commander Broome, who had also received them. The instructions to the senior officer of the destroyers clearly laid down that in the event of an attack on the convoy by a surface force greatly superior to the escort force, it was his duty to shadow the enemy

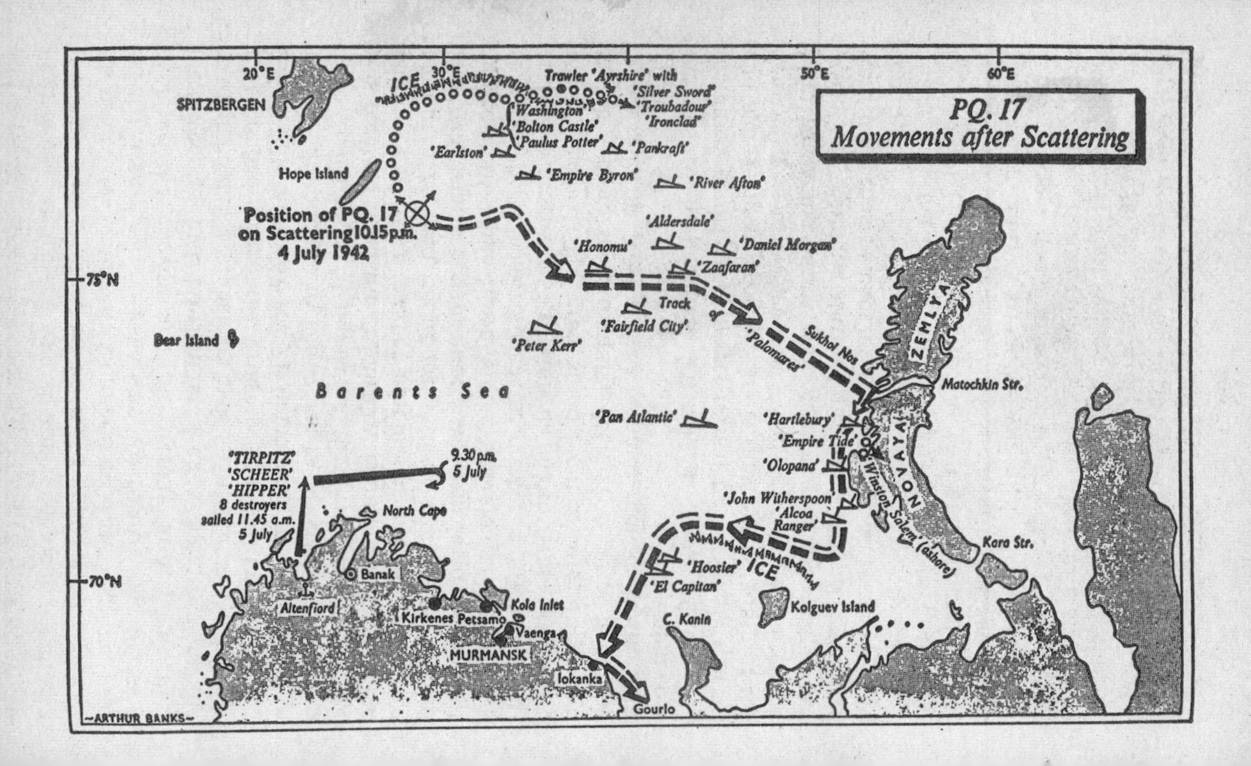
PQ. 17
Movements after Scattering
20°E
30°E
50°E
60°E
75°N
70°N
SPITZBERGEN
ICE
Trawler 'Ayrshire' with
'Silver Sword'
'Troubadour'
'Ironclad'
'Washington'
'Bolton Castle'
'Paulus Potter'
'Earlston'
'Pankraft'
'Empire Byron'
'River Afton'
Hope Island
Position of PQ. 17
on Scattering 10.15 p.m.
4 July 1942
'Aldersdale'
'Honomu'
'Daniel Morgan'
'Zaafaran'
Track
of
'Fairfield City'
'Peter Kerr'
'Palomares'
Sukhoi Nos
ZEMLYA
Matochkin Str.
Bear Island
Barents Sea
'Pan Atlantic'
'Hartlebury'
'Empire Tide'
'Olopana'
NOVAYA
'Winston Salem' (ashore)
'John Witherspoon'
'Alcoa Ranger'
'TIRPITZ'
'SCHEER'
'HIPPER'
8 destroyers
sailed 11.45 a.m.
5 July
9.30 p.m.
5 July
North Cape
Banak
'Hoosier'
ICE
'El Capitan'
Kara Str.
Altenfiord
Kirkenes
Petsamo
Kola Inlet
Vaenga
MURMANSK
C. Kanin
Kolguev Island
Iokanka
Gourlo
~ARTHUR BANKS~

and seize any opportunity favourably presented to attack him; hence he decided that it was incumbent on him to join the cruiser force. So at 10.15 p.m., having passed the order to scatter to Commodore Dowding, he proceeded accordingly. As he said afterwards, the decision to leave the convoy and the weakly armed corvettes, minesweepers and trawlers at such a moment was the hardest he had ever had to make. Unfortunately, the fact that he had joined the cruisers was not known to the Commander-in-Chief for 21 hours and this was the subject of subsequent criticism which is discussed later.

It so happened that just as the first urgent message was received from the Admiralty, Hamilton's flagship the *Norfolk* had flown off her amphibian aircraft on an ice patrol, so he held on to his easterly course for half an hour while unsuccessful efforts were made to recall it. It subsequently came down in the sea alongside the A/A ship *Palomares* who rescued the crew and towed the aircraft to Matochkin Strait, and thence to Archangel where it was beached. The crew stood by their aircraft for two months before the Admiralty decided to write it off, by which time the *Norfolk* had recommissioned, so the pilot (Lieut. (A) R. Wignall, R.N.V.R.) never found out exactly why he had been left behind. It was 10.30 p.m., therefore, before the cruisers turned to a westerly course, and increasing speed to 25 knots they passed south of the convoy so as to be between it and the probable direction from which the enemy was momentarily expected to appear. The visibility at the time was extreme, but there were numerous patches of fog, as well as some icebergs about.

The carrying out of his instructions was as distressing to Admiral Hamilton as it was to Commander Broome, and the former expressed his feelings in a message to his force which read: 'I know you will all be as distressed as I am to leave that fine collection of ships to find their own way to harbour.' He was also disturbed about the possible effect this sudden withdrawal of naval support would have on the morale of the merchant ships' crews. Since they were unaware of the reason for his action he thought it must seem to them as though his ships were 'running away at high speed'. Had he known that the Admiralty's instructions were based on conjecture rather than on positive information, he certainly would not have withdrawn so hurriedly, but the impression conveyed by the messages he had received was one of imminent danger.

The order to scatter his convoy also came as an unexpected and unpleasant surprise to Commodore Dowding, so much so that he twice asked for it to be repeated. When repetition confirmed his worst fears he was led to infer from the suddenness with which it had been given that an attack by enemy surface ships was about to occur. To the masters of the merchant ships who knew nothing of the reasons which had brought about the situation with which they were now faced, it was a moment they would never forget. At the Convoy Conference in Iceland before sailing they had been warned that the going would be tough, but they took comfort from the presence of the escort force which was to protect them in their hour of need. Now they had been ordered to scatter, and the major portion of that force was fast disappearing over the western horizon. Yet when the fateful signal was executed, the 30 merchantmen carried out the manoeuvre with the precision of a well-drilled fleet. Soon some ships were steering north towards the ice, some south towards the enemy's coast, some west to retrace their steps, while others continued in the direction of their destination. Since there were nearly as many ships as there are points of the compass, it was only natural that the less independent among the masters should keep together for mutual support and company, and so it was.

It did not take the enemy long to appreciate the advantage he had been given. His aircraft, no longer obliged to face the concentrated fire of a well-guarded convoy, could now afford to press home their attacks and take deliberate aim. The U-boats, thankful to be rid of the ever watchful destroyers, which had kept them at a distance for the past five days, could boldly surface and use their higher speed to chase after the ships whose positions were reported by their aircraft. In the air and on the sea the hunt was on, the massacre was about to begin.

One of the first victims, the *Empire Byron*, fell to a

U-boat early on 5 July, while to the north of her four ships, *Earlston, Washington, Bolton Castle* and *Paulus Potter*, succumbed to a joint onslaught by dive-bombers and U-boats. Later the *Pankraft*, proceeding alone, shared the same fate. Soon after midday the Commodore's ship *River Afton* was overtaken by a U-boat and sent to the bottom, as was the *Carlton.* In the late afternoon the *Fairfield City*, and the *Daniel Morgan* which had been sheltering in a bank of fog, emerged and were immediately set upon by patrolling aircraft. Three Ju.88's dived on the former and as three sticks of bombs enveloped her, she rapidly started to settle. Her consort fought back fiercely and successfully dodged nine sticks of bombs aimed at her. Her 3-inch gun winged two of her attackers before it jammed, but after two more attacks she started to take in water as a result of a plenitude of near misses, and had to be abandoned. A U-boat promptly surfaced and gave her a *coup de grâce*, and after interrogating the survivors and indicating the course to steer to the nearest land, departed in search of further victims. A group comprising the minesweeper *Salamander*, the tanker *Aldersdale*, the *Ocean Freedom*, and the rescue ship *Zaafaran* was attacked by aircraft and both the tanker and the rescue ship were sunk. Happily the *Salamander* was able to rescue all the crew of the former and some of the latter, immediately the attack was over. Another victim of air attack was the *Peter Kerr*, and U-boats despatched the *Honomu.* In the first 24 hours of their onslaught the enemy sank 12 ships, bringing the total with the three ships previously sunk, to 15, more than twice the losses yet sustained by any convoy to north Russia.

But the end was not yet. The following day German aircraft scouring the area for more targets came across the *Pan Atlantic* steaming alone, and in a matter of minutes she was on fire and sinking. The U-boats, appreciating that by now the surviving ships might be heading for the Novaya Zemlya coast, raced ahead to intercept them, and between 6 and 8 July sank the *Hartlebury, Olopana, John Witherspoon* and *Alcoa Ranger*, all of which appear to have made the land and were heading south for the White Sea.

Meanwhile, an ominous warning signal from the Admiralty to the Senior British Naval Officer, North Russia, informing him that the most likely time of surface attack was the night of the 5th/6th or early on the morning of the 6th, had been intercepted by the two A/A ships *Palomares* and *Pozarica*, each with a small group of corvettes and minesweepers, so they advised any ship encountered to make all possible speed to the eastward, as they themselves set course towards the coast of Novaya Zemlya. The *Palomares* group drew ahead and was joined by the two freighters *Benjamin Harrison* and *El Capitan*, and these were the first ships to reach an anchorage in the Matochkin Strait which separates the two halves of the largest island of the Novaya Zemlya group. They arrived on 7 July and soon afterwards were joined by the *Salamander* escorting the *Ocean Freedom*, and by the *Hoosier*, the *Samuel Chase* and the rescue ship *Zamelek*. When the *Pozarica* arrived nearly the whole of the remaining escort ships were collected in the anchorage. Last to arrive was the corvette *Lotus* which, regardless of the Admiralty's grim warning, had turned back to look for survivors of the *River Afton*. She found Commodore Dowding sitting on a raft in the icy water with two members of the crew and, also in the vicinity, the master and 36 other members of the ship's company.

After a hurried conference on board the *Palomares*, it was decided to vacate the anchorage as soon as possible, for the ships were at the mercy of both aircraft and U-boats should either of these locate them, so that evening the five merchant ships, escorted by the two A/A ships, three minesweepers and three trawlers, formed a small convoy and headed south for the White Sea. Almost at once they ran into dense fog and the *Benjamin Harrison* lost touch and returned to the anchorage. The others pressed on, and during the forenoon of the following day the fog lifted for a short time and course was shaped to pass to the east and south of Kolguef Island which lies only 50 miles north of the Russian mainland. From time to time the little convoy came across boatloads of survivors from ships which had been sunk, and these were taken on board the escort vessels. On the afternoon of the 9th when the south-western point of Novaya Zemlya had been reached, pack ice was seen ahead and course had to be altered to the west to get round it; later that evening it was found possible to resume a more southerly course. They were only about 60 miles off the Russian coast when at 10 p.m. they were attacked by 40 high-level bombers who, in the absence of any opposition on the part of the Russian air force, carried out four hours of systematic precision bombing of the ships below them, as a result of which two more ships, the *Hoosier* and *El Capitan*, were sunk as a consequence of repeated near misses. The *Samuel Chase*, although with many of her steam pipes fractured and her compass blown out of its binnacle, was gallantly kept going by her stout-hearted crew. The little rescue ship *Zamelek*, almost lifted bodily out of the water by the bombs bursting around her, dropped astern but managed to keep on steaming. She was loaded with survivors and had she gone down the loss of life would have been fearful. Urgent appeals for help from Russian fighter aircraft brought no response and the ordeal continued, with the two A/A ships valiantly defending their charges, theirs being the only guns effective against this form of high-level attack. It says much for the accuracy of their fire that four enemy aircraft were destroyed. At 2.30 a.m. the enemy finally withdrew, and half an hour later two Russian flying boats appeared on the scene and circled round while the convoy eased down to let the Zamelek catch up. Commodore Dowding with the *Ocean Freedom, Samuel Chase* and their escort reached Archangel the following day, and his first concern was to discover how many ships had survived the terrible onslaught to which his convoy had been subjected. He was relieved to find that two ships, the *Donbass* and the *Bellingham*, accompanied by the rescue ship *Rathlin* were already in harbour. That made four together with the two he had just brought in. There was still the *Benjamin Harrison* somewhere off the vulnerable Novaya Zemlya coast. Only five ships out of 30—it was hard to believe. Soon news began to arrive that some other ships had successfully reached the same coast, and despite all that he had endured Commodore Dowding at once set about organising an escort force to go out, find them and bring them in.

On 16 July he left Archangel in the corvette *Poppy*, with the *Lotus* (Senior Officer of the Escort Force, Lieutenant H. J. Hall, R.N.R.) and the French *La Malouine*. The calm weather of the past two weeks had now given way to storms and the three corvettes had a rough passage on their way north. They reached Byelushya Bay in the southern half of Novaya Zemlya on the 19th where they found 12 survivors of the *Oleopana* encamped ashore. Proceeding on up the coast they came across the *Winston Salem* which had run aground south-east of North Gusini Nos and was unable to free herself. They had to leave her temporarily while they continued the search. In Moller Bay they found the CAM ship *Empire Tide* with over 240 survivors on board, and running short of food, so these were distributed among the three ships and the ship herself was told to be ready to join the convoy when it returned. The following morning they reached Matochkin Strait where Commodore Dowding found five more ships of his convoy. These were the *Silver Sword, Troubadour* and *Ironclad* who owed their safety to the initiative of the Captain of the trawler *Ayrshire*, whose adventures are recounted later; the *Benjamin Harrison* and the damaged Russian tanker *Azerbaijan*. These had also been joined by a Russian icebreaker, the *Murman*, and a trawler. Commodore Dowding wasted no time in getting the ships under way and it was arranged that he should embark in the *Murman*, which it was hoped would be able to force a passage for the ships through the ice which had obliged the previous convoy to turn to the west where they had been attacked by German aircraft. It was fortunate that the five ships and their escort set out so promptly, for the following morning a U-boat reconnoitred the Matochkin Strait, and finding the anchorage empty, bombarded the Russian signal station.

Having collected the *Empire Tide* the convoy hurried south. Much fog was encountered and the voyage was marked by several U-boat alarms, during one of which the Captain of the *Murman*, much to Commodore Dowding's astonishment, having failed to persuade him to turn the convoy about, increased to full speed and left it far behind, to return later when the panic had subsided. The *Winston Salem* was still aground when they passed her, but two Russian tugs were standing by. On 22 July the escort was reinforced by the arrival of the A/A ship *Pozarica*, with three minesweepers, a corvette and two Russian destroyers, and the whole party berthed safely at Archangel on the evening of the 24th. Thanks to the efforts of the U.S. Naval Attaché who flew to her in a veteran Catalina aircraft, the *Winston Salem* was successfully refloated and reached harbour on 28 July, the last of the ill-starred convoy to do so. Thus the total number of surviving ships was brought to 11. Out of the 35 ships and a tanker which had started the voyage, two had turned back, 13 and one rescue ship had been sunk by aircraft, and 10 had fallen victims to the U-boats, at a cost to the enemy of only six aircraft. It has now been established that the enemy employed 202 aircraft during the attacks on PQ17, of which 130 were bombers, 43 torpedo and 29 reconnaissance aircraft. Of the 156,492 tons of cargo loaded in the ships of the convoy, only 57,176 tons arrived, while 430 tanks, 210 aircraft, and 3,350 vehicles were lost, sufficient to have equipped an army. It was a major disaster.

Before we go on to consider the effects and repercussions resulting from the events described above, the story must be told of Lieutenant L. J. A. Gradwell, R.N.V.R., commanding the trawler *Ayrshire*. By his resource and initiative he preserved three ships from sharing the fate of the 23 others. When the convoy began to scatter he took the *Silver Sword, Troubadour* and *Ironclad* under his protection and set course for Hope Island, which lay 70 miles north-west of the scattering point. Here he hoped to be able to lie up until the unknown danger from which they had been ordered to flee, was past. However, before the island was reached, ice was encountered, which obliged him to alter course to the eastward. By now he was beginning to hear over his radio the dire distress calls of unfortunate ships as one by one they fell victims to the enemy's aircraft and U-boats, so he decided that the only hope of safety lay in forcing a passage into the ice which fortunately was not very thick. This he did, using his ship as an icebreaker. Having penetrated some 20 miles he found further progress impossible, so he made a signal to 'heave to'. The dark hulls of the merchant ships stood out alarmingly against the dazzling white of the surrounding ice, and the mirage conditions prevailing, which enabled objects well below the horizon to be seen hanging inverted in the sky, added to his anxieties, for he knew that once sighted by enemy aircraft the fate of all of them was beyond question. He boarded each ship in turn and finding that between them there was sufficient white paint for each to coat that part of them facing south, he soon set all available hands to 'paint ship'. At the same time he arranged for the guns of a number of tanks carried as deck cargo to be made ready for action, and the necessary ammunition to be broken out of the hold. As a final precaution he ordered fires to be banked in all boilers as even a wisp of smoke might betray their position. For two days the three ships and their escort remained in the ice, and then when no more agonising calls were heard over the radio Gradwell decided it was time to move on. This took some time, for a southerly wind had packed the ice against the ships. When at last they were all free he decided that it was too dangerous to set course directly for Archangel, so he led his charges to a bay in the north of Novaya Zemlya where they anchored while he coaled ship from one of the merchant ships that had some to spare. Thence they proceeded south to the Matochkin Strait where they found the *Benjamin Harrison*, which it will be remembered had lost touch with Commodore Dowding's first convoy and returned to the anchorage. Not daring to use his own radio, Gradwell sent a party ashore to the Russian signal station and with some difficulty a request for their arrival to be reported to Archangel was preferred which, as has been related, in due course reached Commodore Dowding.

Of a no less dramatic but more poignant nature were the stories told by the surviving members of the sunken ships. Two lifeboats containing 46 survivors of the *Washington*'s crew, after enduring a blizzard which lasted for six hours and spending a week at sea, eventually made the Novaya Zemlya coast, suffering acutely from hunger and exposure. On landing they found that seagull soup was the form of nourishment they could expect from this barren land, so they returned to their boats and, continuing south, two days later fell in with four boatloads of survivors from the *Paulus Potter*, one-third of whom were suffering from frost bite. After a meal of hell-diver ducks which they managed to snare, the whole party re-embarked and rowed south and eventually came across the *Winston Salem* aground, where they were able to obtain their first real food for ten days. A Russian whaler transferred them to the CAM ship *Empire Tide*, swelling the number of survivors on board her, as already mentioned, to 240.

Another more fortunate crew made land in the vicinity of a Russian pioneer camp, where they were fed and well looked after.

And so the stories go on, tales of hardship and suffering in the frozen north, where midsummer means merely a slight easing of the normally severe conditions. Altogether some 1,300 survivors of the lost ships were landed at Archangel where most of them were obliged to spend a frustrating period of inactivity in very uncongenial surroundings. The Russian medical authorities tended the sick and injured as best they could, but they were short of drugs and modern equipment and, as we shall see later, their pride prevented a ready acceptance of British and American offers to remedy these deficiencies.

Russian reaction to the disaster was not exactly sympathetic. Godfrey Winn has recounted[1] how Captain Lawford of the *Pazorica,* in which he was a passenger, obtained an interview with the Russian Admiral commanding the White Sea, which lasted for 2½ hours. After having given the Admiral a full and frank account of the voyage and the difficulties which had to be surmounted in running the convoys under present conditions, he elicited the comment: 'You should send bigger convoys, and you should provide better means of protection. There

---

[1] Godfrey Winn, *PQ17* (Hutchinson & Co.), p. 156.

should be fighter cover the whole way.' In this appreciation the Russian Admiral was perfectly right, provided the war at sea had been confined to the Arctic Ocean, but Soviet views on global strategy were understandably myopic at that time. On a higher plane criticism was even more forthright, but of that more later.

Returning now to the German ships in their anchorages at Vestifiord and Altenfiord, as Admiral Tovey's covering force had not been sighted since 3 July, it had not been possible to comply with Hitler's order to put the carriers out of action as a necessary preliminary to the start of the operation. Nevertheless, so anxious was Admiral Raeder to lose no time once permission to sail was obtained, that on 3 July he sanctioned the movement of the *Tirpitz* to join the *Scheer* at Altenfiord which took place on the night of 3/4 July. Thus the three ships and their seven destroyers were ideally placed to pounce on the convoy as it entered the Barents Sea.

It was not, however, until 11.37 a.m. on 5 July that Hitler's permission was obtained for the operation to begin, and then only with the proviso that it was to be a 'tip and run' attack, because although it was then known that the cruiser force had withdrawn to the west and Admiral Tovey's force was some 450 miles from the convoy, steering to the south-west, the Naval Staff had worked out that if the force continued its operations against the convoy after 1 a.m. on the 6th it might be attacked by the *Victorious*'s aircraft.

The German force steered north on leaving harbour and at 5 p.m., when about 30 miles offshore, turned to the east. It was sighted and attacked by the Russian submarine *K21*, at about the time the alteration of course was made, and although two hits were claimed on the *Tirpitz*, she did not in fact suffer any damage. About an hour later it was reported by a reconnaissance aircraft, and finally at 8.30 p.m. the submarine *Trident*, on her way to take up a new patrol station, saw and reported it, but was unable to get within attacking distance. By now, news of the success of air and U-boat attacks on the scattered convoy was reaching the German Command, and at 9.30 p.m. the Naval Staff called the operation off, much to Admiral Schniewind's disappointment. During the night of 5/6 July the Admiralty on three occasions suggested to Admiral Tovey that the *Tirpitz* might be unwilling to go as far east as the convoy if the battle fleet was seen to be steering to the eastward, and that if she had been torpedoed there might be an opportunity for *Victorious*'s aircraft to attack her. Although at 6.45 a.m. on the 6th Admiral Tovey did, in fact, turn his fleet to an easterly course when he heard an enemy reconnaissance aircraft approaching, and endeavoured to attract its attention, his force was not sighted. He was joined by Rear-Admiral Hamilton's cruiser force at 10.40 a.m. on that day. By 12.30 p.m., as the weather had become unsuitable for air reconnaissance, he resumed his south-westerly course, and all ships reached harbour on 8 July. The last report received of the German ships was from a British aircraft operating from north Russia which sighted them on their return to Narvik on 7 July. Submarines attempted unsuccessfully to intercept them and they reached harbour without further incident.

When the extent of the disaster leaked out, the repercussions on both sides of the Atlantic were grave and, because at that time no public pronouncement could be made, the German propaganda machine moved into top gear and made the most of its opportunity. Later, when the tales of prisoners of war and survivors became known, a serious charge of ineptitude on the part of the Royal Navy was formulated, which has never been satisfactorily disposed of. It was said of it that it had left its charges in the lurch at a critical moment, and a totally false inference was drawn from the fact that while 23 merchantmen went down not a single one of H.M. ships suffered loss or even damage. But the lie to these charges is given by the actions of the two A/A ships, the corvettes, minesweepers and trawlers, all of which showed a high sense of duty, and by their courage and resourcefulness were able to rescue survivors and assist the ships which escaped destruction to reach port. As for the rest, we must carefully consider all the facts before reaching a conclusion.

It is necessary to bear in mind that the Germans had

made thorough and complete plans for their surface ships to attack the convoy, and that these did in fact sail with that object in view. When it became evident that the latter in its scattered state could be more effectively dealt with by U-boats and aircraft, the former were recalled.

The only object in ordering a convoy to scatter is to reduce the losses likely to occur as the result of an attack by surface ships. So far as defence against U-boat and air attack are concerned, there is no question that close formation offers the only effective answer. In the case of a convoy threatened with all three forms of attack, as was PQ17, a very difficult decision is called for involving some very accurate timing. To scatter too early, as the event showed, was to invite disaster, just as surely as to do so too late. It should have been obvious that such a perplexing decision could only be taken by the man on the spot. There is no doubt that had it been left to the Commander-in-Chief, he would have ordered the cruisers to withdraw, because this was a policy about which both he and the Admiralty were in agreement and he would have allowed Commander Broome to use his discretion how to act when, and if, the surface ship attack on the convoy developed. Admiral Tovey had long held the opinion that the German Naval Command would be unlikely to allow the *Tirpitz* to attack a convoy, so long as it was escorted by destroyers offering a potential threat of torpedo attack—a view with which the Admiralty did not agree—and that is why he considered that the order to scatter the convoy had been premature. What would have happened if the convoy had not scattered and the destroyers had remained with it, is impossible to guess, as everything would have depended on the way in which the German forces were handled. Admiral Raeder had warned Admiral Schniewind that a naval reverse at this time would be particularly unfortunate, and this and the attitude of Hitler to operations by his surface ships were not such as to encourage that boldness upon which success in war nearly always depends. But to give the Admiralty their due, this weakness in German leadership, even if suspected at that time, could not be counted upon. The strength of the German forces deployed in the north of Norway should have enabled them to achieve complete success.

Referring to the withdrawal of the cruisers, Mr Churchill has commented: 'Admiral Pound would probably not have sent such vehement orders if only our own British warships had been concerned', and he goes on to suggest that the presence and possible destruction of the two U.S. cruisers in Rear-Admiral Hamilton's force 'may well have disturbed the poise with which he was accustomed to deal with these heart-shaking decisions'.[1] But, as has been related, before the convoy sailed Admiral Pound had agreed with Admiral Tovey that the cruisers should not be ordered east of Bear Island unless they were threatened by a surface force which they could engage, and this excluded the *Tirpitz*. Hence, it seems most unlikely that the presence of the two U.S. ships had any influence on the First Sea Lord's decision to withdraw the cruisers.

The Commander-in-Chief was of the opinion that Rear-Admiral Hamilton should have released the destroyers to rejoin the scattered convoy once it became evident that the *Tirpitz* was not in his immediate vicinity. He considered that they would have been valuable for anti-submarine purposes, rounding up ships and delaying any attempt by the *Tirpitz* to attack the convoy. There is no question but that Commander Broome was willing and anxious to return, but Hamilton, crediting the German Naval Command with more initiative than they possessed, fully expected a surface action with the *Tirpitz* group to develop at any moment, as he assumed, now that the convoy had scattered, Admiral Schniewind's force would be diverted to deal with him. In these circumstances, and in default of further information, he decided that the destroyers were a welcome and useful addition to his force and might enable him to fight a delaying action, while leading the German ships towards Admiral Tovey's carrier force. Also, now that the tanker *Aldersdale* had scattered with the convoy, it was highly unlikely that the destroyers, if they returned to the convoy area, would find her again, and they might therefore run out of fuel. She was in fact

---

[1] *The Second World War,* Vol. IV, p. 235.

sunk soon after scattering, and in the event he was obliged to fuel them from his cruisers.

The outstanding lesson of the disaster was the confusion caused in the minds of the Flag Officers concerned by the Admiralty's issue of peremptory instructions without sufficient indication of the reasons which prompted them. This led to premature scattering of the convoy, but not necessarily to an increase in the number of ships lost, which was entirely dependent on the action taken by the enemy. Nevertheless, while the Admiralty were better supplied with intelligence about the enemy than any Flag Officer at sea, the latter was in a far better position to judge what action to take, having regard to the weather conditions prevailing in the area of operations, the state of his forces as regards fuel and armament, and other purely local factors of which the Admiralty could not possibly be aware. As the United States Navy found during the conduct of their many successful operations against the Japanese in the Pacific, it is better for the shore authority to keep a Commander-in-Chief fully primed with information and to leave him conduct the operation in his own way.

Now that all the facts are known, it is evident that the primary cause of the catastrophe was the Government's insistence on the carrying out of an operation which, from the start, had very little chance of success. As Professor Michael Lewis says, 'In the light of previous strategical experience we were undertaking the impossible task of passing convoys along hundreds of miles of enemy-held territory, where the air was completely dominated by the Luftwaffe, the sea patrolled by most of the surviving enemy surface fleet and as many U-boats as Hitler cared to spare.'[1] The success of the strategy of convoy and escort depends on the latter being strong enough to deal adequately with any threat to the former. These conditions did not yet obtain in the case of the convoys to north Russia. The fact that the Admiralty was not prepared to risk the Home Fleet in the waters to the east of Bear Island was a tacit admission of the predominance of

---

[1] *The History of the British Navy*, p. 233.

German air power in that area, which the Royal Navy was not yet in a position to challenge. Napoleon once observed: 'Every Commander-in-Chief who undertakes to execute a plan which he considers bad or ruinous is to blame. He ought to remonstrate, to insist on alternatives, and, if necessary, resign rather than become the means of the defeat of the force entrusted to him.' But to anyone of Admiral Pound's calibre, resignation in time of war would have seemed like deserting his post and completely contrary to his high sense of duty. He had been brought up in the tradition that to attempt the impossible is the prerogative of the Royal Navy.

Before closing the chapter on these tragic events, it is necessary to relate the story of the misfortune which befell the homeward-bound convoy QP13 during the final stage of its voyage. This convoy, consisting of 35 ships under Commodore N. H. Gale, R.N.R., with an escort of five destroyers, four corvettes, two minesweepers, and two trawlers had been sighted by enemy aircraft on 2 July, but had escaped further attention, partly because it ran into fog but mainly because the enemy was concentrating his forces for the attack on PQ17. Arriving off the north-east corner of Iceland on 4 July it was ordered to split, 16 ships including that of the Commodore, with part of the escort being routed to Loch Ewe and the remainder with the rest of the escort along the north coast of Iceland to Reykjavik, Captain Hiss of the *American Robin* being nominated acting Commodore of this section. The weather during the previous two days had been cloudy, and it had not, therefore, been possible to take sights during that time, and as a result the position of the convoy was uncertain. The radar carried by some of the ships of the escort was at that time not very reliable, and as the Iceland section approached the land the weather deteriorated. It was blowing a gale from the north-east, raining, with the visibility down to about a mile. At 8 p.m. Commander Cubison, R.N., the senior officer of the escort in the minesweeper *Niger*, decided to go ahead and make the land. Two hours later he sighted an iceberg, which he apparently mistook for the North Cape of Iceland, so he altered the course of the convoy to west. This took the ships straight into a British minefield of the position of which Captain Hiss was not aware. The first indication he received of its existence was when it was referred to in a signal from the senior officer, ordering the convoy to form two columns in order to pass between it and the land. At 10.40 p.m. the *Niger* struck a mine. Too late Commander Cubison realised that they were too far to the north, and hurriedly made a signal to the Commodore to alter back to the south-westward. The *Niger* quickly sank with heavy loss of life, including that of Commander Cubison, and within a brief space of time four ships of the convoy had struck mines and foundered, and two more were seriously damaged. One of those lost was the Russian ship *Rodina* carrying wives and families of Soviet diplomats stationed in London. The French corvette *Roselys*, under the command of Lieutenant Bergeret, and the trawlers *Lady Madeleine* and *St Elstan*, with complete disregard for their own safety, steamed about in the minefield for 6½ hours rescuing survivors, which included some from the cruiser *Edinburgh*. Between them they picked up 211, some of whom later died of exposure. It was indeed a case of 'one woe treading upon another's heel'.

8

A Fighting Destroyer Escort

In cases of defence 'tis best to weigh
The enemy more mighty than he seems;
So the proportions of defence are fill'd
Shakespeare

AFTER THE DISASTER TO PQ17 the Admiralty urged the Government to agree to a suspension of the north-Russian convoys until the days of perpetual light were over, by which time the ice would have receded to its northern limit, thus enabling the convoys to give the German airfields a wider berth. The Prime Minister's reaction to this suggestion, as he has recorded[1] was 'to raise the stakes on

[1] *The Second World War*, Vol. IV, p. 238.

the principle of "In defeat defiance"' and marshal our full naval strength to fight it out with the enemy, but for the reasons given in the last chapter the Admiralty was firmly opposed to such a course of action. Mr Churchill was, therefore, obliged to acquaint Stalin with what he was well aware would be most unwelcome news, and this he did in a telegram dated 17 July 1942. 'The crux of the problem', he told the Russian Premier, 'is to make the Barents Sea as dangerous for German warships as they make it for ours. This is what we should aim at doing with our joint resources.' But Stalin did not see it in that light, and in his reply he dismissed the presence of the German heavy ships and strong air forces in northern Norway as 'wholly unconvincing' reasons for refusing to continue the convoys. It is easy to understand the Russian point of view. The great German offensive on a 200-mile front towards the Don was making headway despite the frantic efforts of the Russian Commanders to halt it, and at a tremendous cost in human life. What were 23 ships and a few hundred men weighed against the sacrifices being made by his own people? The victories of Japan in the Far East, of the Axis forces in North Africa and of the U-boats in the Atlantic seemed of minor importance compared with the grip which the enemy was tightening around his country's throat.

But even if the unacceptable losses in PQ17 had not obliged the Admiralty to interrupt the sailing of the convoys, the urgent need to reinforce the island of Malta most certainly would, because as has been mentioned, the forces required for this had to come from the Home Fleet, the strength of which had been weakened by the gradual withdrawal of the United States ships attached to it, these now being required for operations in the Pacific. An opportunity was thus provided for taking stock of the situation and considering plans for a resumption of the convoys when conditions would be more favourable.

The German Naval Command was elated by the success of the operations against PQ17, which was ascribed to 'exemplary cooperation between aircraft and U-boats', the results being in every way commensurate with those expected from the surface warships. They failed to appreciate the fact that it was the presence of the heavy ships and the *Tirpitz* in particular, which caused the Admiralty to scatter the convoy, thereby simplifying the task of the air and submarine forces. As a result of this false conclusion, and also of the limitations imposed by Hitler on the operation of his surface ships, it was decided in future not to employ these for attacking the loaded PQ convoys, which would be left to the Luftwaffe and the U-boats, but rather to use them for attacking the returning QP convoys in the Barents Sea which they could do with a minimum of risk. These operations would be backed up by minelaying in the area bounded by Franz Josefs Land, Novaya Zemlya and the Russian mainland.

On 21 July preliminary steps were taken to intercept PQ18, which it was expected would sail towards the end of the month, by the despatch of five U-boats to patrol areas north of Bear Island, and by keeping others at readiness to proceed to stations between Iceland and Jan Mayen Island. So anxious were the Germans not to miss an opportunity of repeating their previous success that every report of British movements in the area put them on the alert. The sighting on 22 July of four destroyers south-west of Spitzbergen which were carrying stores and ammunition to Archangel to replace those lost in PQ17, was taken as an indication that these islands were to be used as a fuelling base for the next convoy. Then on 6 August *U405* on patrol in the Denmark Straits sighted and reported a small convoy, and immediately Admiral Klüber, who had just relieved Admiral Schmundt in command of Navy Group North Norway, ordered ten U-boats to sea to intercept the supposed north-Russian convoy. The weather at the time was foggy and unsuitable for air reconnaissance, but when it cleared six days later, 140 aircraft scoured the area in a vain search for it, and it was not till then that the enemy realised that they had been on a wild goose chase.

Air Marshal Sir Philip Joubert, Commander-in-Chief Coastal Command, whose previous proposal to transfer aircraft to north Russia had been turned down by the Admiralty, had meanwhile returned to the charge. He pointed out that had torpedo aircraft been stationed in north Russia the Admiralty might not have considered it necessary to scatter convoy PQ17, and finally he obtained agreement to make arrangements for the temporary transfer of a balanced force of both search and strike aircraft to Russian airfields during the period of the next convoy operation. The force eventually selected for this duty comprised four photographic reconnaissance Spitfires, No. 210 Catalina reconnaissance squadron, and Nos. 144 and 255 Hampden torpedo-bomber squadrons, all under the command of Group Captain F. L. Hopps, R.A.F. At the same time two staff officers of Bomber Command waited on Admiral Tovey at his request to discuss the possibility of an attack by heavy bombers on the German ships at Narvik. Since these were beyond the range of the bombers then in service, they would be obliged to land in north Russia and refuel before returning. Admiral Tovey offered to send the necessary ground staff and stores by sea, but it was not found possible to obtain Russian agreement to the use of any of their airfields for this purpose, so the idea had to be shelved.

On 13 August the U.S. cruiser *Tuscaloosa*, one of the two still attached to the Home Fleet, left the Clyde with 300 tons of stores and 167 members of the ground staff with the equipment required for the maintenance of the two Hampden squadrons. She was accompanied by the destroyers *Rodman, Emmons* and *Onslaught*, each carrying 40 tons of stores. The ground staff and stores for the Catalina squadron had to be flown in later, as there was such a heavy demand for the services of these aircraft that they were obliged to keep operating until the very day of their transfer. The *Tuscaloosa* also had on board a medical unit and stores which it was hoped would be able to help in alleviating the primitive conditions in Russian hospitals, disquieting reports about which had reached Admiral Tovey. In his view it was intolerable that British seamen wounded while carrying supplies to Russia should be exposed unnecessarily to the mediaeval treatment prevailing in Russian hospitals. Vice-Admiral Sir Ian Campbell, who as Captain (D) of the Third Destroyer Flotilla saw as much service as anyone with the Russian convoys, has recorded this impression of the situation:

> Conditions in the hospitals at Polyarno, Murmansk and Archangel, on which depended the care of our sick and wounded, were indeed parlous. When the Petsamo front was active or when there had been heavy convoy sinkings, the hard, uncomfortable beds with their bedclothes of dubious cleanliness, were packed close in the wards. The staff wore dirty overalls and scorned to make use of gloves.
>
> In the airless, squalid wards, boards nailed over the windows as a blackout were a permanent fixture, leaving little outlet for the varied smells. From seven in the morning till eleven at night, loudspeakers blared unceasingly in Russian. Drugs were short and pain regarded with Oriental indifference by surgeons and physicians. Dull, monotonous food did nothing to comfort men lying in fear and pain, unable to make their simplest needs or symptoms known. British surgeons did what they could, but owing to professional jealousy were permitted only to visit the patients and attend operations as laymen. They were neither consulted nor allowed to advise.[1]

When the *Tuscaloosa* arrived, word came from Moscow that the medical unit was not to be allowed to land, but the Russians did not disdain to accept the stores which it had brought. Despite the strongest protests made by Admiral Tovey and also by the Head of the British Military Mission in Moscow, it was not until the matter was raised to the level of the Prime Minister—Stalin, that the *ukase* was modified.

On 26 August, after an interval of 2½ months, Hitler held a conference with Grand Admiral Raeder, at which the PQ17 operation was discussed. The latter suggested that the 'total' destruction of the convoy might have 'forced the enemy to give up this route temporarily, or even fundamentally to change his whole system of supply

---

[1] I.M.R. Campbell and D. Macintyre, *The Kola Run*, p. 176.

lines', and he went on to point out that 'supplies to northern ports of Russia remain decisive for the whole conduct of the war waged by the Anglo-Saxons'. At the same time Raeder was not blind to the danger of 'an attempt of [by] the Anglo-Saxons to occupy north-west Africa and get a foothold in North Africa with the aid of the French', which he considered 'a very great danger to the whole German war effort'. No attempt was made to assess the relative importance of the Russian convoys and operations in the Mediterranean, and although Hitler is recorded as having concurred in Raeder's views regarding the last-named danger, he still considered Norway as the weak spot and insisted on all the larger units of his fleet being kept available for operations in the north. He has been criticised on this account both by Admirals Dönitz, Rüge and others, but had Mr Churchill had his way, a landing in north Norway would have been attempted. It is perhaps natural that the Germans should have regarded Russia as a more important ally of Britain than the United States. While the contribution made by the Red Army to the final victory was both enormous and decisive, that made by the Americans was equally so, but in a more diverse way.

At the end of August Mr Churchill returned from Moscow whither he had set out immediately after the PQ17 disaster. The visit, he says, inspired him 'with new resolve to aid Russia to the very limits of our power'.[1] Stalin had impressed him by his solid confidence that he would win the war, and the Prime Minister busied himself with his customary energy in devising schemes for aiding the Red Armies in the gigantic conflict in which they were engaged. On 6 September he sent Stalin a long message outlining the steps being taken to protect PQ18, the next convoy to Russia, preparations for the sailing of which were now in full swing. Early in September Group Captain Hopps' mixed air group began to move to north Russia, a far from easy task for the two Hampden squadrons whose limited range and poor navigational facilities left no margin for error in a trip of 1,500 miles across

[1] *The Second World War,* Vol. IV, p. 505.

the sea and enemy-held territory. Of the 32 aircraft which took off from Britain, only 23 completed the flight successfully: six crashed in Norway and Sweden and one of these as we shall see, with unfortunate consequences; two ran out of fuel and made forced landings in Russia, one being damaged beyond repair; and one was shot down by a Russian fighter while flying over a prohibited area. Those that arrived safely earned a well merited tribute from the Prime Minister. The Spitfires and the Catalinas arrived without incident. The former, together with the Hampdens, were to operate from Vaenga, and the latter from Grasnaya, both airfields adjacent to the Kola Inlet.

As far as the Admiralty could judge, the enemy threat to PQ18 appeared to be similar to that which pertained during the passage of its predecessor. Unfortunately, however, the Home Fleet was now without a carrier, the *Victorious*, on her return from the operation for the relief of Malta, having had to go into dockyard hands for a refit. This fact severely restricted the cover which the battle fleet would be able to give the convoy, although in Admiral Tovey's opinion this had always been 'more threatening than real'. In any case he considered that some changes were desirable in the dispositions employed for protecting the convoy. He had no doubt whatever that in the face of air and U-boat attacks it would always be possible to fight a convoy through—albeit with heavy losses—but if the Germans were to use their surface ships properly, the risk of a repetition of a disaster on the scale of PQ17 could not be ignored. He was, nevertheless, strongly of the opinion that 'In the variable visibility which prevails in those latitudes, the presence of a strong force of destroyers would constitute a threat which the enemy, in spite of the longer range of his guns, would probably be reluctant to face', and if he did press home his attack, such an escort force would be strong enough to defeat him. By taking the long-endurance destroyers normally allocated to screen the battle fleet, he could provide the convoy with a 'fighting destroyer escort' of between 12 and 16 ships, and this he considered outweighed the resulting disadvantage of having to allocate short-endurance destroyers to screen his heavy ships. Since it was desirable that the 'fighting destroyer escort' should remain with the convoy during its passage through the Barents Sea, where surface attack was most likely, the practice hitherto adopted of sailing both homeward- and outward-bound convoys simultaneously would have to be changed, the former being delayed until the latter had reached the final stage of its journey. This meant that the length of the whole operation would be greatly increased, both on this account and also because of the more northerly route now possible, the ice barrier being at its greatest distance from the Norwegian coast. Even so, it was not possible to keep beyond the range of German aircraft operating from airfields in north Norway. The longer route also called for elaborate fuelling arrangements, no less than four tankers being required to ensure that this formidable flotilla was kept topped up with fuel throughout the voyage. It was decided to send two of these ships under separate escort to Lowe Sound in Spitzbergen, while another two would sail in the convoy. But what was to give this convoy better protection than any yet sailed, was the inclusion for the first time of an escort carrier, the *Avenger*, with a complement of 12 Sea-Hurricane fighters and three Swordfish A/S aircraft. These vessels which had been ordered in the United States under Lend Lease a year previously, were just coming into service, and as will be seen their presence with the Arctic convoys was to tip the scale in favour of the defence. Finally, Admiral Tovey decided not to go to sea with the battleship covering force as he had done previously, but to conduct the operation from his flagship *King George V* at Scapa Flow, where it will be remembered, he was directly connected with the Admiralty by telephone. His second-in-command, Vice-Admiral Sir Bruce Fraser, flying his flag in the *Anson*, with the *Duke of York* and the cruiser *Jamaica* in company, moved to Akureyri in Iceland which was to be their base for the duration of the operation. From there they could cruise for short periods to the north-west of Jan Mayen Island. Closer cover was to be provided by a force of three 8-inch-gun cruisers under Rear-Admiral Bonham-Carter which would operate in an area to the west of Spitzbergen. The operation also provided an opportunity to reinforce and resupply the Norwegian garrison at Barentsburg on those islands, two cruisers and a destroyer being detailed for this task.

The German reconnaissance aircraft were keeping a close watch on Iceland whence nearly all the previous convoys had sailed, so in order to delay its sighting as long as possible it was decided to sail the convoy from Loch Ewe on the north-west coast of Scotland with a separate escort provided by the Western Approaches Command, the ocean escort relieving it off the east coast of Iceland.

At last the day came for all this careful planning to be put to the test, and on 2 September PQ18, consisting of 40 ships, under Rear-Admiral E. K. Boddam-Whetham, D.S.O., serving as a Commodore R.N.R., weighed anchor and headed north through the Minches. In company were the two tankers *Gray Ranger* and *Black Ranger* for refuelling the escorts, four motor minesweepers bound for Russia and the rescue ship *Copeland*. As soon as the long line of ships cleared the Outer Hebrides, they encountered the full force of an Atlantic gale which so delayed their progress that they were 36 hours late at the rendezvous with the ocean escort. This comprised the two A/A ships *Ulster Queen* and *Alynbank*, three destroyers, four corvettes and four trawlers all of which joined on 7 September. Soon after the wind began to moderate and wet weather with patches of fog set in. On the 9th Rear-Admiral Burnett in command of the 'fighting destroyer escort', flying his flag in the cruiser *Scylla*, joined the convoy with the escort carrier *Avenger* and 10 of the 18 destroyers detailed for the operation. Burnett, who from now on plays an outstanding part in the history of the Arctic convoys, belonged to that select company of officers known in the Royal Navy as 'springers'. In other words, he had made physical training his speciality. In his youth he had excelled in every form of sport, and his service had been mainly in small ships. He was at this time holding the post of Rear-Admiral Destroyers in the Home Fleet, one for which he was particularly fitted. Unfortunately, it was mainly an administrative one, with little opportunity of getting to sea, but the decision to form a 'fighting destroyer escort' gave him the chance for which he had been waiting. The other eight destroyers of his command had gone ahead to fuel from the tankers *Oligarch* and *Blue Ranger* which had been sent to Spitzbergen for the operation. Also with the escort force were three minesweepers and two submarines; four more of the latter were established on patrol off the Lofoten Islands, and a further three off the north coast of Norway. Altogether 51 warships, of which 25 were destroyers, were thus employed on the operation; it was by far the most heavily defended convoy yet to sail to north Russia.

On 5 September, by an unfortunate mischance, the enemy obtained valuable information about the convoy operation from one of the six Hampden aircraft which, as related, crashed in Scandinavia. This particular one had the misfortune to be winged by a German patrol vessel off the Norwegian coast and was forced to land near Vardsoe. Secret documents found on board contained the radio-communications organisation to be used during the passage of the two convoys. With the help of this and a decyphered Russian order to the 95th Naval Air Regiment, the enemy obtained a fairly accurate picture of the route being followed and the time schedule of the various phases of the operation, which were of considerable assistance to him in making plans to attack the two convoys. However, this information did not alter his decision to employ only U-boats and aircraft to attack the northbound convoy and to keep his surface ships for operations against the homeward bound one during its passage through the Barents Sea. The German Air Force, whose torpedo bomber strength had increased to 92, was ready and anxious to try and repeat its success against the previous convoy.

PQ18 was located by German reconnaissance aircraft late on the 8th, but they lost it and did not find it again until 1.20 p.m. on the 12th, because of the presence of cloud and low visibility in the area. However U-boats managed to gain and maintain contact during this period, although they were kept at a respectful distance by the *Avenger*'s A/S aircraft, which made several attacks on them and assisted ships of the escort force in doing so.

1. PQ18 under air attack, September 1942. H.M.S. *Eskimo* in foreground

2. Admiral of the Fleet Sir Dudley Pound, First Sea Lord 1939-1943

3. Admiral Sir Louis Hamilton, Rear-Admiral Commanding 1st Cruiser Squadron

4. JW57, February 1944. Swordfish from H.M.S. *Chaser* on patrol

5. Admiral of the Fleet Lord Tovey, Commander-in-Chief Home Fleet 1940-1943, with Commodore J. C. K. Dowding, R.N.R.

6. Admiral Sir Stuart Bonham-Carter, Flag Officer Commanding 18th Cruiser Squadron

7. U-boat at high speed

8. Reconnaissance aircraft catapulted from a German warship

9. German destroyer and sinking British merchant ship

10. Grand Admiral Erich Raeder, Commander-in-Chief German Navy 1928-1943

11. General Admiral Otto Schniewind, Flag Officer Battle Group 1941-1943 and Commander-in-Chief Group North 1943-1944

12. Grand Admiral Karl Dönitz, Flag Officer U-boats and Commander-in-Chief, German Navy 1943-1945

13. Admiral Otto Ciliax, Admiral Commanding Battle-cruiser Force 1941-1942, Admiral Commanding Norway 1943-1945

14. Ju.88s on a north Norwegian airfield

15. Clearing snow from the quarterdeck of H.M.S. *King George V*

16. The forward 6-inch guns of H.M.S. *Belfast* in Arctic waters

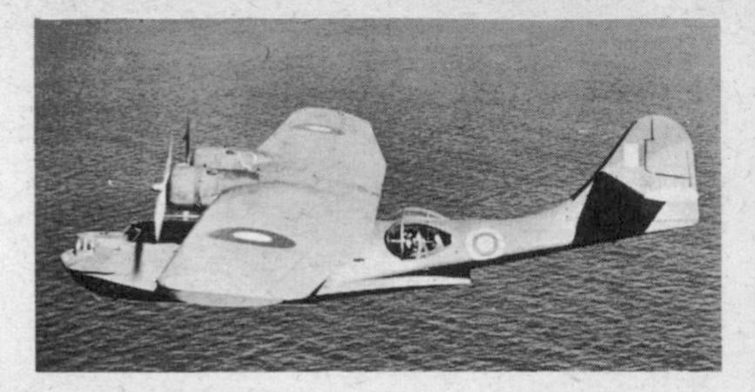
17. Catalina

18. Heinkel 115 seaplane

19. Swordfish

20. Russian naval tug assisting an escort carrier's motor boat through ice in an Arctic port

21. The escort carrier H.M.S. *Nairana* seen in heavy weather from the flight deck of H.M.S. *Campania*

22. The sloop H.M.S. *Magpie* on escort duty

23. Anti-aircraft crews at action stations in a German destroyer

24. The corvette H.M.S. *Lotus* on escort duty in the Arctic

25. Midget submarine (X-craft) of the type used in the attack on the *Tirpitz*

26. H.M. trawler *Northern Pride*

27. Survivors of the American freighter *Carlton* after rescue by German patrol vessels

28. Convoy in pack ice (seal in foreground)

29. The battle-cruiser *Scharnhorst* sunk by H.M.S. *Duke of York* on 26 December 1943

30. The battleship *Tirpitz* surrounded by anti-torpedo nets

31. Rear-Admiral R. R. McGrigor and Lieut.-Commander G. R. O. Watkins on the bridge of the escort carrier *Campania* during an air attack

32. Commander A. G. West in Arctic clothing on the bridge of H.M.S. *Inglefield*

33. The heavy cruiser *Hipper*, flagship of Admiral Kummetz during the attack on Convoy JW51B

34. A convoy arrives in Kola Inlet

35. The German destroyer Z25

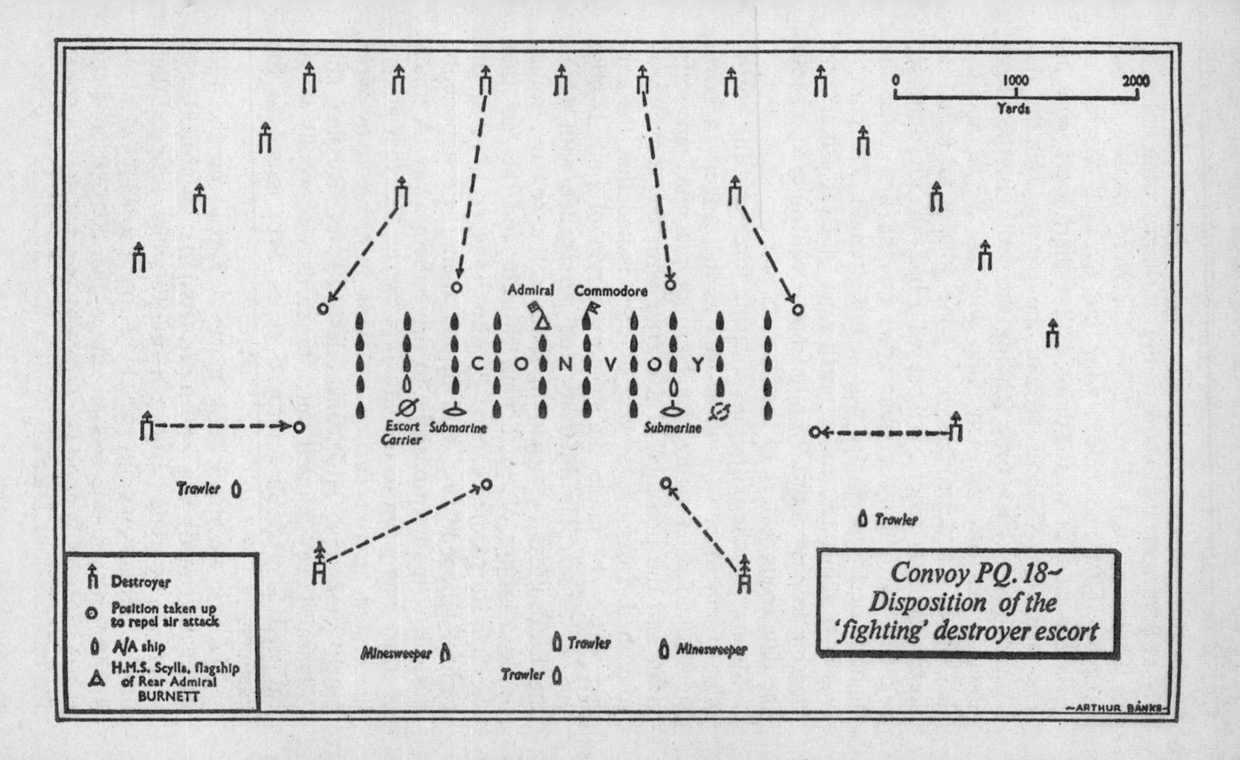

Convoy PQ. 18– Disposition of the 'fighting' destroyer escort

One of these, by the destroyer *Faulknor* on *U88* at 9 p.m. on the 12th was crowned with success, but the following day at 8.55 a.m. two ships in the starboard wing column, the *Stalingrad* and *Oliver Elsworth*, were torpedoed and sunk by *U408* and *U589*, who thus avenged the loss of their comrade. It was estimated that there were now no less than eight U-boats around the convoy and the destroyers had a busy time fending them off. In the afternoon of that day, Burnett, who with the *Scylla* and the first group of destroyers had gone ahead to refuel at Spitzbergen, on relief by those who had already done so, rejoined the convoy so that now, for the first time, the 'fighting destroyer escort' was at full strength. The convoy was now about 150 miles north-west of Bear Island and steering to pass about 90 miles north of it and so on into the dangerous waters of the Barents Sea.

Meanwhile, the battleship covering force cruising north-west of Jan Mayen Island as well as the tankers in Lowe Sound, had been sighted by German reconnaissance aircraft, and the presence of a carrier with the convoy was confirmed. Instructions were at once issued that the carrier was to be made the primary target of both U-boat and air attack. The intensity and persistence with which the Luftwaffe now began to shadow the convoy, sometimes in groups of up to nine aircraft, and the fact that the Sea Hurricanes carried by the *Avenger* were of the earliest type and less well armed than their opponents, made it virtually impossible to drive them away. A touch of irony was given to the situation by the fact that among the crated aircraft carried by ships in the convoy were much later type Hurricanes destined for Russia. This Admiral Tovey pointed out afterwards was wholly illogical, and as a result improved types were issued to the carriers.

The first air attack took place at 3 p.m. on the 13th when the convoy was 450 miles from Banak airfield, and was made by some half-dozen Ju.88's which dropped their bombs through gaps in the clouds from a height of about 4,000 feet, without loss to either the convoy or themselves. But this was only a foretaste of what was to come, for half an hour later 30 Ju.88's and 55 He.111 torpedo bombers carried out a mass attack, the latter employing what was known as the 'Golden Comb' technique by which they approached in line abreast, 100 to 150 yards apart at a height of about 35 feet above the sea in perfect formation. Each aircraft carried two torpedoes and all were dropped simultaneously so the convoy was threatened by 110 torpedoes racing towards it, the tracks of which looked like the ever-lengthening teeth of a giant comb. It was an awe-inspiring sight and one calling for instant action. The Commodore executed an emergency turn of 45° to starboard together which would bring the ships parallel to the course of the advancing torpedoes. Unfortunately the signal was either not seen or misunderstood by the two starboard columns which turned in succession and six of the seven ships in them were hit, one of them disintegrating with a terrific explosion. Two more ships in the middle of the convoy were also hit and all subsequently sank. The enemy had struck hard, and he was to keep on striking. Three-quarters of an hour later, another torpedo attack took place, this time by a handful of He.115 seaplanes, fortunately without success, and then at 8.35 p.m. when it was almost dark, 12 more He.111's came in from ahead in small groups, but like the previous attack they failed to score a hit. All these attacks were met by an intense barrage of gunfire from both the merchant ships and the escorts. During the first big torpedo attack, the cruiser *Scylla* went on to full speed, and racing ahead of the convoy to give her rapid-firing 4.5-inch guns clear arcs of fire, had the satisfaction of seeing several aircraft hit and plunge into the sea in flames. In the three attacks the Germans lost eight aircraft, all of which were accounted for by gun-fire, because the *Avenger*'s fighters having been employed in a vain attempt to drive off the shadowers, were not ready to meet the enemy's main attack when it was delivered. This led her Captain, Commander Colthurst, to alter his tactics and decide to employ his fighters to break up large formations of aircraft threatening the convoy, rather than in fruitless attempts to drive off shadowers. Moreover, he realised that he must maintain a continuous combat air patrol over the convoy with sections of fighters landing to refuel, re-arm, and taking off again in rotation.

At 3.30 a.m. on the 14th the convoy lost another ship to the U-boats, the freighting tanker *Atheltemplar* falling a victim to *U457*. Because of the number of U-boats around the convoy it was pointless to try and take her in tow and she had to be sunk. Considering that she was stationed at the end of the middle column of the convoy, credit must be given to the captain of the U-boat for this attack. Seven and a half hours later the loss was avenged when one of the *Avenger*'s Swordfish aircraft in co-operation with the destroyer *Onslow* sank *U589* after a hunt lasting an hour and a quarter.

The Admiralty was not of course aware of the enemy's decision not to employ his surface forces against PQ convoys, so a very careful watch was being maintained by Catalina aircraft operating from both Britain and Russia on the movements of these vessels. The pocket battleship *Scheer*, with the cruisers *Hipper* and *Köln*, had left Narvik on the 10th for Altenfiord, and this movement had been reported by the submarines stationed off the coast, one of which, the *Tigris*, had made an unsuccessful attack on the *Scheer*. But up to the 14th the *Tirpitz* had been reported in her usual berth near Trondheim. Then on that day a Catalina aircraft from Britain reported that she was no longer there, and this naturally caused the Admiralty considerable anxiety, especially when it was found that she had not joined the other ships in Altenfiord. The Hampden torpedo striking force at Vaegna was therefore despatched to look for her but they sighted nothing and returned to base. The mystery was not solved until the 18th when she was seen to be back at her mooring. She had in fact been exercising in the Vestfiord.

The air battle over PQ18 was resumed at 12.35 p.m. on the 14th when about 20 torpedo aircraft were sighted on the starboard bow. They had managed to approach low enough not to be detected by radar. Half of them concentrated on the *Avenger* and the other half on the *Scylla* and the screening destroyers. This change of tactics was evidence of the enemy's dislike of the presence of fighter aircraft as well as the greatly increased fire-power of the escort. This time the carrier was ready for them. With her two escorting destroyers conforming to her every movement, like pilot fish with a shark, she steamed out at high speed in front of the convoy to gain room to manoeuvre, and flew off six fighters to meet the enemy. The A/A ship *Ulster Queen* also stood out from the convoy to give her the support of her six 4-inch guns. 'It was a fine sight', Burnett afterwards recorded, 'to see *Avenger* peeling off Hurricanes while streaking across the front of the convoy . . . and then being chased by torpedo-bombers as she steamed down on the opposite course to the convoy to take cover.' The attack cost the enemy 11 aircraft and not a single ship was hit. But no sooner had the discomfited torpedo bombers disappeared over the horizon, than a dozen Ju.88's appeared overhead and started dive-bombing. Several ships, including the *Avenger*, had narrow escapes, but no damage was done and the enemy lost another aircraft. Hardly had this action ceased when 25 torpedo aircraft came in from ahead, dividing as before, into two groups, one of which made a dead set for the *Avenger*. By now *Avenger* had ten fighters in the air, and these together with the ships' guns accounted for nine more enemy aircraft, but one ship, the *Mary Luchenback*, in the starboard wing column was torpedoed and blew up with a terrific explosion which covered her next in line, the *Nathaniel Greene*, with débris and burst open the crates of her deck cargo. Many ships carried between 2,000 and 3,000 tons of T.N.T. and their crews well knew that there was every possibility of their being 'blown to glory', depending on where the torpedo struck. During this action three Hurricanes were shot down by the ships' guns, but the pilots were saved. The final attack of the day began at 2.30 p.m. when about 20 aircraft approached from astern and bombed intermittently through gaps in the cloud for about an hour. Despite the difficult conditions which provided only fleeting glimpses of the target, another aircraft was shot down. Then, mercifully, the sky became overcast and gave the defenders a welcome respite from almost three hours of continuous air attack.

The next day the cloud still persisted, but between 12.45 p.m. and 3.35 p.m. some 50 aircraft flew over the convoy looking for holes through which to bomb. Whenever they were sighted they were subjected to an intense burst of fire while the *Avenger*'s fighters chivied them from above. The enemy lost three more aircraft to the ships' guns and although several ships were near-missed, no damage resulted. By now the convoy was 400 miles from the nearest enemy airfield, and in the prevailing weather conditions the Luftwaffe were obliged to halt their attacks. Although they had sunk nine ships they had lost 34 aircraft, a balance which Reichsmarschall Göring did not regard as at all satisfactory.

But PQ18 was not yet out of trouble. Three U-boats were still in contact, and as many as 12 were in the area. Two had betrayed their presence on the surface by the smoke of their exhausts during the last air attack, and had been put down by the destroyer *Opportune*. At 3 a.m. on the 16th, one was successfully attacked by the *Impulsive* as she was diving under the screen on the port bow of the convoy. This was subsequently confirmed as *U457* which had torpedoed the *Atheltemplar*, but that afternoon after the *Opportune* and *Offa* had carried out an unsuccessful attack on yet another one sighted on the surface, Group North ordered all U-boats in contact with PQ18 to transfer to the homeward-bound convoy QP14 which had sailed from Archangel on the 13th and was now emerging from the White Sea; its story is told in the next chapter.

That afternoon Burnett began the transfer of his forces from PQ18 to QP14. This he did gradually in three groups so as to make it less obvious to the enemy. In addition to the *Avenger* and the 'fighting destroyer escort' he took with him the A/A ship *Alynbank*, the tankers *Gray* and *Black Ranger*, and the two submarines. PQ18 was therefore left with one A/A ship, the *Ulster Queen*, and its own escort of three destroyers, three minesweepers, four corvettes and four trawlers. Next morning, however, two large Russian destroyers joined and two smaller ones the day after. The former mounted four 5-inch guns with a 45° elevation besides two 3-inch A/A guns, and their fire proved of great value when the convoy was again attacked from the air when rounding Cape Kanin at 8.20 a.m. on the 18th. Twelve He.111 torpedo aircraft delivered an attack from the starboard quarter of the convoy dropping their torpedoes at between 3,000 and 4,000 yards range, and although in the Commodore's opinion ships had a good opportunity to avoid them, one ship, the *Kentucky*, was hit. A similar attack an hour later was unsuccessful, but on this occasion it was synchronised with a bombing attack by Ju.88's, during which the *Kentucky* received a hit which sealed her fate. The Hurricane aircraft in the CAM ship *Empire Morn*, which hitherto had been a spectator during all these air attacks, now came in very handy and contributed to the German loss of three aircraft with another one damaged. The pilot then flew on and successfully landed at a Russian airfield with only four gallons of fuel left in his tank. The convoy reached the Dvina bar on the evening of the 19th, but before the ships could be berthed a strong gale sprang up and the following afternoon while they were seeking more sheltered anchorages, a dozen Ju.88's came over and bombed them for an hour, fortunately without result. On the 21st three ships which had run aground and were being guarded by the *Ulster Queen*, entered harbour, but still determined to try and avenge their losses the Luftwaffe had a final but unsuccessful fling at the stranded ships before they were refloated and moved to their unloading berths.

Of the 40 ships which had set sail from Loch Ewe on 2 September, 13 had been lost, and this despite the much stronger escort with which the convoy had been provided. At the same time no previous convoy had endured such persistent air attacks amounting in all to over a hundred by torpedo bombers, and slightly less than that by high-level and dive-bombers. But what was important was the enemy's disillusionment about his ability to bring about the scattering of a convoy by the threat of torpedo-bomber attack. He found that the carrier's fighters made it impossible to approach her in order to launch an effective attack, and that the wide screen of warships made the launching of torpedoes against merchant ships in the inner columns an extremely hazardous undertaking. So although Burnett was dubious at the time whether the operation had been a success or a failure, if he had been able to see into the enemy's mind he would have known that his 'fighting destroyer escort' had proved its worth.

9

The End of the Beginning

This is not the end. It is not even the beginning of the end.
But it is, perhaps, the end of the beginning
W. S. Churchill. 10 November 1942

WE MUST NOW FOLLOW the fortunes of QP14 as it headed west under the capable leadership of Rear-Admiral Burnett, a tough, rugged seaman and very much in his element in a fight against odds.

Since it was composed mainly of the remnants of PQ17, this was a small convoy of only 15 ships. It was in charge of the indomitable Commodore J. C. K. Dowding, who hoisted his broad pendant on board the *Ocean Voice* which, as Commodore's ship in PQ16, it will be remembered had closely escaped destruction by bombing. The close escort of the two A/A ships *Palomares* and *Pozarica*, two destroyers, four corvettes, three minesweepers and three trawlers, was under the command of Captain J. F. Crombie, R.N., the Senior Officer of the flotilla of minesweepers which made a contribution to the safety of the Russian convoys out of all proportion to their size, for they were only little ships of 1,000 tons with a complement of 100 officers and men, and never designed for the arduous conditions under which they were now obliged to operate.

The reader will recall that the German Group North intended to use surface ships to attack this convoy during its passage through the Barents Sea, and to that end the pocket battleship *Scheer* and the cruisers *Hipper* and *Köln*, with four destroyers, had been assembled in Altenfiord. But on 13 September, the day that QP14 left Archangel, Hitler telephoned Admiral Raeder and warned him to avoid as far as possible sustaining losses without corresponding results. Confronted with the strength of the fighting destroyer escort, the presence of British submarines off north Norway, as revealed by the unsuccessful attack on the *Scheer*, the existence of the Hampden torpedo striking force in north Russia, the knowledge that a British battleship force was at sea, and the constant watch on his ships being maintained by reconnaissance aircraft, the Grand Admiral not surprisingly reached the conclusion that the risks were too great, so he cancelled the intended operation by the surface force. It is of interest to note that Admiral Pound had told the Prime Minister that if he had had the handling of the German surface, submarine and air forces, he would guarantee the complete interdiction of the convoys to and from north Russia, and there is little doubt that had it not been for Hitler's ignorance regarding the use of maritime forces, and the restrictions with which he circumscribed the actions of his Naval Commander-in-Chief, the latter would have shown much greater enterprise.

The weather during the convoy's passage through the Barents Sea was thick with patches of fog and intermittent snow squalls, which favoured the defenders and hampered the work of the enemy shadowing aircraft, although these did succeed in making contact from time to time. It was bitterly cold too, and severe icing conditions impeded the work of the *Avenger*'s A/S aircraft in their endeavours to maintain constant air patrols around the convoy. In this they were assisted by Catalina aircraft working from the Kola Inlet. Through not having an accurate plot of the convoy's movements, the enemy's submarine dispositions initially went awry. Instructions had been given to eight U-boats to patrol along a line 200 miles to the east of the passage between Bear Island and the South Cape of Spitzbergen, but by the time this line was established, the convoy was well to the west of it. When this was discovered from a report of a shadowing aircraft which caught sight of the convoy at 11 a.m. on the 18th, the U-boats took up the chase at full speed, and three of them were sighted astern and to the north-east of the convoy, one ship of which was unsuccessfully attacked that afternoon; although *U435* made contact later that night, she soon lost it again.

The tankers *Gray* and *Black Ranger* which had supplied the escorts with 5,600 tons of fuel since the start of the operation, had now exhausted their stock. Admiral Burnett being unwilling to weaken the 'fighting destroyer escort' at such a critical period of the convoy's passage, sent two destroyers into Lowe Sound to fetch the tanker *Oligarch*. This, with the *Blue Ranger*, constituted a valuable reserve of fuel both for his force and also for the destroyers screening Admiral Bonham-Carter's cruisers. The thick weather seemed to offer an excellent opportunity to throw the enemy submarines and aircraft off the scent, and Burnett decided that when the convoy passed the South Cape of Spitzbergen on the morning of the 19th, he would alter its course to take it up the west coast of Spitzbergen which would increase its distance from the enemy airfields in north Norway and also take it towards the approaching tanker. To prevent any shadowing submarine from observing the alteration of course, an hour before it was due to take place he stationed destroyers and minesweepers astern and on either quarter of the convoy and gave the destroyers orders to continue on the original course for six miles after the turn to the north-west was made, and then to rejoin him at high speed. He also ordered a special search by two aircraft astern of the convoy to ensure that any U-boats on the surface would be kept down while it was taking place. This precaution paid off for three of those racing to overtake their quarry were sighted and obliged to dive. All would have been well except for the appearance of a shadowing aircraft during the final phase of the movement which occurred at 8.20 a.m. but there is no evidence to show that the intruder noticed the change of direction, as it was not until 12 hours later that the U-boats were firmly on the convoy's trail.

Two ships had straggled from the convoy after it cleared the White Sea, and during the day one of them appeared out of the mist in the direction from which an attack by the German surface ships might be expected to materialise, thus giving Burnett a very anxious moment, since the threat of such an attack was naturally in the fore-front of his mind. The other straggler was found later that aternoon and as she was still not certain of being able to maintain convoy speed, she was sent to join the *Blue Ranger* in Lowe Sound, with whom she later reached the United Kingdom.

So far the U-boats could only claim three successes against the two convoys with which they had been engaged during the last ten days, then suddenly their luck changed and during the next three days they managed to sink two ships of the escort force, three merchant ships and one of the tankers. Their first victim was the minesweeper *Leda* stationed astern of the convoy, which was torpedoed and sunk by *U435* at 5.20 a.m. on the 20th in mistake for a destroyer, with the loss of some 14 of her company. It was estimated that there were now five submarines in contact with the convoy, and counter-attacks by destroyers and aircraft continued throughout the day, but without success. At 3.20 p.m. *P614*, one of the two British submarines with the convoy which had earlier been detached to patrol for a few hours to the south of it before returning to base, caught a fleeting glimpse of *U408* between snow squalls and stalked her until in a position to attack, but unfortunately her torpedoes missed. Then at 5.20 p.m. *U255* obtained three torpedo hits on the 5,000-ton American *Silver Sword*, one of the ships of Convoy PQ17 which Lieutenant Gradwell of the trawler *Ayrshire* had preserved from destruction. It was tragic that a ship which had survived such great dangers should have been stricken when she was two-thirds of the way back. The loss of this ship, despite the strong escort surrounding the convoy, backed up by A/S air patrols, was certainly a feather in the cap of the U-boat commander, although it was largely due to the very poor asdic conditions prevailing, caused by the melting of the ice during the summer, a fact not fully appreciated at that time.

As the convoy was now beyond the range of heavy air attack Burnett decided to detach the carrier *Avenger* and his flagship, the cruiser *Scylla*, to return to base independently. He had requested aircraft from Coastal Command to take over the A/S air patrols and so relieve the

Avenger's pilots who were sorely in need of rest after a gruelling ten days of continuous operating under extremely severe conditions. He also considered that the U-boat threat was such that it was inadvisable to retain these two valuable ships any longer. Unfortunately, unknown to the Admiral, Coastal Command was fully stretched providing aircraft for a convoy battle developing in the North Atlantic. So having transferred his flag to the destroyer *Milne* (Captain I. M. R. Campbell, R.N.) the two ships parted company, but hardly had they disappeared over the horizon when *U703* succeeded in torpedoing the *Tribal*-class destroyer *Somali*, commanded by Lieutenant-Commander C. D. Maud, R.N., who was temporarily replacing the ship's captain who was sick ashore. As the weather at the time was calm there seemed to be a good chance of saving her, so she was taken in tow by a sister ship, the *Ashanti* (Captain R. Onslow, R.N.), while three more destroyers and the trawler *Lord Middleton* were detailed to escort her. This left the convoy with 12 destroyers and the close escort of nine ships. The next forenoon the appearance of a Catalina from Coastal Command seemed to indicate that the Admiral's request was being met, but unfortunately after only a few hours with the convoy the aircraft was shot down by a U-boat it was trying to attack, and no replacement was available.

At daylight on the 22nd, having assured himself that the *Ashanti* with her tow was making satisfactory progress, Burnett turned over his command to Captain Scott-Moncrieff, R.N., in the destroyer *Faulknor*, and set course for Scapa Flow. An hour after his departure, at 6.30 a.m., *U435* succeeded in penetrating the screen and torpedoed three ships within five minutes of each other. They were the tanker *Gray Ranger*, the *Bellingham* (another survivor from PQ17), and the Commodore's ship *Ocean Voice*. Once again Commodore Dowding found himself waiting to be picked up out of an icy sea. Fortunately, rescuing ships were soon on the scene, and he with most of the officers and men of the luckless vessels were saved. This was the last attack, as soon afterwards the U-boats were ordered to withdraw. But now another hazard beset the convoy in the shape of a northerly gale, which swept down upon the ships riding high in ballast and tossed them about making steering and station-keeping a torment. It was with thankful hearts that they reached the sheltered waters of the Minches and thence Loch Ewe where they berthed on the 26th.

But what of the damaged *Somali*, slowly making her way south under tow? The torpedo had struck her in the engine-room, one of the largest compartments in the ship, and both this and the adjacent boiler room were flooded, so that there were several hundred tons of water in her and a consequent loss of a considerable amount of buoyancy. As she slipped awkwardly along at a speed of about five knots, both captains realised that everything depended on the continuance of calm weather, since despite every effort to limit the area of the flooding, water was gradually seeping through to other compartments and was only kept under control by a constant pumping. When, therefore, the diesel generator which had been supplying power for the pumps broke down, an acute situation arose which was only saved by the passing of a power cable from the *Ashanti*, which was done with great difficulty by a boat's crew who worked in the icy water lashing it to the towing cable. Meanwhile the crew of the *Somali* were busy lightening ship by the transfer of stores to the trawler *Lord Middleton*, and throwing overboard all moveable gear. Thus for the next two days steady progress was made, and hopes began to rise that the damaged ship might be brought safely to port. Providentially, on the 22nd the tanker *Blue Ranger*, on her way back from Spitzbergen, hove in sight just as Captain Onslow was beginning to get anxious about his fuel. With a fine display of seamanship he accomplished the difficult task of securing astern of the tanker without slipping his tow, and, to use his own words, 'We presented the somewhat unusual sight of three ships towing in line ahead while oiling was in progress.' Then, on the evening of the following day a falling barometer and flecked cirrus cloud sweeping across the sky gave warning of the approach of the Atlantic gale already mentioned. All but two officers, one of whom was the Commanding Officer, Lieutenant-Commander Maud, and 80 ratings had been taken off the *Somali*, since by that time everything possible had been done to make her seaworthy, but as the wind increased and the rising sea caused the water-logged ship to labour more and more, the towing hawser sprang taut out of the sea one moment, only to fall back slack the next, and it became obvious that disaster was in the offing. The captains of the two ships conferred over the telephone line that had been run between them. It was a battle against lengthening odds. Lieutenant-Commander Maud ordered all hands on deck, as a precaution. It was well that he did so, for the end came with dramatic suddenness. Early on the morning of the 24th, with the wind howling through the darkness and the angry hiss of the waves rolling up from astern, there was heard the ugly, frightening sound of rending metal as the ship broke in half. This was followed by the shattering thud of bursting bulkheads as the two sections drifted apart, slowly turned over and sank. Only 35 out of the 80 men on board were picked up out of the icy water, including Lieutenant-Commander Maud, who was unconscious when rescued. He was able to vouch from his trying ordeal that death from freezing is mercifully preceded by a state of unconsciousness and is therefore painless.

Reviewing the result of the two convoy operations in which 16 merchant ships had been lost out of a total of 55 convoyed, together with a large destroyer, a minesweeper, a fleet tanker and four fighter aircraft (three of whose pilots were rescued), the Commander-in-Chief, Admiral Tovey, did not consider the losses excessive in view of the scale of air and submarine attacks to which they had been subjected. The Germans lost 33 torpedo, six Ju.88 dive-bombers, and two long-range reconnaissance aircraft—a total of 41; three U-boats had been lost and five damaged, and another had been sunk by a Catalina aircraft off Iceland while lying in wait for QP14. Some 250 aircraft torpedoes had been fired in order to sink ten ships. Both the German Naval and Air Commands were disappointed with the results. The former attributed the U-boats' lack of success against PQ18 to the *Avenger*'s A/S aircraft and the strong destroyer escort round the convoy, and the latter accounted for its heavy losses by reference to the better gunnery equipment of the fleet destroyers as compared with that of the ocean escort type, coupled with improved methods of radar control as well as the more powerful A/A defences carried by the merchant ships themselves. By failing to use his surface ships as planned, the enemy had, of course, lessened his chances of achieving a real success, and it is difficult to understand why he did not attack the tankers in Lowe Sound which, although beyond the reach of air attack, were vulnerable to that by U-boat. The loss of these ships would have been serious, as the success of the operations depended to a large extent on the fuelling arrangements. But the outstanding feature of the cycle of events recorded above was the way in which the ships' companies of the destroyers stood up to the immense physical strain which 18 days of prolonged operating under severe climatic conditions imposed upon them. During the whole time they were constantly on the go, as Admiral Burnett remarks in his report: 'When there was no air attack in progress there were countless A/S hunts, counter-attacks and investigations, continuous zig-zagging in formation, moving positions on a large screen to fill gaps of others away chasing contacts, and during lulls, topping up with oil or running alongside to take on or transfer survivors.' Above all, it was on the commanding officers of the ships that the burden fell most heavily for they had to be 'on call' during the whole of the time, and virtually lived in a stout wooden chair fixed alongside the binnacle, in which they could doze when things were quiet, but from which they could instantly spring into action.

As mentioned in the last chapter, on his return from Moscow Mr Churchill had immediately taken steps to ensure that aid to Russia was given high priority in all departments. In a message to the Chiefs of Staff Committee dated 16 September, he stressed the importance of keeping up a continued stream of supplies to the Russian armies in the field, whose defeat he pointed out would 'let loose the whole mass of the German armies upon us'. But, once again, operations in other theatres claimed priority, and this time they were of such a nature as to mark a turning point in the whole of the war against the Axis powers. Plans for an invasion of North Africa, known as 'Torch', were well advanced and these involved the use of the major part of the Home Fleet; the operation being scheduled to take place in late October or early November. Although Mr Churchill had intimated to Stalin that its launching would affect the running of the Russian convoys, he had not made it clear that an interruption of the convoys was inevitable, because he hoped that some means would be found of continuing them. Stalin's reactions to any alteration in the convoy cycle, as previous experience had shown, were churlish, and the Prime Minister was anxious not to do anything which might injure the good relations he had so painstakingly established with the Russian leader. In this he was fully supported by President Roosevelt, as the messages exchanged between them clearly show. But added to all this, there was in Mr Churchill's mind a passionate desire to do something to help the Russians, whose willingness to carry on the struggle in the face of appalling losses both of men and territory and whose determination to win, cost what it may, evoked in him the strongest feelings of admiration and emotion. Therefore, he returned once more to an idea over which he had wrestled unsuccessfully with the Chiefs of Staff earlier in summer—the eviction of the Germans from northern Norway by a sudden descent, which he had aptly christened 'Jupiter'. 'When we consider the losses attendant on the sailings of these convoys,' he minuted to the Chiefs of Staff on 16 September, 'that they have to take place three times in every two months, and the grievous consequences of announcing on the other hand that we can send no more, it may well be that "Jupiter" with all its cost and risk, will be found not only necessary, but the cheapest in the long run.'[1]

Bold and imaginative as the plan undoubtedly was, it met with strong opposition from the British Chiefs of Staff, while the American ones, with the immense logistic problem on their hands of fighting a two-ocean war, showed no enthusiasm for the idea. Whatever its military

[1] *The Second World War*, Vol. IV, p. 511.

merits, it was the shortage of shipping which made it wholly impracticable. Every ton over and above that needed to bring in essential supplies to Britain was required to carry supplies and reinforcements to the armies in the Middle East and to prepare for the North African landing. Nevertheless, it was with the greatest reluctance that the Prime Minister set aside a plan to which he has recorded he was still faithful.

During the last two weeks of September and the first week of October Mr Churchill conferred by telegram with the President as to the best means of breaking the news to Stalin about the temporary suspension of the convoys. Neither relished the prospect, and the President suggested employing a new technique for sailing ships along this dangerous route in which evasion and dispersion were to be the guiding factors, and by this means it was hoped Stalin would have less cause for complaint. In the end the President's suggestion was adopted in a modified form. At the beginning of November in Latitude 76° N. the sun ceases to appear above the horizon during the whole 24 hours, and what with this, the favourable ice conditions, and the bad weather to be expected, it was considered that ships sailing singly had a reasonable chance of getting through unnoticed. Some trawlers were stationed at intervals along the route and two submarines were sent to patrol north of Bear Island, all to act as rescue ships in case of need, but even so it was not easy to obtain volunteers for this hazardous enterprise, despite the bonus of £100 offered to every man who undertook to make the voyage. Out of 13 ships which sailed on the outward voyage, three turned back, one was wrecked on Spitzbergen and subsequently bombed, two were sunk by U-boats, two were destroyed by aircraft, and five arrived safely. Out of eight ships which sailed home from Russia, only one was lost. On the outward voyage, British and American ships sailed alternately and as the latter were generally faster than the former, they sometimes overtook one another.

While waiting for the President's agreement to the wording of a telegram to Stalin informing him of the reasons why PQ19 could not sail as scheduled, the Prime

Minister took up with Mr Molotov the subject of the Russian refusal to allow the landing of a British hospital unit which was referred to in the last chapter. Although Mr Molotov sent a reply which Mr Churchill characterised as 'a good example of how official jargon can be used to destroy any kind of human contact, or even thought itself', permission was eventually granted and the opportunity was taken of sending the unit in the cruiser *Argonaut*, escorted by two destroyers, which sailed on 13 October to bring home the crews of the two squadrons of Hampden aircraft which had been turned over to the Russians. The force reached the Kola Inlet on 21 October having once been sighted by enemy aircraft, but without any consequential action.

News began to filter through British intelligence sources of a marked reduction in the strength of the German Air Force in north Norway as General Montgomery's Eighth Army moved forward in pursuit of General Rommel's defeated Afrika Korps, and the 'very great danger to the whole German war effort' which Admiral Raeder had foreseen was about to materialise. An added reason for the movement of the Luftwaffe was the onset of winter which made operating conditions in north Norway very unprofitable. Since a large number of empty merchant ships had accumulated in White Sea ports which would be frozen in unless evacuated before mid-December, the Admiralty decided to run a special convoy to bring them home. Admiral Tovey requested that the convoy be limited to 20 ships, but the shortage of shipping was such that the Admiralty decreed that 30 must be accepted. In the event one ship grounded and one failed to sail, so that only 28 ships under Commodore W. C. Meeks actually sailed on the date fixed, 17 November. The convoy escort force was to be reinforced during its passage through the Barents Sea by five destroyers which were to be relieved by five others west of Bear Island. A force of two cruisers and three destroyers under Rear-Admiral L. K. Hamilton provided cover against surface attack west of Bear Island. One Russian and three British submarines were stationed on patrol off Altenfiord, where the cruiser *Hipper* and four destroyers were lying in wait for the convoy. On 15 November the enemy had decyphered an intercepted signal from which he became aware of the intention to sail the convoy, and in addition to placing the surface force under orders to sail, he established a patrol line of eight U-boats 240 miles to the east of Bear Island to intercept it. However, a succession of gales thwarted both the British and the German plans for the operation. In the absence of air reconnaissance reports, the *Hipper* force did not sail, while the ships of the convoy became so scattered that all semblance of cohesion was lost. Neither of the two destroyer escort forces made contact with the convoy, which was diverted to pass south of Bear Island to avoid a suspected concentration of U-boats to the north of it. Some of the ships did not receive the signal, and ironically of those which did two, one British and one Russian, fell victims to U-boats on 23 November. The remaining 26 ships reached Icelandic waters safely, where they were collected and convoyed to Loch Ewe.

Two days after convoy QP15 sailed from Archangel, Hitler conferred with Grand Admiral Raeder. It was not a very encouraging report which the latter had to give him. British aerial minelaying was taxing the mine-sweeping forces to the limit, fleet movements were hampered by a shortage of oil fuel, the *Tirpitz* was having trouble with her engines and was in need of a refit, and the withdrawal of Luftwaffe units from Norway had exposed the weakness of the coast defences in that area. The Commander-in-Chief of the Navy once again stated his view that operations against Russian convoys should be undertaken when there was actual proof that the objectives were worthwhile and, as an instance of such, he cited QP convoys 'since it is expected that they will not be heavily guarded; therefore good results may be obtained'. The destruction of supplies destined for Russia does not appear at that stage to have been considered worthwhile! The Grand Admiral reported that the 8-inch-gun cruiser *Prinz Eugen*, a sister ship of the *Hipper*, and the pocket battleship *Lützow* were both ready for transfer from the Baltic to Norway, but in view of the fuel shortage Hitler decided that only the diesel-engined *Lützow* was to be moved. Once again the Führer recorded his fear of an invasion of Norway during the Arctic night, and he ordered the strengthening of the light forces there and the building up of supplies in the area. He further stipulated that the number of submarines in the Arctic ocean was not to be allowed to fall below 23. Still not aware that the tide was beginning to turn, he instructed his staff to consider the invasion of Iceland using transport submarines, which he desired should be constructed for the purpose.

But slowly and surely the initiative which had been Germany's for just over three years, was passing to the Allies. It was perhaps fitting that this should be the moment chosen to change the designation of the Russian convoys from PQ-QP to JW-RA, ostensibly for reasons of security, but as we shall see, it was to usher in a new and brilliant series of operations by the Royal Navy in their defence.

10

To the Sound of the Guns

With the New Year, new luck
Russian Greeting

THE RUNNING OF CONVOYS to north Russia in midwinter, as previous experience had shown, called for a different technique from that employed during the summer. The darkness which settles over the Arctic regions from mid-November to mid-January made air reconnaissance virtually impossible, and because of the violent storms which occur with marked frequency at this time of the year, it was desirable in Admiral Tovey's view to limit the size of the convoys to what could be reasonably handled and kept together. Under these conditions, he considered that there was 'an excellent chance of evading both U-boat and surface attack and even of completing the passage without the enemy knowing of the convoy's existence'. When the time came for him to discuss the resumption of the convoys with the Admiralty, the latter turned down his suggestion of a small convoy of six ships escorted by three trawlers, at a time when the U-boats were clustered round convoy QP15. Instead, they proposed to wait until 22 December and sail a convoy of 31 ships with a strong escort similar to that given to PQ18, which had made the passage under summer conditions. To this proposal Admiral Tovey was opposed on two counts. Firstly, large convoys were likely to be split up by the weather into a number of small groups covering a wide area and these would not only be more liable to detection by U-boats but they would present the enemy's surface forces with an opportunity to carry out a most rewarding sweep. Secondly, by waiting until the 22 December to restart the convoys, the first half of the favourable dark period would be lost. After a good deal of discussion, he was ordered to sail the convoy in two sections of about 16 ships, each one being escorted by seven destroyers and some smaller craft. To permit of cruiser cover being given to the convoys along the dangerous Barents Sea stretch of the voyage, the Home Fleet was reinforced by two additional 6-inch-gun cruisers. Contrary to Admiral Tovey's considered opinion, the Admiralty insisted that the cruisers should go right through with the convoy to Kola Inlet, instead of turning back on reaching the longitude of the North Cape. As the loss of the *Edinburgh* had shown, there was a considerable risk from U-boat attack to cruisers accompanying a slow convoy, but as Admiral Tovey subsequently admitted, this insistence was fully justified in the event.

The first section of the convoy, known as JW51A, consisting of 15 ships and a tanker, escorted by seven fleet destroyers and four smaller vessels, sailed on 15 December, close cover being provided by the cruisers *Sheffield* and *Jamaica* with two destroyers, under Rear-Admiral R. L. Burnett who flew his flag in the first-named ship. The Commander-in-Chief in the *King George V* with the 8-inch-gun cruiser *Berwick* and three destroyers sailed to provide distant cover. Four submarines were disposed to watch the exits to Altenfiord where the cruisers *Hipper* and *Köln* were lying. The pocket battleship *Scheer* had gone to Germany to refit, and her relief, the *Lützow*, reached the anchorage on 18 December, although this changeover was not known to the Admiralty at the time. The convoy had a fine and completely uneventful passage, the enemy having no inkling of the movement. Admiral Burnett, who had been instructed not to approach within 50 miles of the convoy unless it was attacked, kept some 60 miles to the south of its route after it passed Bear Island, and reached Kola Inlet on 24 December, a day ahead of the convoy, five of whose ships went on through the White Sea to Molotovsk.

The second half of the convoy, JW51B, consisting of 14 ships, sailed on 22 December. The escort comprised the six fleet destroyers, *Onslow* (Captain R. St V. Sherbrooke, Senior Officer of the Escort Force), *Obedient, Orwell, Obdurate, Oribi* and *Achates*, the corvettes *Rhododendron* and *Hyderabad*, the minesweeper *Bramble*, and the trawlers *Vizalma* and *Northern Gem*. Distant cover was provided by the battleship *Anson*, flying the flag of Vice-Admiral Sir Bruce Fraser, with the 8-inch-gun cruiser *Cumberland* and three destroyers, which sailed from Akureyri in Iceland on 26 December. The first six days of the convoy's passage were also uneventful. On the 27th the destroyer *Oribi* had a gyro-compass failure, lost touch which she never regained, and reached Kola Inlet independently. That night, when the convoy was half way between Jan Mayen and Bear Islands a great gale overtook it and the five ships of the port wing column lost touch, as did also the trawler *Vizalma*. The next afternoon the minesweeper *Bramble* (Commander H. T. Rust, D.S.O., R.N.) was detached to look for the missing merchantmen, three of which rejoined the convoy the next day. The *Vizalma* fell in with a fourth ship the *Chester Valley*, and the two proceeded in company. The fifth ship reached Kola independently two days after the rest of the convoy.

By the morning of the 31 December the storm had abated, the wind had dropped to force 3, the sea was slight with no swell, the sky overcast with occasional snow squalls, and the thermometer registered 16° of frost, in consequence of which the masts, rigging and upper works of all ships were coated with ice. In the semi-twilight which passes for day at that time of the year, the visibility was about seven miles to the northward and ten to the southward. The only indications so far received of enemy activity had been direction-finder bearings of a U-boat well ahead of the convoy, of another well to the south, and of an enemy destroyer off the North Cape. However, unknown to Captain Sherbrooke, on the previous day *U354* had sighted and reported the convoy, which she described as comprising six to ten ships steaming eastward at 12 knots and weakly escorted. As for some time the German Naval Staff had not received any reports of British forces operating in the Arctic, and as most of the reconnaissance aircraft and dive-bombers had been transferred to France and North Africa, it was decided to despatch the pocket battleship *Lützow* on a shake-down cruise in Arctic waters where with the help of her radio installations she might be able to pick up some information about British intentions. Preparations for this had just been completed when *U354*'s report was received. This seemed to offer the sort of easy success that Raeder considered worthwhile, so instructions were immediately issued for a force consisting of the *Lützow*, the *Hipper*, wearing the flag of Vice-Admiral Kummetz, and six destroyers, to sail as soon as possible to attack the convoy. Operational command was to be exercised by the Flag Officer Northern Waters, Admiral Klüber, at Narvik. Tactical command was, of course, vested in Vice-Admiral Kummetz. The latter's instructions included: the destruction of the convoy; avoidance of action with superior forces; time not to be wasted rescuing enemy crews and the enemy to be prevented from so doing; the capture of a few captains for interrogation—or even of a single ship was desirable. He was informed that at midnight on the 30th/31st the convoy was within an area 240 miles north and 120 miles east of position 71° 30′ N., 36° 00′ E., steering east at between 7 and 12 knots, and that *U354* and *U626* were in its vicinity. As it turned out these two U-boats were of no help to him in finding the convoy. He was also warned, 'It is suspected that the two British cruisers and escorts which left Kola Inlet on 27 December are with the convoy', and that there were three to four enemy submarines at sea. A comparison of the strength of the British forces guarding the convoy and the German one under Admiral Kummetz reveals that the latter was much the more powerful. It mounted a total of six 11-inch, eight 8-inch, 23 5.9-inch, 15 5-inch, and 12 4-inch guns, compared with the British total of 24 6-inch, six 4.7-inch and 36 4-inch guns. Moreover, the German ships were all first-rate fighting units, whereas the destroyer *Achates*, the minesweeper *Bramble*, the corvettes and the two trawlers were quite definitely not, so there was nothing but the restrictions placed upon him by his superior officers to prevent the German Admiral from achieving his object.

The German ships left Altenfiord at 6 p.m. on the 30th and by making a slant to the north-west they avoided the submarines lying in wait for them and their departure was not, therefore, observed. No sooner were they clear of the land than Kummetz received a signal from Klüber, which must surely rank as one of the most discouraging messages ever sent to an Admiral sailing to carry out an operation of war—it read: 'Contrary to the operational order regarding contact against the enemy, use caution even against enemy of equal strength because it is undesirable for the cruisers to take any great risks.' It shows the extent to which Hitler's restrictive policy had permeated the German Naval Command. Yet Kummetz had evolved a plan which, had it been carried through with dash and determination, might well have brought him a resounding success.

There were about 2½ hours of feeble twilight during the forenoon, during which the visibility was normally sufficient to distinguish ships at distances of up to ten miles, and this was the time during which he proposed to attack the convoy. He particularly wished to avoid night action because that would be favourable to the launching of torpedo attacks on his ships by enemy destroyers, and further, it would be easier to pick out the ships of the convoy during the twilight period. Moreover, since the convoy's speed of advance was not known with any accuracy, he decided to approach it from astern, aiming to reach its furthest back position at dawn and then sweep eastward with his destroyers spread 15 miles apart and so overtake it, if it was further on than expected. He also decided to divide his force so as to attack the convoy from two directions in the hope that the escort forces would be drawn to whichever force first made contact, leaving the field clear to the other one. During the night therefore, he ordered the *Hipper* and the *Lützow* to open out so as to be 75 miles apart at dawn, the former to the north and the latter to the south. He kept the six destroyers with the *Hipper*, intending to spread them about 8 a.m. the next day, and subsequently to allocate three to each force.

Meanwhile Admiral Burnett, whose force had spent a restful if dreary Christmas in the Kola Inlet, enlivened by sporadic air raids from a German airfield near Petsamo, sailed on the 27th and steered west towards the advancing convoy until 10 a.m. on the 29th, when he reached a position which he estimated to be about 20 miles west of it, though he did not actually sight it. After detaching his two destroyers to return to Iceland, he turned to the south-east, and later to east, keeping generally to the south of the convoy route. At 6 p.m. on the 30th, when he was once again to the north of the Kola Inlet, from which a west-bound convoy of 13 ships, RA51, had just sailed, he turned to the north-west, hoping to pass astern of convoy JW51B because, as he rightly surmised, any attack by enemy surface ships on the latter would now be most likely to come from astern. He also decided that if he were to the north of the enemy, he would gain the advantage of such light as there was, and this also was to prove a correct conclusion. The fact that he would no longer be between the convoy and the enemy was offset by virtue of his position on the northern flank of the line between Altenfiord and the convoy, from which he was well placed to cut the enemy off. Unfortunately, as a result of the gale, the convoy was nearly 30 miles south and 60 miles west of the position in which Burnett expected, and the Commander-in-Chief estimated it to be, so that instead of taking up a position astern of it he was in fact 30 miles due north of it. This misapprehension was

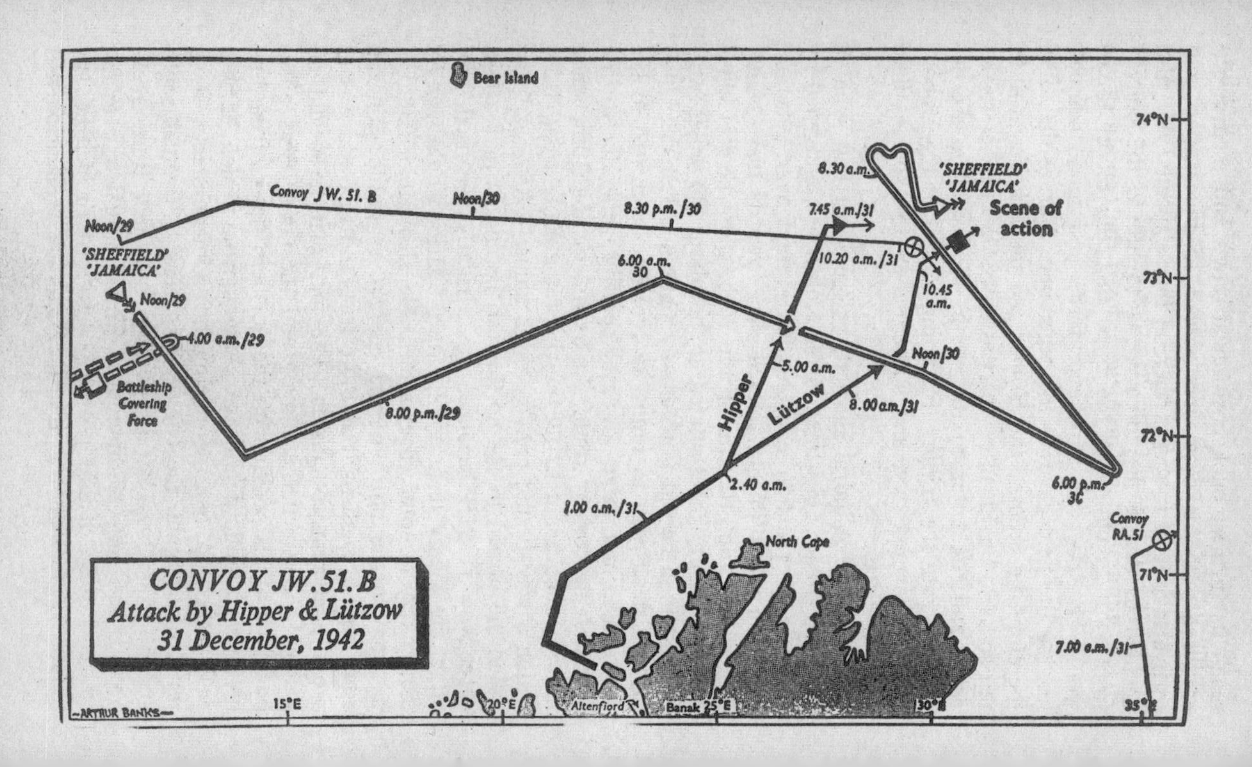
Bear Island
Convoy JW. 51. B
Noon/29
Noon/30
8.30 p.m./30
7.45 a.m./31
8.30 a.m.
'SHEFFIELD'
'JAMAICA'
Scene of action
10.20 a.m./31
10.45 a.m.
'SHEFFIELD'
'JAMAICA'
Noon/29
4.00 a.m./29
Battleship Covering Force
8.00 p.m./29
6.00 a.m. 30
5.00 a.m.
Noon/30
Hipper
Lützow
8.00 a.m./31
2.40 a.m.
6.00 p.m. 30
1.00 a.m./31
Convoy RA.51
7.00 a.m./31
North Cape
74°N
73°N
72°N
71°N
15°E
20°E
25°E
30°E
35°E
Altenfiord
Banak
ARTHUR BANKS
CONVOY JW. 51. B
Attack by Hipper & Lützow
31 December, 1942

to have an important bearing on the Admiral's decisions during the action which was about to begin.

At 7.15 a.m. the *Hipper*, still steering to the north-east at high speed, passed some 20 miles astern of the convoy. A few minutes later Kummetz ordered the captain of the destroyer *Eckholdt*, senior officer of the flotilla, to investigate two silhouettes which had just been sighted from the flagship's bridge. The *Hipper* turned towards them so as to reduce her own silhouette and there followed some anxious moments such as surround all night encounters in time of war. No report having been received from the *Eckholdt*, at 7.42 a.m. the German Admiral told his flag-captain to steer more to the eastward and reduce speed to ten knots, as it was not yet light enough to put his plan into effect. Soon afterwards, more and larger silhouettes could be seen and Kummetz now felt certain that this was the convoy he had been sent out to destroy, so he ordered the course to be reversed and in so doing he lost touch with his destroyers, while he bided his time waiting for a lightening of the darkness which still surrounded him. The investigation which the *Eckholdt* had been ordered to carry out led her away to the south-east and it appears that the other destroyers followed. They were organised in two divisions of which the first comprising the *Eckholdt, Beitzen* and *Z29* were to work with the *Hipper*, while the second comprising the *Riedel, Z30* and *Z31* were to work with the *Lützow*. They had not yet been detached but in anticipation of this, the *Riedel* group moved over towards the pocket battleship, while the *Eckholdt* group continued to shadow the convoy, which they had now been instructed to do.

At 8.30 a.m. on that very cold and frosty morning of New Year's Eve, the situation in the area was as follows: Convoy JW51B temporarily reduced to 12 ships and escorted by five destroyers, two corvettes and a trawler, was about 220 miles north-west of the Kola Inlet, steering to the eastward at a speed of about eight knots; 30 miles to the north was Burnett with his two cruisers; 15 miles north of him was the trawler *Vizalma*, escorting the *Chester Valley*; 15 miles north-east of the convoy was the minesweeper *Bramble*, still looking for missing merchant ships. None of these four groups was aware of the other's relative position, and in addition, somewhere in the area was the fifth missing merchant ship. Lurking on the port quarter of the convoy was the *Hipper* with her six destroyers, and closing it from the starboard bow was the *Lützow*.

Just about this time the destroyer *Obdurate* on the starboard beam of the convoy sighted and reported two destroyers to the west of her steaming slowly north, and a minute or so later a third ship was seen. The German ships turned away to the north-west and in the patchy visibility they were temporarily lost to sight. On receipt of the *Obdurate*'s report Captain Sherbrooke ordered her to investigate, but it was not until 9.30 a.m. that the latter once again sighted the enemy ships at a range of about four miles, and they immediately opened fire, then turned away and once again disappeared from view. On seeing the gun flashes Captain Sherbrooke immediately turned his ship in their direction and ordered *Orwell, Obedient* and *Obdurate* to join him.

Kummetz decided that the time had come to launch his attack and at 9.33 a.m. he ordered his destroyers to join their respective ships. He was now to suffer for having allowed them to lose touch, for as it grew lighter and more ships could be seen, some of which were obviously destroyers, he was quite unable to tell friend from foe. His flag-captain, Hartman, suggested challenging the nearest destroyer, and this was done. There was no answer, but it was always possible that it was one of his own ships and that the signal on the shaded lamp had not been seen, so he did not dare open fire. A message was now received from the *Eckholdt* saying that she and her division had formed up round the convoy, and one from the *Lützow* stating that she was steering to the north-east at 26 knots. Suddenly the yellow gun flashes of the German destroyers' brief engagement with the *Obdurate* flickered on the horizon and at the same time the dark hulls of the merchantmen could be seen standing out against the faint glimmer of the eastern sky. But even as they looked a black curtain of smoke billowing from the funnels of a British destroyer streaking across the sky line, blotted out the ships of the convoy. This was being laid by the *Achates*, the only destroyer now remaining with them. There was no doubt that this was an enemy ship and Captain Hartman asked and was given permission to open fire on her. The cruiser turned to port to bring all four of her 8-inch-gun turrets to bear and at 9.42 a.m. she opened fire, but although several broadsides were loosed, she failed to find the small, fast-moving target.

As Captain Sherbrooke steamed west to the support of the *Obdurate*, the dark outline of a large ship loomed up on his starboard bow. He had so far only been joined by the *Orwell*, the *Obedient* being on the far side of the convoy and not yet having had time to do so.

The turn to port which the *Hipper* had made before opening fire had presented Sherbrooke with a beam silhouette, which immediately disclosed her identity to him. He at once gave the order to open fire, the range being about 5½ miles. At the same instant the *Hipper* saw the destroyers and assuming that they were delivering a torpedo attack on her, she put her helm hard over and turned away to the northward. During the next half hour a fitful action ensued, the British ships firing by radar and the *Hipper* replying with random fire from her after-turrets. The sudden turn away confirmed Captain Sherbrooke's opinion that the threat of torpedo attack was his strongest weapon, and so long as he could maintain it he would retain the initiative over his much more powerful enemy. If he could have been certain of hitting her, he would undoubtedly have fired his torpedoes, but a cruiser steaming at high speed and having complete freedom of movement is a difficult target, and he could not possibly afford to miss because then he would have shot his bolt and been completely at the mercy of the cruiser's greatly superior gun armament. At 9.55 a.m. the *Obedient* joined him, and soon afterwards he sighted the *Obdurate* approaching from the south-west, but still had no idea of the position of the German destroyers, which might be working round to attack the convoy, so he ordered the *Obedient* and *Obdurate* to return to it while with *Onslow* and *Orwell* he kept the *Hipper* at bay. At 10.8 a.m. the *Hipper*, whose occasional lunges at the convoy were successfully frustrated by Captain Sherbrooke's aggressive tactics, appeared to break off the action and retire to the north. This was partly because Sherbrooke had succeeded in preventing Kummetz from discovering what was going on behind the smoke and partly in pursuance of his plan to draw the escorts away from the convoy so as to give the *Lützow* a clear run. But five minutes later he must have changed his mind for he made a somewhat ambiguous signal to his forces: '*Hipper* to north of convoy and there are four enemy destroyers between us and the convoy'; and at the same time he told Captain Hartman to turn back to the south-east and try and drive off his persistent opponents. After a few inaccurate salvos the *Hipper* found the destroyers' range and scored four hits on the *Onslow* in rapid succession, which caused considerable damage. The two foremost guns were put out of action, the forward super-structure and mess decks were set on fire, the main aerials and both radar sets were destroyed, and the engine-room was holed. Casualties too were heavy, and included Captain Sherbrooke who was severely wounded in the face and temporarily blinded. But despite his wounds he continued to direct his flotilla until satisfied that the next senior officer, Commander D. C. Kinloch in the *Obedient*, had taken over. On being hit Sherbrooke had ordered his navigating officer to put the helm hard to starboard, make smoke and ease to 15 knots, for he knew that his ship had had as much as she could take for the moment and it was essential to try and get the fires under control. Providentially a snow storm descended, reducing the visibility to about two miles and touch with the *Hipper* was lost for the time being. The first phase of the battle was over.

We must now return to Burnett and his two cruisers away to the north of the convoy. Just before 9 a.m. the *Sheffield*'s search radar picked up an echo seven miles to the north and both cruisers immediately went to Action Stations. After further ranges and bearings had enabled a plot to be made it was found that the echo, now appearing as one large and one small ship, was moving east at a speed of about ten knots. Unknown to the Admiral they were the *Vizalma* and the *Chester Valley*. Then just after 9.30 a.m. the southern horizon was illuminated by gun flashes. Believing that the convoy was ahead of him, there was no ready explanation for these two events, but it was thought that the gun flashes might possibly be the result of anti-aircraft fire. When, however, a short while later the flashes became more vivid, indicating the discharge of heavy guns, he realised that something more was afoot. He had just received Captain Sherbrooke's report of the sighting of three enemy destroyers, which had been sent off just before he caught sight of the *Hipper*, so Burnett now knew that there were German surface forces in the vicinity of the convoy, but the mystery ships to the north still puzzled him. He therefore, held to his north-easterly course while he discussed the possibilities with his staff, then at 9.55 a.m. he decided that the convoy must be much further south than he surmised and that the ships to the north must be stragglers, so he turned his force to the south, increased speed to 25 knots and steamed towards the gun flashes, an application of the time-honoured principle of war—when in doubt steer for the sound of the guns. It has been suggested that he might well have taken such action some 20 minutes earlier when he first observed the gun flashes to the south. His primary responsibility was 'the safe and timely arrival of the convoy', of whose position he was not at all certain, but which he believed to be to the east, that is ahead of him. It was quite possible for the enemy deliberately to stage a diversion in order to draw him away from it, and he had therefore to be careful not to fall into such a trap. It was the flashes from the evidently heavier guns which decided the issue, and once having made up his mind he lost no time in coming to the assistance of the hard-pressed destroyers. As soon as he was able, he increased the speed of his squadron to 31 knots and the bows of the two cruisers cut through the water throwing up a shower of spray which froze as it fell on the ice-coated decks, super-structures and guns so that they had the appearance of ghost ships racing through the Arctic twilight.

At about 10.30 a.m. the *Sheffield*'s radar picked up two ships one almost ahead and the other on the port bow at ranges of 12 and 15 miles respectively. The battle between the *Onslow* and the *Hipper* was drawing to a close and the flash and thunder of the guns soon ceased, but in the smoke which hung over the area it was not possible to distinguish one ship from another, so Burnett turned his squadron to an easterly course. Hardly had he done so than a new burst of firing occurred on his starboard bow. This was the *Hipper* engaging the unfortunate *Bramble*, which it will be remembered was alone to the north of the convoy. Before she was overwhelmed by the cruiser's gun-fire at close range, the minesweeper managed to despatch an enemy report which only the *Hyderabad* received, but failed to pass on. At 10.45 a.m. officers on the *Sheffield*'s bridge caught a momentary glimpse of 'a ship larger than a destroyer'. This was in fact, the *Hipper* and the south-easterly of the two radar contacts which were being tracked, and a few minutes later the plot showed that she was altering course to starboard, so Burnett immediately led his squadron round in pursuit. He had no margin of speed over his adversary, who was still some ten miles ahead of him and also travelling at 31 knots.

The convoy had meanwhile altered course to the south, oblivious of the fact that in turning away from one enemy it was steering straight towards an even more powerful one. Commander Kinloch, now senior officer of the escort force, in the *Obedient* with the *Obdurate* in company, was three miles north of the convoy and steering to close it, his object being to keep between it and the last known position of the *Hipper*. The *Orwell*, which had been standing by the damaged *Onslow*, was five miles to the north-east of the two destroyers and steering to join them. The *Achates* was still busy laying smoke to the west of the convoy, and the *Onslow* was seeking to get ahead of it to enable her to 'home' the cruisers of whose whereabouts the destroyers had no means of knowing. Suddenly the corvette *Rhododendron* on the port quarter of the convoy reported smoke to the south-west and this was followed two minutes later by a report of a large vessel two miles away steering to the north-east. The corvette *Hyderabad* also saw the ship and two destroyers as well, but most unfortunately she failed to report them. Had she done so Commander Kinloch might have attached greater credence to the *Rhododendron*'s report, but as it was he continued to the southward waiting for corroboration of it. The ship sighted was none other than the *Lützow* with her three destroyers coming up to attack the convoy as Kummetz had planned. Her Commanding Officer, Captain Stänge, had seen the gun flashes of the action between the *Hipper* and the destroyers, and had received a report from the *Hipper* to this effect, but as he approached he experienced the same difficulty as all the participants in this confused action, that of distinguishing friend from foe. Added to the obscurity caused by funnel and gun smoke there were recurrent snow squalls, so when at 10.50 a.m. he sighted an unidentified ship on his port hand, which was in all probability the *Rhododendron*, he turned to an easterly course and reduced speed, waiting for the visibility to improve before making his attack. He had in fact, crossed a short distance ahead of the convoy, which had just altered back to a south-easterly course. He was now on the latter's port beam at a distance of about five miles, and ideally placed to encompass its destruction.

After disabling the *Bramble*, the *Hipper* ordered the destroyer *Eckholdt* to finish her off and at 11.15 a.m. as she sped southward she encountered the destroyer *Achates*, which had just received orders from Commander Kinloch to join the *Onslow* ahead of the convoy. Emerging from behind the smoke screen which she had been laying, the unlucky ship came into full view of the *Hipper* who, with a few well-aimed salvos damaged her severely, killing her captain, Lieutenant-Commander A. H. J. Johns, and 40 more of her company. Her second-in-command, Lieutenant Peyton Jones, promptly took over and as soon as he was able to do so, resumed laying smoke to shield the convoy. This the crippled ship continued to do until the action was over, when the damage she had received caused her to capsize and sink, 81 of her crew being skilfully rescued by the trawler *Northern Gem*. The actions of her former captain and of Lieutenant Peyton Jones were described by Admiral Tovey as 'gallant in the extreme'. The *Hipper* now turned to the north-west and shifted her fire to the *Obedient* who with her two consorts had taken station between the convoy and the menacing cruiser. The range was just over four miles and all three ships might well have been sunk, but once again the fear of torpedo attack assailed the German Admiral, and after firing a few salvos, which put *Obedient*'s radio out of action, the *Hipper* swung round to the north and straight into the gun sights of the advancing British cruisers.

Burnett's assumption that by keeping to the northward he would have the advantage of the light was now fully justified, for whereas his ships could see the *Hipper* plainly, the latter did not see them until first the *Sheffield* and then the *Jamaica* opened fire on her. It was not until these had fired four salvos that the *Hipper* managed to reply, and by that time she had received three hits, the first of which put a boiler-room out of action and reduced her speed to 23 knots. Turning almost a complete circle to starboard, a manoeuvre not conducive to accurate shooting, the *Hipper* became obscured by smoke, and firing ceased. The British ships conformed to the enemy's movements and at one time the range fell to only four miles, a punishing one for the guns of both sides had they been able to see each other; then at 11.43 a.m. when both sides were heading south, two enemy destroyers suddenly appeared on the *Sheffield*'s port bow in a good position to fire torpedoes at her. Her captain promptly reversed his helm and headed for the leading ship with the intention of ramming. This was the *Eckholdt* which had mistaken the *Sheffield* and *Jamaica* for the *Hipper* and *Lützow*, and was trying to take station on them. As the range came down to point blank, the *Sheffield* poured a devastating fire with all her armament into the hapless destroyer, which was soon a blazing wreck. There was now no need to ram her. The *Jamaica* meanwhile had engaged the *Beitzen* which turned away under smoke. This diversion allowed the *Hipper* to withdraw to the west at her best speed and at 11.37 a.m. Kummetz signalled to all his ships to break off the action and retire to the west. But watching the battle from a distance was *U354*, whose sighting report of the convoy had brought it about. She certainly could not have had much idea of what was going on, nevertheless at 11.45 a.m. her captain made a signal which read, 'According to our observation, the battle has reached its climax. I see nothing but red.' Whatever impression those last five words were meant to convey, at Hitler's headquarters they were misconstrued as indicating that the operation was going according to plan.

We left Captain Stänge in the *Lützow* marking time to the east of the convoy and allowing a golden opportunity to slip through his fingers. Ten minutes before his Admiral decided to call off the operation, he made up his mind to join him and hauled round to a north-westerly course. Soon afterwards some ships of the convoy came into sight so he opened fire on them, slightly damaging one ship, the *Calobre*. Commander Kinloch thereupon turned his destroyers to the eastward and began to make smoke, which caused the *Lützow* to transfer her fire to the destroyers. The *Obdurate* was damaged by a near miss, so the destroyers turned away to keep between the convoy and the German ship, which by now had received the order to withdraw.

After the action with the German destroyers, Burnett turned west again in pursuit of the *Hipper* who was 12 miles away fine on his port bow. Then at 12.23 p.m. he sighted the destroyers *Beitzen* and *Z29* some four miles away to the southward and in a good position for firing torpedoes, so he turned towards them and was about to engage them when the *Lützow* hove in sight, so fire was opened on her instead. She replied immediately and the *Hipper*, who was now only seven miles away, joined in, her fire being much more accurate than that of the battleship. To avoid being caught between two fires, Burnett was obliged to turn away to the north, and by 12.36 p.m. firing had ceased and the action was over. He continued to shadow the enemy until 2 p.m. but as it was now quite dark and the latter was clearly retiring and as he did not want to get too far away from the convoy, he turned back to the eastward. After covering the westbound convoy RA51 for two days he returned to Iceland, the Commander-in-Chief having ordered another cruiser force to sea to relieve him. Meanwhile the *casus belli*, convoy JW51B, reached its destination intact.

Kummetz, for his part, concluded that Burnett would be obliged to return to the convoy and would not be able to continue shadowing him, and therefore it was unlikely that he would be intercepted on his return passage to Altenfiord. In this he was correct, but the submarines which he had successfully avoided on sailing, were still in their patrol positions. The westernmost one, *Graph*, formerly *U570*, which had been captured intact in August 1941, sighted the *Hipper* just after 1 a.m. on 1 January. Unfortunately she was too far off to attack, but the captain knew there were other ships to follow, so he moved to the west and three hours later made an unsuccessful attack on two of the destroyers, one in tow of the other. That was the last seen of the enemy.

The result of the action was admirably summed up by Admiral Tovey in his report to the Admiralty: 'That an enemy force of at least one pocket battleship, one heavy cruiser, and six destroyers with all the advantage of surprise and concentration, should be held off for four hours by five destroyers and driven from the field by two six-inch cruisers, without any loss to the convoy, is most creditable and satisfactory.'

Captain Sherbrooke's gallant action in defence of the convoy and his outstanding devotion to duty earned him the award of the Victoria Cross.

The British force lost a destroyer and a minesweeper, the German a destroyer, but the *Hipper* was severely damaged and although repaired she was never again employed in an operational capacity.

The reason for the British achievement was an application of the time-honoured maxim 'offence is the best means of defence', which it will be remembered governed Commander Richmond's actions in the defence of convoy QP11 and which was applied in this instance with conspicuous success. The Germans, on the other hand, although carrying out an offensive operation, were hampered by defensive restrictions. Further, whereas throughout the action the British forces' primary aim—the safety of the convoy—governed all their actions, as when Captain

Sherbrooke sent two of his ships back to the convoy while holding off the *Hipper* with the other two, the German ships whose aim was the destruction of the convoy were constantly being deflected by other considerations, paramount among which was the avoidance of damage to themselves. The six powerfully-armed destroyers showed a singular lack of initiative for which Kummetz afterwards tried to shoulder the responsibility. 'As the action developed', he said in his report, 'I should no longer have been able to assemble our own destroyers round the *Hipper* before darkness, and would thus have left her without destroyer protection at a difficult period.' He also told Klüber that it would have been wrong to send the destroyers away, otherwise the perspective would have been lost. Captain Stänge of the *Lützow* agreed with these views, yet there can be no doubt that a resolute attack on the convoy by the three destroyers attached to him when he was marking time waiting for the visibility to improve, would have paid a handsome dividend.

The action brought home to the German Naval Command the fact that so long as Flag and Commanding Officers were bound by such crippling restrictions, success would remain beyond their grasp, but before the partial lifting of these could take effect the Battle of the Barents Sea was to have repercussions in the German High Command far beyond anything which Admiral Kummetz could ever have imagined.

11

A Significant Series of Events

Events are sometimes the best calendars
Lord Beaconsfield

AS ADMIRAL KUMMETZ WAS leading his dispirited force back to Altenfiord, tension at Hitler's headquarters was rising. After *U354*'s seemingly hopeful message there had been silence, except for a short routine signal announcing the return of the force to base. When that evening the German Radio monitoring service picked up a Reuter's message from a British source claiming that an enemy cruiser had been damaged and a destroyer left in a sinking condition, the Führer wanted to know why Kummetz had not yet transmitted a report of the action. He was told that radio silence was mandatory for all forces at sea, and even Raeder, when told of Hitler's growing impatience, refused to allow the rule to be broken. It was not until 4.10 a.m. on 1 January, when the *Hipper* was safely inside the fiord, that Kummetz despatched a brief report in which no mention was made of the convoy and a rather tendentious account was given of the action. Hitler, who had been hoping to announce a great New Year's Day victory, was ill-satisfied with this information and demanded to be given a more detailed account, adding that it was disgraceful that he, as Supreme Commander of the Armed Forces, should be kept in such ignorance, whereas the British had been able to make an announcement the previous evening. Kummetz's excuse for his silence was the simple one that he had nothing to report, but he was not aware of the false hopes raised by *U354*'s signal. However, at about midday, when he had received Captain Stänge's account of the proceedings of the *Lützow*, he sent off an amplifying report. Later that afternoon when the destroyers' reports had come in, he sent off yet another message giving more details of the affray. As this last message was rather long it was marked for despatch by teleprinter, whereas the first two reports had been transmitted by radio. Owing to trouble with the engine of the boat taking the message ashore, to a change of cyphers and to a breakdown in the teleprinter line, it was 7 p.m. before Raeder received the message in Berlin. He at once telephoned a paraphrased version to Hitler's headquarters, but by then the latter's impatience had overstepped the bounds of reason. In an outburst of anger he decreed that all the heavy ships were to be put out of commission and ordered Raeder to report to him immediately, so that he could be informed personally of this 'irrevocable decision'. This irrational action marked the culmination of a growing feeling of impatience with his navy that Hitler had evinced even before the failure of this operation, and which undoubtedly stemmed from Reichsmarschall Göring's malicious propaganda regarding the number of fighter aircraft tied down for the protection of the big ships, and the paucity of results achieved by the latter.

Raeder did not hasten to comply with Hitler's command to report to him, hoping that after a cooling-off period he might be in a more reasonable frame of mind. The meeting took place on 6 January, and the Grand Admiral has given a full account of it in his memoirs.[1] After delivering what he calls 'a spiteful and quite unobjective attack on the Navy', Hitler handed him a list of points for consideration based on the premise that all battleships, battle-cruisers, and heavy cruisers were to be paid off. Nine days later Raeder presented his reply together with a memorandum on the use of sea-power. 'If Germany destroys her warships,' he said, 'then Britain, whose whole war effort stands or falls with the control of the seaways, will regard the war as practically won.' But Hitler was not open to argument, and so in a private meeting after the conference Raeder tendered his resignation which was accepted. Thus his long and unsuccessful struggle to make Hitler understand the value and importance of sea-power came to an end. On 30 January he was succeeded by Admiral Dönitz who until then had been the Flag Officer Submarines.

When he became head of the German navy, Dönitz was only 51, and he was not only younger than his predecessor, but a very different type of man. He had the ruthlessness which Raeder lacked and which particularly commended him to Hitler, with whom he was soon on very good terms, so much so that even the flamboyant head of the Luftwaffe, Göring, was induced to treat him with deference. For the moment we must leave Dönitz as he gets to grips with his new responsibilities, and return to the Russian convoys, on which his influence was soon to be felt.

Despite the fact that in Britain the sailing of these con-

---

[1] Grand Admiral Raeder, *Struggle for the Sea,* p. 227 *et seq.*

voys under the prevailing favourable conditions was being expedited, the Russians themselves were not satisfied with what was being done. They claimed that they had been promised 30 ships in both January and February, yet only 14 had been assembled for the next convoy due to sail on 17 January. When the Russian Ambassador, M. Maisky, lodged an official complaint on the matter, the Prime Minister told the Foreign Secretary, Mr Eden, 'I am getting to the end of my tether with these repeated Russian naggings.'[1] As already mentioned, the Russians took very little stock of what was going on in the rest of the world, and pressed their claims with monotonous insistence, but now that operations in the Mediterranean were in full swing and the Battle of the Atlantic was working up towards a crisis, shipping was at an even greater premium. Nevertheless, as Admiral Tovey had pointed out, and as the success of convoys JW51A and B had shown, there was everything to be gained by making the best possible use of the 'dark' period.

The Admiralty were, of course, ignorant of the facts related above attending on Raeder's resignation, and in view of the lack of success which the enemy had had during his operations against convoy JW51B, it seemed likely that a more powerful force, which would include the *Tirpitz*, might be used against the next convoy. It was also thought that the carrier *Graf Zeppelin* might be nearing completion, although this was not so. These views were strengthened when on 10 January the battle-cruiser *Scharnhorst* and the heavy cruiser *Prinz Eugen* were sighted by reconnaissance aircraft off the Skaw steering north-west. Steps were taken to intercept them but when the German ships knew that they had been sighted they reversed their course and returned to the Baltic. It is of interest to note that Hitler did not cancel this move, which he had authorised on 22 December before the outburst which led to Raeder's resignation.

The British Home Fleet was still without a carrier, but it now included three battleships of the *King George V* class, eight cruisers, and about 20 destroyers, an adequate

---

[1] *The Second World War*, Vol. IV, p. 825.

force for covering the next convoy. Thus on 17 January convoy JW52, consisting of 14 ships, sailed from Loch Ewe. The weather was fine and once the Commodore had ordered a particularly slow ship to return to Iceland, excellent progress was made. The convoy was sighted by aircraft on the 23rd and, when it was still west of Bear Island, U-boats made contact, but thanks to the increasing number of escort vessels equipped with high-frequency direction-finding apparatus, which enabled them to obtain bearings of any U-boat making a signal, all the latter's attempts to attack were foiled. The U-boats' habit of chattering to each other and of reporting their position at frequent intervals to the Flag Officer under whom they were operating, enabled the senior officer of the escort to alter the course of the convoy so as to avoid the areas in which they were patrolling. But these movements were unknown to the Flag Officer commanding the cruiser covering force who, as we have seen, generally kept some 40 or 50 miles on the flank of the convoy and avoided the dangerous area astern of it where the U-boats generally congregated. He was, therefore, disturbed to find afterwards that on one occasion his force in fact had been occupying such a position when he believed it to be on the convoy's port bow. Commenting on this, Admiral Tovey emphasised the importance of all forces seizing the opportunity of reporting their position each time they were sighted or reported by the enemy, when radio silence was of no value. Had this been done in the instance quoted, the cruiser Admiral would not have been placed in such an awkward predicament. At the same time, navigational difficulties during the dark period were such that long periods of dead reckoning were inevitable, and as is well known, cumulative errors may result in positions so obtained being inaccurate.

The good fortune which favoured the passage of convoy JW52 continued to the end. An unsuccessful attack by four He.115 torpedo carrying aircraft was driven off, two of the attackers being shot down, and the convoy arrived intact in the Kola Inlet on 27 January. Two days later the return convoy RA52 sailed. Because of delays in unloading, only 11 ships were ready, so that the escorts, which included the damaged *Onslow*, well outnumbered the ships in convoy. However this time the U-boats managed to sink one ship, the American S.S. *Greylock*, fortunately without the loss of a single life, and the remaining ten ships reached Loch Ewe safely.

The next convoy, JW53, should have sailed on 11 February, but due to loading delays it did not do so until the 15th, and then only 28 of the 30 ships allocated to it were ready. The dark period was now over, and by the end of the month there would be nearly seven hours of broad daylight in every 24. It was therefore planned to give this convoy a strong escort similar to that with which PQ18 had been provided. Unfortunately the convoy encountered very bad weather for the first four days after sailing, during which the escort carrier *Dasher* was damaged, and the cruiser *Sheffield* lost the roof of her foremost turret. There was no relief for the carrier who was obliged to return to harbour, but a cruiser was sent to take the *Sheffield*'s place. Several of the destroyers and merchant ships were damaged, one of the latter putting into Scapa and five more returning to Loch Ewe, while the convoy itself became badly scattered. Fortunately the battleship *King George* V passed within radar range of it and was able to plot the positions of the ships, which were transmitted to the senior officer of the escort force, who once again was Captain I. M. R. Campbell, R.N. With the help of this information, he succeeded in rounding them up and getting them back into formation. Once again U-boats made contact with the convoy west of Bear Island, but so effective were the counter-measures taken by the destroyers, with the help of high-frequency direction finding, that the enemy failed to bring off a single attack. On the 28th fourteen Ju.88's came in to attack the convoy, but the escort which included the A/A cruiser *Scylla*, gave them such a hot reception that they dropped their bombs wide of the target. Similarly another attack by 11 aircraft the following day was equally ineffective, and the convoy again arrived safely, 15 of the ships going to Murmansk and the other seven to White Sea ports.

Again after a brief respite of only 48 hours, on 1 March the escorts of convoy JW53 set out with the west-bound convoy RA53, which consisted of 30 ships. The U-boats were soon in contact, and this time they sank one ship, the *Porto Rican*, and damaged another, the *Richard Bland*, both on the morning of the 5th. That afternoon an attack by 12 Ju.88's was successfully repulsed, and then the following day the convoy ran into a full gale. As always, ships began to straggle and this gave the U-boats their chance, two more ships being sunk. The weather also claimed a victim when the American Liberty ship *J. L. M. Curry* broke in half and foundered, while another, the *J. H. Latrobe*, sprang a leak and had to be taken in tow by the destroyer *Opportune*, which by a fine display of seamanship brought her safely into the harbour of Seidisfiord in Iceland. Fuelling at sea in the prevailing weather was out of the question, and Captain Campbell, anxious about the dwindling amounts remaining in his destroyers, was obliged to send half of them on ahead to fuel in Iceland, with instructions to rejoin as soon as they had done so, when the rest would follow suit. The U-boats were still lurking round the convoy and almost in sight of Iceland they succeeded in putting a second torpedo into the *Richard Bland*, which spelt her doom; fortunately most of her crew were rescued.

The Admiralty had reason to feel satisfied with the result of the January and February convoys. The losses were comparatively small and, as Admiral Tovey remarked, they were mainly due to the weather rather than to action on the part of the enemy. But the periods of daylight north of the Arctic circle were lengthening rapidly, and that in itself was a sound reason for reviewing the policy of sailing the Russian convoys. Early in March, however, the Germans provided another and much more cogent one.

On 8 February Dönitz had submitted a plan to Hitler for paying off the big ships, and as he said, he 'refrained from raising any objection to his [Hitler's] decision'. Hitler approved the plan which provided *inter alia* for the paying-off of the *Hipper* and *Köln* in March, the *Scharnhorst* in July and the *Tirpitz* in the autumn. But at the conference at which the matter was discussed, time did not permit, or possibly he was reluctant to raise it himself, the clarification of the important question of the restrictions which Hitler had placed on the actions of Flag Officers and which had prevented decisive results from being obtained in operations against the Russian convoys. Dönitz, therefore, instructed his representative at Hitler's headquarters, Vice-Admiral Krancke, to obtain Hitler's views on the future commitments of the heavy ships, as at all costs he was anxious to avoid a repetition of the Barents Sea fiasco. He wanted a clear understanding that he had the responsibility for ordering the heavy ships to sea as soon as a worthwhile chance of success presented itself. Further, that once ordered to sea, the officer in command would have to act and fight entirely on his own responsibility, according to the tactical situation without awaiting special instructions from a higher echelon. He warned that in such circumstances losses would have to be expected. Such was Hitler's weather-cock nature that he now expressed 'complete and definite approval of this interpretation' by his Grand Admiral. This decision was to have an important bearing on subsequent events.

Although Dönitz, in his capacity as Flag Officer Submarines, had confidently expressed the view that the war at sea could be won by the U-boat arm alone, when he had had time to examine Hitler's order to pay off the big ships, he reached the same conclusion as his predecessor. At his next meeting with the Führer, which took place on 26 February, he bravely returned to the charge, pointing out that the Archangel convoys would make excellent targets for the large ships, and that in view of the heavy fighting taking place on the Eastern Front, he considered it his duty to exploit these possibilities to the fullest extent. He therefore proposed sending the *Scharnhorst*—which after two unsuccessful attempts to leave the Baltic was still languishing there—to join the *Tirpitz* and the *Lützow* in northern Norway, where they would form a 'fairly powerful' task force with the addition of six destroyers. Hitler's reaction to the proposal, as Dönitz has recorded, was 'at first extremely immoderate . . . but in the end he grudgingly agreed'.[1] In reply to Hitler's ques-

---

[1] *Memoirs of Grand Admiral Dönitz*, p. 310.

tion how long it would be before a suitable target was found, Dönitz replied 'in the next three months', which exacted the prophetic retort, 'Even if it should require six months, you will then be forced to return and admit that I was right.'

The *Scharnhorst* left Gdynia on 8 March and, favoured by thick weather and snow squalls, this time she escaped observation and reached Narvik on the 14th, where she was joined by the *Tirpitz, Lützow* and *Nuremberg*. Eight days later the last named returned to Germany to refit, while the other three ships sailed for Altenfiord in foggy weather, during which a collision between two of them was narrowly averted.

When news of the concentration reached Admiral Tovey, his argument for suspending the Arctic convoys during the summer months was strongly reinforced, and he so informed the Admiralty. He pointed out that the only counter to the enemy's move was for the battle fleet to accompany the convoys into the Barents Sea and this would be a foolhardy adventure unless a really powerful carrier force were available to accompany it. However, while the matter was still under discussion, it was decided by events taking place in the Battle of the Atlantic. Dönitz had thrown the full weight of the U-boat arm into the struggle in a desperate attempt to reach a decision. In January there had been a big drop in the number of merchant ships sunk there, in February and March losses rose steeply, but these were not achieved without loss to the U-boats, 12 of which were destroyed in March. It was now *la guerre à l'outrance* and realising that a crisis was approaching, the Admiralty saw that every available reinforcement would be needed to defeat the enemy's intentions, and this ruled out a continuation of the Russian convoys. On 30 March Mr Churchill broke the news to Stalin in a telegram in which he cited the German concentration of ships in northern Norway as the primary reason for suspending the March convoy, and warned him that offensive operations in the Mediterranean in May would take every single escort vessel. As always, Stalin took the news with bad grace, referring to 'a catastrophic diminution of supplies of arms and military raw materials to the U.S.S.R.',[1] but after a further telegram from the Prime Minister on 6 April which outlined the way in which the Allies were bringing pressure to bear on Germany, both on land and in the air, Stalin became more amenable.

About this time Dönitz decided to remove one link from the cumbersome chain of command in north Norway, which it will be remembered had been established after the invasion of that country. He gave as his reason for so doing: 'With the situation in the war at sea as it was at the beginning of 1943, any large scale naval operations such as would have required an organisation of this nature, were no longer to be expected',[2] but the primary cause of the change was undoubtedly the way in which the reports of the Barents Sea battle had been handled. As mentioned in Chapter 2, the post of Flag Officer Northern Waters was now amalgamated with that of Group North, and Admiral Schniewind was appointed to it with the title of Commander-in-Chief Northern Group, with his headquarters at Kiel.

The long days of perpetual light dragged slowly by for the crews of the German ships as they lay idly at their moorings in Altenfiord with no worthwhile targets to lure them to sea. But by their presence alone they were bringing greater relief to their brothers-in-arms on the Russian front than they had hitherto succeeded in doing by their sorties into the Barents Sea. The shortage of oil fuel at that time precluded even such a modest diversion as going to sea for target practice. However, at the end of August enough fuel had been saved to permit of a minor operation being carried out against Spitzbergen, which was bombarded by the *Tirpitz* and *Scharnhorst* on 8 September. News of the movements of the Germans ships reached London early that morning, and although the Home Fleet put to sea immediately, there was, of course, no hope of intercepting the enemy ships. On 22 September a Catalina aircraft reached the depleted and harassed garrison, bringing them new radio equipment and supplies.

---

[1] *The Second World War,* Vol. IV, p. 676.
[2] *Memoirs,* pp. 367-8.

The Spitzbergen sortie had used up almost all the available supply of oil fuel, but Captain Hoffmeier of the *Scharnhorst* was not at all satisfied with the performance of his gun crews during the operation and requested permission from Admiral Kummetz to carry out further high- and low-angle target practice. This was eventually approved and he put to sea for the purpose on 21st, anchoring for the night off the island of Aaroy with the intention of continuing with the practices the following day. He was therefore surprised when the next morning the sleeve target which he had ordered failed to appear and still more so when at about 11 a.m. he received orders to await the arrival of two destroyers which were

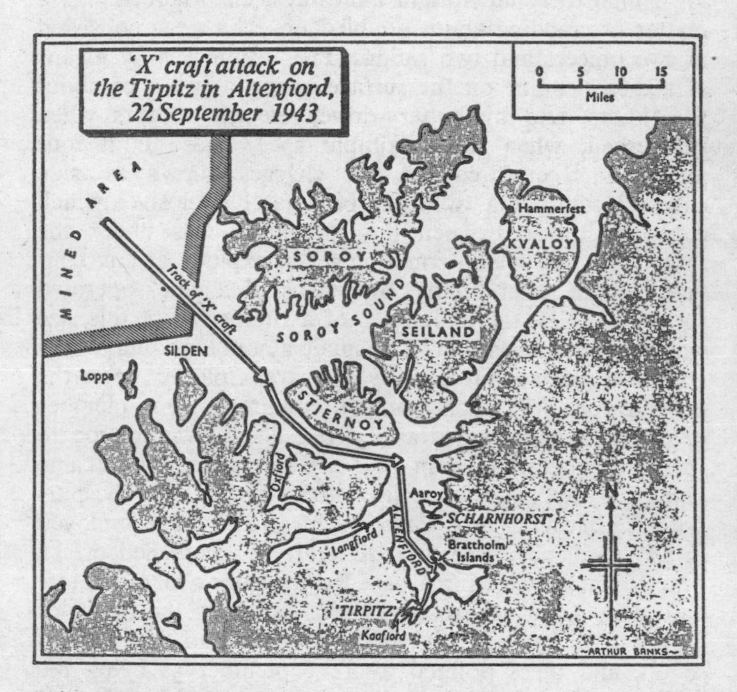

being sent to join him and escort him back to the anchorage, where he was to occupy the berth recently vacated by the *Lützow*. It was not until his ship was safely berthed inside the zareba of nets that he heard of the stirring events which had occasioned the change in his programme.

On the morning of 10 September an R.A.F. photographic reconnaissance aircraft which had been specially flown to North Russia for the purpose, observed that the *Tirpitz* was back in her usual berth in Kaafiord, a branch of Altenfiord. This information was anxiously awaited by Rear-Admiral C. B. Barry, the Flag Officer Submarines. It had been decided to stage an attack on the German heavy ships menacing the Russian convoys, using midget submarines known as 'X' craft. These vessels were 50 feet long and 5½ feet in diameter in the middle, tapering off towards the bow and stern. There was just room for a man to stand upright amidships, elsewhere it was a matter of crawling about doubled up. The crew consisted of two officers and two ratings. Propulsion was by means of a diesel engine on the surface giving a speed of about 6½ knots, and by battery-driven electric motors when submerged, when the maximum speed was about four knots. Each craft carried two charges known as 'side cargoes' containing two tons of amatol explosive, which could be released when the submarine was under the target ship and which could be set to explode at any convenient time after laying, by means of a clock-operated fuse. Naturally, the endurance of a submarine of this size was limited not only by the small amount of fuel which could be carried but also by the strain placed upon the crew living under such cramped conditions. One member of the crew was trained as a diver, and it was his job to free the submarine from any net in which she became entangled, by using a special cutter provided for the purpose. This was a very tricky business and only employed in an emergency. The first 'X' craft was launched on 15 March, but in selecting a date for the attack many factors had to be taken into consideration, such as the hours of darkness, the phases of the moon, the state of the tide and so on, and these pointed to 22 September as being the earliest and most suitable date. Because the 'X' craft had insufficient endurance to reach north Norway on their own, arrangements were made for the six craft selected for the operation to be towed there by six ordinary operational submarines which were specially fitted out for the purpose. These were the *Thrasher* towing *X5*; the *Truculent, X6*; the *Stubborn, X7*; the *Seanymph, X8*; the *Syrtis, X9*; and the *Sceptre, X10*. They sailed at intervals from their base in the west of Scotland on the night of 11/12 September, and before the aerial photographs of Altenfiord had been received. These had to be flown in by a Catalina aircraft which had been sent to north Russia for the purpose. Two days later, when these had been received and evaluated, Admiral Barry made a prearranged signal to the six submarines and their tows which confirmed the plan that *X5, X6* and *X7* were to attack the *Tirpitz, X9* and *X10* the *Scharnhorst*, and *X8* the *Lützow*, which was still in her berth when the photograph was taken although she sailed before the attack took place,[1] and the *Scharnhorst* left for exercises. The weather which during the first three days of the passage had been fine and calm, now became overcast with a nasty short sea, and in the early hours of the 15th the *Seanymph* parted her tow, a fact which was not noticed until she surfaced for ventilation some two hours later. The unfortunate *X8* was thus left on her own, but eight hours later she fell in with the *Stubborn* towing *X7*, with whom she remained in company until dusk, when she lost touch through misreading a course signalled. The *Stubborn* contacted the *Seanymph* early the next morning, but it was not until 5 p.m. that the latter again had *X8* in tow. However, the midget submarine's troubles were not yet over; she developed mechanical defects which led to the jettisoning of her side cargoes, one of which fired prematurely, causing further damage which made her of no further use for the operation, so she was scuttled. Early on the 16th the *Syrtis* discovered that her tow had also parted, but although she searched diligently for *X9*, the latter was never sighted again, and it was presumed that when the two parted she nose-dived below her safe depth and that the hull collapsed. There were

[1] Note: according to Captain Roskill (*The War at Sea*, Vol. 3, p. 69) the *Lützow* did not leave Altenfiord until the 23rd, but she had vacated her berth before the attack took place.

now only four of the six 'X' craft left. The crews which made the passage were due to be relieved on arrival off Altenfiord by others who would carry out the assault, but the former contributed every bit as much to the success of the enterprise, as Admiral Barry said afterwards[1]: 'The passage crews of the "X" craft deserve great credit for the way they stuck the long and weary passage and for the efficient state of the craft when they were turned over to the operational crews.' The transfer took place on the evening of the 19th, after the parent submarines had all made successful landfalls; then with their charges still in tow, they closed the land. *Stubborn* had an anxious moment when the mooring wire of a floating mine got entangled in the tow rope and the mine become impaled on *X7*'s bow, but the captain of *X7*, Lieutenant B. C. G. Place, R.N., with a well aimed kick, succeeded in dislodging it. On the evening of the 20th the four 'X' craft cast off their tows and proceeded on their great adventure. The captains of the other three were: *X5*—Lieutenant H. Henty-Creer, R.N.V.R.; *X6*—Lieutenant D. Cameron, R.N.R.; and *X10*—Lieutenant K. R. Hudspeth, R.A.N.V.R. Their first hazard was to cross the minefields guarding the entrance to the fiord (see plan) which was successfully accomplished on the surface during the night of the 20th/21st, and during daylight the next day *X5*, *6* and *7* made their way up the fiord, but *X10*, which had developed a number of defects, put into a small fiord off the island of Stjernoy, where she endeavoured to make them good, unfortunately without success, and she was unable to take any further part in the operation. At about 4.30 p.m. *X7* sighted the *Scharnhorst* anchored under the lee of Aaroy island on return from her first day's gunnery practices, but she was not her target, so together with *X6* she carried on up the fiord and the two craft spent the first part of the night of the 21st/22nd among the Brattholm group of islands, only four miles from where the unsuspecting battleship *Tirpitz* was lying. *X6* was having trouble with her periscope, which made her subsequent achievements all the more remarkable. It was just after

---

[1] See *London Gazette*, No. 38204 of 10 February 1948, para. 68.

midnight when Lieutenant Place set out in *X7* for Kaafiord, followed about an hour later by Lieutenant Cameron in *X6*. They cut their way through the anti-submarine net guarding the entrance to the fiord, but in going deep to avoid a patrolling motor boat, *X7* got caught in a spare section of net, formerly part of the zareba round the *Lützow*, from which it took him over an hour to extricate his craft. At 7.05 a.m. *X6* passed through the boat entrance in the anti-torpedo nets surrounding the *Tirpitz* and which had been opened to admit a motor boat, and closed a few moments after *X6* passed through. Unfortunately, she then ran aground and in freeing herself broke surface for a moment, and was observed by one of the *Tirpitz*'s crew, who were busy at their quarters for cleaning guns. Luckily it took some time for the information to reach someone in authority, by which time after being again forced to the surface by a rock and getting entangled in the nets on the far side of the *Tirpitz* Cameron managed to release both his charges set to detonate in one hour abreast the battleship's forward turrets. The time was 7.15 a.m.

Realising that escape was hopeless, he ordered the scuttling of his craft, making sure that all secret equipment had first been destroyed. He and his crew were picked up by the captain of the *Tirpitz*'s motor boat which was alongside when he first broke surface and which had been sent to investigate the sighting.

X7, less fortunate than her sister ship, got caught in the nets surrounding the battleship, but after a short time managed to wriggle clear and Lieutenant Place was surprised to find that he was inside them, with the *Tirpitz* right ahead only 30 yards away. He went ahead, slid under the battleship's keel, released one charge under the forward turrets and the other one some 200 feet further aft. Having succeeded in his mission, Place tried to make good his escape, but in so doing once again became entangled in the nets, and clearing these he ran into others. With his air pressure running low and his compass out of action, he was considering his next move when at 8.12 a.m. there was a tremendous explosion, which freed him from the net, and although there did not appear to be any structural damage to his craft, depth-keeping had become impossible and there seemed to be no way of controlling her porpoise-like behaviour. Further, each time she surfaced she was greeted by heavy automatic fire. Place managed to put her alongside a gunnery practice target on to which he scrambled, but before the other three members of the crew could get clear she sank. Two and a half hours later his First Lieutenant, Sub-Lieutenant Aitken, broke surface, wearing his escape helmet. He had tried valiantly to save the other two members of the crew and stayed down until all his oxygen was expended, but it was of no avail.

Before describing the effect of these happenings on board the *Tirpitz* it is necessary to finish the story of *X5* which we last heard of heading up Altenfiord in company with *X6* and *X7*. Although neither of the last-named craft sighted her again, it seems likely that she was the one which the Germans claim to have sunk outside the nets at 8.42 a.m. on that fateful morning. There were no survivors and nothing more is known of her end.

It seems to have taken a little time for those on board the *Tirpitz* to appreciate the threat to their ship, indicated by the sighting of *X6*, for it was not until 15 minutes later that watertight doors were closed. However, when Captain Meier, her Commanding Officer, was informed, he immediately signalled for a tug and ordered steam to be raised. Realising however, that it would be some time before these measures could take effect, he ordered the ship to be slewed as much as possible by heaving in on the port cable and veering on the starboard one. This had been accomplished when the explosion took place and undoubtedly helped to minimise the damage. All four charges exploded simultaneously, the first two counter-mining the others, and the effect on the ship of the explosion of eight tons of amatol beneath her was tremendous. She was lifted bodily some five to six feet, and men on deck were knocked off their feet; all lights went out, and she took on a list to port of five degrees. An examination of the damage revealed that all three sets of main engines had been put out of action, the fire control equipment was wrecked, two turrets were immobilised, electrical and radio equipment was damaged, and the port rudder had been twisted. She was quite definitely out of action for many a long day. It was as Admiral Barry recorded 'a daring attack which will surely go down in history as one of the most courageous acts of all time'.[1] Both Lieutenants Place and Cameron were awarded the Victoria Cross for their outstanding and remarkable display of bravery and both they and the other four survivors spent the rest of the war as prisoners of the Germans. But while the work of the officers and men who took part in this expedition was praiseworthy in the extreme, the failures in the technical equipment with which the crews of the 'X' craft had to contend, indicate that it had not been sufficiently tried out. At the same time, more than a year previously, Mr Churchill had pointed out how this one ship was able to dominate the naval situation throughout the world, and the need to cripple her was urgent. Although after the midget submarine attack she was still afloat, she was no longer an effective fighting ship, and a respite had been gained which was to ease the difficulties of running the Russian convoys.

12

The Scharnhorst's *Last Sortie*

One out of suits with fortune
Shakespeare

IT IS NOW NECESSARY to retrace our steps for a short period to the early summer of 1943 and consider what was happening in the British Home Fleet. On 8 May, after an arduous, eventful and successful 2½ years as Commander-in-Chief, Admiral Sir John Tovey handed over his command to Admiral Sir Bruce Fraser, previously his second-in-command, an officer of great experience whose technical knowledge and tactical skill were

[1] *London Gazette,* No. 38204 of 10 February 1948.

outstanding. But the forces available to the new Commander-in-Chief to control the Northern Approaches and to provide cover for the convoys to Russia, were as slender as those with which his predecessor had had to make do. In particular, the absence of a carrier was very hampering to fleet operations. The *Victorious* had gone to assist the U.S. Navy in the Pacific, and he had only the veteran *Furious* which was nearing the end of her useful life and even then was in dockyard hands for urgent repairs. However, in August the U.S. carrier *Ranger*, too slow for the high speed operations of the Pacific war, was loaned to the Home Fleet command, together with the heavy cruisers *Augusta* and *Tuscaloosa*, and a division of destroyers, but this did little to relieve the chronic shortage of the last-named category which still persisted. When in June Admiral Fraser considered the prospect of an autumn resumption of the Russian convoys, he could see only two sound reasons for doing so; first that the flow of supplies to Russia by the northern route was essential to the successful prosecution of the war; second, that the convoys might result in bringing the German surface forces to action. He was doubtful if the first premise could be substantiated and, as for the second, he did not think that the German squadron would venture out unless it were given the chance to destroy a weakly escorted convoy, or of attacking a damaged carrier or battleship. However, before the Admiralty could pass an opinion on these views, the events described in the previous chapter took place, and the strategic picture in the Far North was changed. Also, at the end of August Admiral Sir Dudley Pound was obliged to resign his post as First Sea Lord on account of ill health and he was succeeded by Admiral Sir Andrew Cunningham. Tribute has already been paid to Admiral Pound's great qualities and achievements and the way in which he upheld the traditions of the Royal Navy during the first four gruelling years of war, but it was fortunate indeed that such a brilliant and experienced leader should be available to take his place. If Mr Churchill had any doubts about the compatibility of the new First Sea Lord, they were soon dispelled. Cast in the Nelsonic mould and every inch a fighter, Admiral Cunningham was just the man to lead the Royal Navy during the offensive phase on which the war had now entered.

Mr Churchill has recorded how on 21 September the Russian Foreign Minister, Mr Molotov, sent for the British Ambassador to Russia and 'insisted' upon the urgent resumption of the convoys. He has also set out the text of a telegram which he sent to Stalin in which he made it clear that the intention to resume the convoys was 'no contract or bargain, but rather a declaration of our solemn and earnest resolve'.[1] In reply Stalin rejected such an enfranchised assertion, and again linked the arrival of supplies by the northern route with the operations of the Soviet armies. This very pertinent question of the true value of the Arctic convoys to Russia will be examined later, but it is interesting to note that at the time there was a general feeling among both the British and American Chiefs-of-Staff, that Stalin's assertions on that score were made more for the purposes of propaganda than out of dire necessity. On the present occasion the Russian leader's reply was couched in such uncivil terms that Mr Churchill refused to accept it, and this action, as he records, profoundly impressed the Soviet government. As further evidence of his disapproval, Mr Churchill temporarily stopped the sailing of the destroyers detailed to restart the cycle of the Arctic convoys by fetching back empty ships from Russia. The Foreign Secretary, Mr Eden, who was in Moscow at the time, took the matter up with a chastened Mr Molotov, who hastened to assure him that the convoys were very greatly appreciated. Soon afterwards the ban was lifted, and the Russian convoys sailed again.

In the Admiralty, ever since intelligence reports had confirmed that serious damage had resulted from the midget submarine attacks on the *Tirpitz*, plans were being evolved to restart the convoys. Although the most serious part of the surface ship threat had been eliminated for the time being, there were still the battle-cruiser *Scharnhorst* and a number of destroyers at anchor in Altenfiord,

---

[1] *The Second World War*, Vol. V, p. 235.

and the *Scharnhorst* especially was capable of doing a lightly protected convoy grave injury.

Mr Churchill had told Stalin that he hoped to send four convoys to Russia, each of approximately 35 ships, during the four months November to February inclusive. To allow for non-starters, the Ministry of War Transport increased the number of ships to 40, a figure which the Admiralty felt obliged to accept. Admiral Fraser, like his predecessor, and for the same reasons, protested against the sailing of such large convoys during the winter months, and it was finally agreed that they should be sailed in two parts, each of about 20 ships, at intervals of a fortnight. This schedule put a great strain on the slender resources of his command, but there was no better solution in the prevailing circumstances.

The first of the new series of operations involved the return of 13 merchantmen which had spent the summer in the Kola Inlet, waiting for a return convoy. An escort of nine destroyers, two minesweepers and a corvette under Captain I. M. R. Campbell, R.N., was sent to fetch them and took with them five Russian minesweepers and six motor launches. Captain Campbell has recorded how on arrival, for the first time, his flotilla was allowed to berth at the Russian naval base of Polyarnoe instead of having to anchor in Vaenga Bay, and how despite brave attempts on his part and on those of his officers to establish friendly relations with the Russian naval officers, the ever-present political commissars cast an aura of gloom over every convivial occasion. The convoy, numbered RA54A, left on 1 November, and shielded by thick fog most of the way reached the United Kingdom intact. The first half of an outward-bound convoy, JW54A of 18 ships, sailed from Loch Ewe on 15 November, followed a week later by the other half, JW54B of 14 ships. As unloading at the Russian ports was a slow business, only eight ships were ready for the return convoy RA54B which sailed on 26 November. All these three convoys had a normal destroyer escort and were given close and distant cover by cruiser and battleship forces respectively, and all of them reached their destinations without loss or interference on the part of the enemy. The weather, too, generally to be reckoned a formidable adversary at this time of the year, was unusually complacent; it was hardly likely that such a state of affairs would continue. The enemy's radio intelligence, on which he now relied mainly to detect convoy sailings, had in fact sensed that some movement was afoot when convoy JW54A sailed, and the U-boat patrol line in the Bear Island passage was extended by three boats to the north and south; also the Battle Group in Altenfiord was brought to three hours' notice for steam. However, on 27 November, nothing having been sighted, normal patrols were resumed. On 12 December the first half of that month's convoy, JW55A comprising 19 ships, sailed from Loch Ewe, escorted and covered in a similar manner to the previous convoys of this series. On the 18th a report by *U636* of the sighting of an escort vessel, coupled with radio intelligence, suggested to the German naval staff that another convoy was at sea, and three U-boats which were about to sail on patrols in the Atlantic, were placed under the control of the Flag Officer Commanding the Fleet. Once again the information was too late for effective action to be taken, and the convoy reached Kola Inlet and Archangel without loss. Admiral Fraser, who in his flagship *Duke of York* was providing heavy cover for the convoy, on learning through radio intelligence that the enemy was aware of the movement, which he thought indicated that the convoy had been sighted by enemy aircraft, concluded that action by the battle group in Altenfiord was a possible consequence. He accordingly decided that the *Duke of York* should go right through to Kola Inlet with the convoy, thereby setting a precedent, since it will be remembered that both the Admiralty and his predecessor had been agreed on the undesirability of risking the heavy ships east of the North Cape. The circumstances now, however, were different. The threat offered by the German air force in north Norway was very much diminished, and during the dark period air reconnaissance was less effective. Moreover, with the *Tirpitz* out of action, an encounter with the *Scharnhorst* or any of the cruisers was to be welcomed. The risk of U-boat attack was acceptable, because these generally congregated round the convoy. The *Duke of York*, with the cruiser *Jamaica* and four destroyers in company, reached Kola Inlet on 16 December, and sailed again on the 18th, so that the small force was well placed to counter any attempt on the part of the German surface ships to interfere with the convoy. During his brief stay in Russia, Admiral Fraser met the Soviet Commander-in-Chief, Admiral Golovko, and acquainted himself with the general situation in the area. After leaving Kola he returned with his force to Akureyri on the north coast of Iceland whence, as soon as the ships had replenished with fuel, he sailed again to cover a double convoy movement which was now in progress.

It will be recalled that soon after he took over as Commander-in-Chief of the German Navy, Dönitz had extracted from Hitler an understanding about the operation of the heavy ships. Obviously, when it was given, neither of the parties to it had any notion that nearly 12 months would elapse before its terms would be invoked. But Dönitz's desire to vindicate his judgment in Hitler's eyes had never left him. In the spring he had laid down the principles on which the Battle Group would operate against the convoys:

> The conditions required for successful operations by surface ships against traffic in the Arctic will occur very seldom, since the enemy, to judge from past experience, will deploy for the protection—immediate and indirect—of his convoys, forces of such strength as will undoubtedly be superior to that of our own forces. Nevertheless there may occur opportunities for attacking unescorted or lightly escorted ships or small groups of ships sailing independently. Whenever such an opportunity occurs, it must be seized with determination, but with due observance of tactical principles.
>
> It may also sometimes be considered necessary to attack heavily escorted convoys with all available forces; orders to deliver such an attack will be given if the convoy in question is deemed to be of such

value that its destruction is of primary importance to the situation as a whole.[1]

When he first heard that the convoys had been resumed, he seized the opportunity during a meeting with Hitler on 19/20 December to inform him of his intention to sail the *Scharnhorst* and the destroyers of the Battle Group to attack the next Allied convoy headed from England for Russia, if a successful operation seemed assured.[2] It does not appear that Hitler had any comment to offer. He had lost faith in the operations of his heavy ships, and even the knowledge of the deteriorating situation of his armies on the Eastern Front evidently did not lead him to clutch at such a straw. In making this statement, Dönitz must have been aware of the change in operating conditions which had taken place with the onset of winter. The long periods of darkness advantaged his opponent's destroyers, in delivering torpedo attacks on capital ships, and the brief period of twilight at that time of the year was barely sufficient to enable an effective attack to be delivered on a convoy, especially if it were guarded by an aggressive escort. There was also the weather, characterised by violent storms and blinding snow squalls, with mountainous seas and intense, bitter cold, which increased the difficulties of locating the convoy and reduced the efficiency of air reconnaissance. But more important than all these factors, was the knowledge that British superiority in radar, of which as the *Führer Naval Conferences* show, Dönitz was fully aware, was likely to prove decisive in a night encounter.

On 22 December a German reconnaissance aircraft reported a convoy of 40 ships off the Faroe Islands, which was in fact the B section of the outward-bound convoy JW55, comprising 19 ships, which had sailed two days previously. The Flag Officer Group North, Admiral Schniewind, thereupon concentrated the eight available U-boats in the Bear Island passage to await its arrival, and he brought the Battle Group to three hours' notice for steam. This was a routine precaution when enemy

[1] *Memoirs,* p. 373.
[2] *Führer Naval Conferences,* 1943.

forces were reported entering his area. He assumed that the convoy would be covered by a battleship force, although this had not yet been located, and he regarded the operation as a trap to lure the Battle Group out and destroy it. In this appreciation he was correct, as subsequent events were to show. Meanwhile, on 23 December air reconnaissance provided a more accurate report of the convoy, now stated to consist of 17 ships in a position 300 miles south-east of Jan Mayen Island. The next day a further report placed it 220 miles east of that island, whereupon Schniewind moved the U-boat patrol line 100 miles to the west. The Fifth Luftflotte had no strike aircraft available with which to attack the convoy, and it was stated that continuous air reconnaissance could only be maintained if confirmation were received of the intention to use the Battle Group to attack it. Even so, it would only be possible to search to a depth of one day's steaming by a battleship (about 480 miles) from the convoy. This information confirmed Schniewind's opinion that the chances of success for the Battle Group were slight and the risks great, but he telephoned the Naval Staff in Berlin to find out the Grand Admiral's intentions. Dönitz was in Paris, but due back the following day, and it was decided that the matter would have to wait until his return. A factor which was also to influence the dramatic events about to take place, was the absence on sick leave of Vice-Admiral Kummetz, Flag Officer Commanding the Battle Group, and his temporary replacement by the Flag Officer Destroyers, Rear-Admiral Erich Bey. In contrast to Kummetz, a torpedo specialist, and a good tactician, but, as we have seen, not a very forceful leader, Bey was a bluff, hearty destroyer man, who had seen action at the second battle of Narvik in April 1940. An insight into his character is provided by his views on the operations of the Battle Group, which he submitted to Schniewind at the end of November, a fortnight after relieving Kummetz. In general he agreed with his predecessor's opinion that during the dark winter months, raids by destroyers on the convoys were all that should be attempted, but because he was a man with an optimistic temperament, he ended his report with these words: 'Any prospect of success must necessarily depend mainly on chance, or on some failure or major mistake by the enemy. Yet despite our weakness, the war has given us many favourable opportunities, and experience justifies the hope that luck will be on our side.' Bey's appreciation did not reach the naval staff in Berlin until shortly before the events about to be described took place, but meanwhile, when information about the resumption of the convoys had been received, they had issued a directive which modified the previous view that sorties by the Battle Group during the dark period should be abandoned, and cautiously suggested that such operations might be considered so long as they were 'compatible with our strength' and on condition that satisfactory air reconnaissance could be provided. This last, as we have seen, was not forthcoming, but in any case it is difficult to read into Bey's hopeful statement, support for the use of the *Scharnhorst*. It seems more likely that like Admiral Kummetz, he was thinking mainly in terms of attacks by his destroyers.

We left Admiral Fraser in the *Duke of York* with the cruiser *Jamaica* and four destroyers in company, heading northward to cover the movement of convoys JW55B outward, and RA55A homeward-bound. The latter, comprising 22 ships, had sailed from Kola Inlet on 22 December, and the following day Vice-Admiral Burnett in the cruiser *Belfast* with the cruisers *Norfolk* and *Sheffield* in company, who had been covering the movement of the previous convoy to Russia, also left Kola, to provide cover in the dangerous area east of Bear Island, for the two convoys now at sea. At noon on the 24th convoy JW55B was 240 miles east of Jan Mayen Island and about 400 miles west of Altenfiord. It was also nearly 400 miles ahead of Admiral Fraser's battleship covering force, and therefore in a very vulnerable position. So concerned was the Commander-in-Chief for its safety that at 2 p.m. he decided to accept the risks inherent on breaking radio silence in order to direct the Escort Commander to reverse its course for three hours, while he increased the speed of his force from 15 to 19 knots. These measures resulted in closing the gap by 100 miles. This interval between the outward-bound convoy and the battleship covering force, which had arisen partly as a result of the latter's unscheduled visit to Kola Inlet with the previous convoy, and partly as the result of the limited endurance of the destroyers screening it, was to play a significant part in the events of the next two days.

It had been Admiral Fraser's intention to advance at a speed of 15 knots to reach a position between Jan Mayen and Bear Islands when the convoy was just east of the latter, when he would have been able to spend about 30 hours in the area, but at the high speed at which he was now obliged to proceed his destroyers would burn more fuel, and this would mean that his stay in the covering position would be that much shorter. On Christmas Day, as the force sped northwards, a south-westerly gale swept into the area, raising a heavy sea and bringing snow squalls, which further impeded the already poor visibility. Great white-crested waves rolling up from the port quarter, picked up the destroyers and swung them off course, keeping the helmsmen hard at work counteracting the vicious movements of the sea by a plentiful use of the rudder. Even the great 30,000-ton *Duke of York* was lifted and tossed around with a corkscrew motion, which becoming more pronounced as the gale increased in fury, resulted in a night which Admiral Fraser was to describe as 'most uncomfortable'. As it now seemed that the enemy had not sighted the homeward convoy RA55A, Admiral Fraser again broke radio silence to direct Admiral Burnett to divert it further to the northward and to transfer four destroyers of its escort force to reinforce that with convoy JW55B. This brought the strength of the latter to 14 destroyers, a sufficiently powerful force to ensure that if the German surface ships were sent to attack it, they would meet with formidable opposition of a kind which they most feared.

Although previously German radio intelligence had proved more efficient than the Admiralty suspected, it does not appear to have intercepted either of Admiral Fraser's two messages referred to above, but the conditions for radio transmission and reception in the Arctic were notably uncertain. Hence on the morning of Christmas Day when, on his return from Paris, Dönitz came to review the situation, this is how he says it appeared to him: 'A convoy carrying war material for Russia and protected by a cruiser escort that was no match for our battleship, was sailing through an area within easy reach of our battle group. Its position, course and speed were known. Because of ice in the vicinity of Bear Island which prevented evasive action and the superior speed of the German ships, it could not hope to avoid our attack.'[1]

From this it must be assumed that he was quite prepared for his ships to engage the British cruisers, yet one of the salient features of his orders regarding the attack was: 'Engagement will be broken off at your discretion In principle you should break off on appearance of strong enemy forces.' Although, as we have seen, air reconnaissance was inadequate both because of the paucity of aircraft and the conditions of weather and light, yet he assumed that if there were a battleship covering force at sea, 'it must have been a long way from the convoy', and from this he deduced that 'the *Scharnhorst* seemed to have every chance of delivering a rapid attack'. But in the back of Dönitz's mind was the worsening situation on the Russian front which seemed to call for some heroic gesture on the part of the navy, and he uses this also as an argument in support of his decision to sail the Battle Group. He claims that in making it he was supported by both Admiral Schniewind and the Naval Staff, but it seems clear that the former was not quite so enthusiastic about the operation as his Chief would have us suppose.

In his headquarters at Kiel, Schniewind was receiving reports of the convoy's progress from time to time. At 9 a.m. *U601* in contact reported that it had just passed over her; at 10 a.m. its position was reported by an aircraft, which soon afterwards returned to base. At 12.15 p.m. he was still without word from Berlin about the sailing of the Battle Group, so he brought it to one hour's notice for steam. At 2.15 p.m. he received the prearranged message conveying Dönitz's order to sail the Group—'Eastern Front 1700', the figures indicating the

---

[1] *Memoirs,* p. 375.

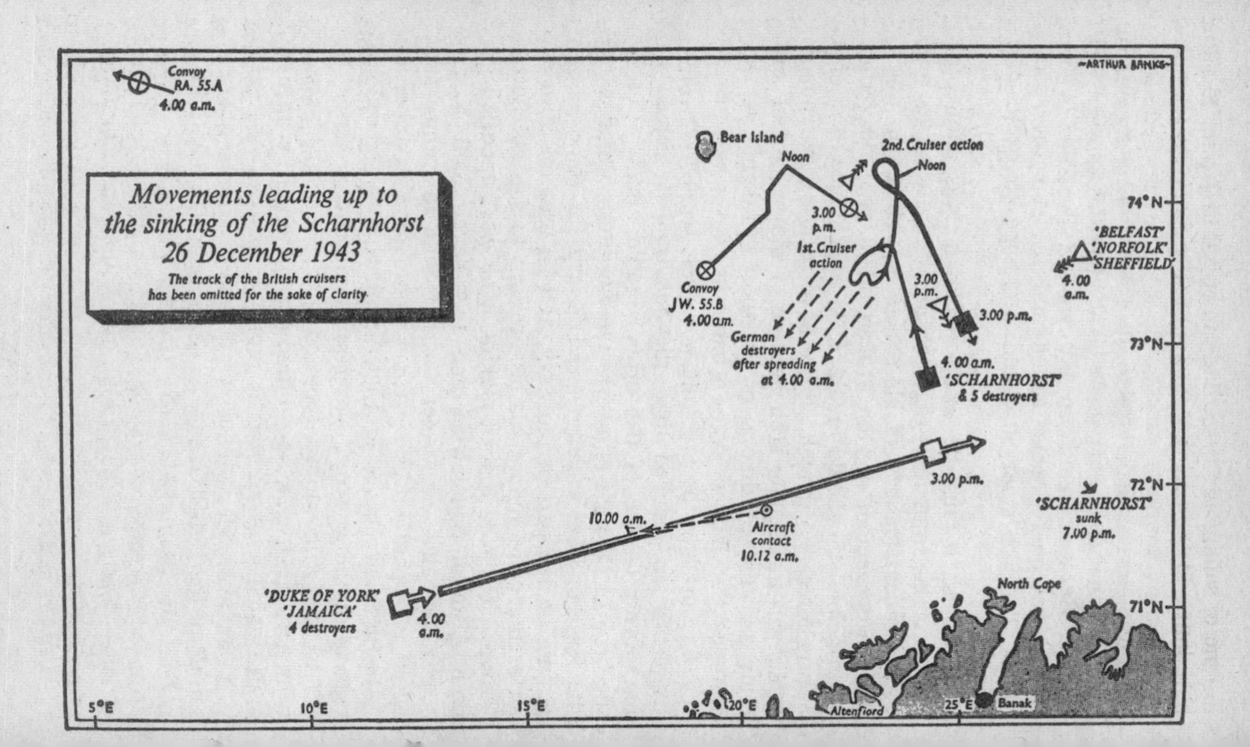
Movements leading up to
the sinking of the Scharnhorst
26 December 1943
The track of the British cruisers
has been omitted for the sake of clarity
Convoy
RA. 55.A
4.00 a.m.
ARTHUR BANKS
Bear Island
Noon
2nd. Cruiser action
Noon
3.00
p.m.
1st. Cruiser
action
Convoy
JW. 55.B
4.00 a.m.
German
destroyers
after spreading
at 4.00 a.m.
3.00
p.m.
3.00 p.m.
4.00 a.m.
'SCHARNHORST'
& 5 destroyers
'BELFAST'
'NORFOLK'
'SHEFFIELD'
4.00
a.m.
74° N
73° N
72° N
71° N
3.00 p.m.
'SCHARNHORST'
sunk
7.00 p.m.
10.00 a.m.
Aircraft
contact
10.12 a.m.
'DUKE OF YORK'
'JAMAICA'
4 destroyers
4.00
a.m.
North Cape
Altenfiord
Banak
5°E
10°E
15°E
20°E
25°E

time of sailing as 5 p.m. later amended to 7 p.m. to allow Admiral Bey and his staff to transfer from the damaged *Tirpitz* to the *Scharnhorst*. The fact that he had not already done so, seems to indicate that he was not expecting that the order to sail would be given. At 2.20 p.m. *U601* again reported the convoy's course and speed and included a weather report which read: 'Wind south force 7 (up to 33 knots), rain, visibility 2 miles.' On receipt of this report Schniewind telephoned Berlin and suggested a postponement of the operation because of the lack of air reconnaissance and the unfavourable weather. He suggested that the destroyers should attack the convoy, while the *Scharnhorst* remained in the offing as cover, but Dönitz would not agree to any alteration of the plan. Despite this rebuff, it is interesting to note that Schniewind's operation orders gave Bey considerable latitude, as an examination of them reveals:

> (1) Group attack on the convoy will be delivered by *Scharnhorst* and five destroyers on 26 December at first light (approx. 11 a.m.).
> (2) Concerted attack will only be delivered if conditions are favourable (weather, visibility, accurate information regarding enemy).
> (3) If conditions do not suit *Scharnhorst*, destroyers will attack alone, battle cruiser to stand off and observe, or if decided advisable, to be in readiness in the outer fiord.

But the one essential prerequisite for success, 'accurate information about the enemy', was lacking.

The Battle Group sailed as ordered and once clear of the land, set course to the northward at 25 knots. With the sea almost astern, it was not bad going for the *Scharnhorst*, but the destroyers with their heavy 5.9-inch guns rolled badly. Just before midnight Bey broke radio silence to report to Group North that he was in the operation area, that action by the destroyers was severely restricted by the weather, and that he was obliged to reduce speed. Schniewind replied that if the destroyers were unable to keep the sea, Bey was to consider the possibility of cruiser action by the *Scharnhorst* alone. The term 'cruiser action' was intended to denote the tactics employed by cruisers in ocean warfare, and hardly seems applicable to an attack on a well-defended convoy. The message ended, 'Decision left to Group Commander's discretion'. About the same time he received a long valedictory message from Dönitz, which enjoined him to 'exploit the tactical situation with skill and daring—to avoid a stalemate—to attack in force and make use of *Scharnhorst*'s superior fire power—to use his judgment about breaking off the action—and to disengage if a superior enemy is encountered'. It is possible to question the need for these instructions if Dönitz had the confidence in Bey that he professed to have.[1] The inclusion of an order to disengage if a superior enemy is encountered, had an unfortunate similarity to that which had tied the hands of his predecessor Kummetz a year before.

But Bey had already made his first mistake when he broke radio silence to send the message referred to above, and from which he gained nothing. The watchful British radio intelligence service heard the transmission and deduced from it that the *Scharnhorst* was at sea. This information was immediately passed to Admiral Fraser and reached him at 3.39 on the morning of the 26th. The situation in the area of operations at 4 a.m. on that critical day was as follows:

(a) The westbound convoy RA55A was some 220 miles to the west of Bear Island steering west at 8 knots. Its presence was unknown to the enemy.

(b) The eastbound convoy JW55B was about 50 miles south of Bear Island steering E.N.E. at 8 knots. It was being trailed by *U601*.

(c) Vice-Admiral Burnett's cruiser force was 150 miles to the east of convoy JW55B and steering S.W. by W. at 18 knots.

(d) Admiral Fraser with the battleship force was 220 miles to the S.W. of convoy JW55B steering to the east-

---

[1] He was an extremely efficient officer of very considerable war experience and he had done well in all the appointments he had held (*Memoirs*, p. 374).

ward at 24 knots. Speed had been increased immediately on receipt of the information about the *Scharnhorst*.

(e) About 100 miles south-east of the convoy and steering to the northward at 25 knots was the *Scharnhorst* with the destroyers *Z29, 30, 33, 34* and *38* in company.

At 4.01 a.m. Admiral Fraser again broke radio silence to order Vice-Admiral Burnett and the Senior Officer of convoy JW55B's escort force to report their positions and at the same time he gave them that of his own force. Under the prevailing conditions of darkness, poor visibility and bad weather, the advantages of the three groups knowing the whereabouts of each other clearly outweighed the possible disadvantage of betraying his position. As it happened the enemy does not seem to have intercepted this transmission. At 6.28 a.m. Admiral Fraser sent another signal directing the convoy to steer N.E. in order to increase the *Scharnhorst*'s difficulties in finding it, and he also ordered the cruisers to close it.

During the night Bey had received several very delayed aircraft reports about the convoy, and from one timed 3.10 p.m. of the previous day he learned that a radar sweep round the convoy had failed to detect any enemy force within 50 miles of it. From the information with which he had been supplied, he estimated that by 6.30 a.m. he would be within 30 miles of his objective, so at 7 a.m., possibly acting on a U-boat report and certainly on a false estimate of the convoy's position, he turned to the S.W. and ordered his destroyers to spread 10 miles ahead and 5 miles apart to search for it. As they were now heading into the full force of the gale, speed had to be reduced to 10 knots. He would of course, have done better to have made for the most likely westerly position of the convoy and searched for it with the wind and sea astern.

At 8.40 a.m. Burnett's flagship, the *Belfast*, which 25 minutes earlier had altered to the N.W. and increased to 24 knots to close the convoy, picked up the *Scharnhorst* on her radar at a range of 17½ miles, bearing W. by N. She appeared to be between the cruisers and the convoy and some 30 miles to the eastward of the latter. For some reason which will never be known, at 8.20 a.m. Bey had altered the *Scharnhorst*'s course to the northward and increased her speed, without however informing his destroyers of his action, so that she was now on a converging course with the British cruisers, and the range between them fell rapidly. At 9.21 a.m. when the *Sheffield* reported 'Enemy in sight', the range was 6½ miles; three minutes later the *Belfast* opened fire with starshell, and at 9.29 a.m. Burnett ordered his squadron to open fire, and turned his ships to close the range, but in so doing the arcs of fire of the two leading ships were temporarily blanked and only the *Norfolk* was able to comply. She hit the battle-cruiser with her second and third salvos, one shell destroying her forward radar set. The *Scharnhorst* was taken completely by surprise and she at once increased speed and turned away to the S.E. As soon as she had drawn clear of the cruisers she returned to a north-easterly then northerly course with the intention it must be assumed, of working round the cruisers to get at the convoy. To forestall this move, Burnett, who had followed her to the S.E. and who appreciated that in the prevailing weather the enemy ship could maintain a much higher speed into the wind and sea than his cruisers could, turned back towards the convoy, adjusting his course so as to approach it from a south-westerly direction and to avoid having to steam head on into the sea should the *Scharnhorst* suddenly reappear as he approached.

Dönitz is critical of Bey's action during this first encounter with the enemy on two counts. First, he says: 'There is every justification for considering that when contact had been established in the morning the ensuing battle should have been fought out to its conclusion.'[1] Secondly, for not ordering the destroyers to join him. There is an element of hindsight in this criticism. Bey was evidently in doubt as to the strength of the opposition which he had encountered, and in the back of his mind must have been Dönitz's admonition not to become engaged with superior forces. At the same time, the *Scharnhorst* had nine 11-inch, twelve 5.9-inch and fourteen 4.1-inch guns as well as two sets of triple torpedo tubes. She

---

[1] *Op. cit.*, p. 380.

had 12 inches of side armour over her vital spaces and two armoured decks of 4.3 and 2.4 inches of specially hardened steel. She could give and take a lot of punishment. Her opponents were far more lightly armed and armoured; the *Belfast* and the *Sheffield* each carried twelve 6-inch guns and the *Norfolk* eight 8-inch guns. But had Bey kept his five destroyers with him, each armed with five 5.9-inch guns, the odds would have been very much in his favour and Admiral Burnett's task would have been a great deal harder. At 10.9 a.m. Bey asked the senior officer of his destroyer division, Captain Johanneson in *Z29*, to report on the situation. He replied that he was proceeding according to plan, steering to the S.W. at 12 knots, and gave his position; 18 minutes later he received an order to steer E.N.E. at 25 knots.

Meanwhile, at 9.30 a.m. Admiral Fraser had ordered the convoy to and steer north instructed the escort commander to detach four destroyers to join Admiral Burnett. This was done with commendable despatch in the prevailing weather and by 10.25 a.m. the senior officer of this destroyer division, Commander R. L. Fisher, R.N., had reported to the cruiser Admiral, and 25 minutes later he had formed an anti-submarine screen ahead of the cruisers which were now in station ten miles ahead of the convoy. It was evident to the Commander-in-Chief that unless the cruisers succeeded in regaining contact with the *Scharnhorst*, he was unlikely to be able to bring her to action with the *Duke of York*. However, throughout the operation both British Admirals fully appreciated that the safety of the convoy was their primary consideration. Such a strategy has sometimes been dubbed defensive, but the reverse is in fact the case, for there is no more certain way of contriving an engagement with a reluctant enemy than by escorting a convoy through waters which he considers it imperative to control. In the present instance Burnett was confident that the *Scharnhorst* would return to the convoy, and if he kept his force concentrated he knew that he would be able to drive her off, but if he dispersed his ships to look for her, individually they would be too weak to do so. Again, if instead of returning to the convoy he had endeavoured to maintain radar contact with the *Scharnhorst*, with her superior speed when steaming into the wind and sea, she might well have eluded him and reached the convoy before him. This last aspect was subsequently considered by the Admiralty, but the correctness of his action in the existing circumstances cannot be assailed and was supported by Admiral Fraser in his despatch.

At 10.12 a.m. a German reconnaissance aircraft transmitted a report of a radar contact of several ships which appeared on the screen as one large and several small ones. Because of the darkness, visual identification was not possible. The position given was 49 miles E.N.E. of the true position of Admiral Fraser's force and 107 miles S.W. of the *Scharnhorst* at that time. Because of the strong south-westerly wind blowing, the error in position is possible, especially with aircraft not specifically trained for operations over the sea. Whether or not the *Scharnhorst* picked up this report we do not know; it would depend on her having a set available for listening out on the aircraft frequency. Either way, Bey continued with his attempt to locate the convoy, but the suggestion that he did receive it is supported by the statement of P.O. Gödde, a survivor from the *Scharnhorst*, that between 11.00 and 11.30 a.m. the ship's company were informed that a British heavy battle group had been sighted 150 miles to the west.[1] Other reports suggest that this message was not broadcast until 3 p.m. when dinner was piped. The probability is that this was a re-broadcast of an earlier message. At 11.58 a.m. after a further exchange of positions with the senior officer of his destroyers, Bey ordered him to attack the convoy in the position in which it had been reported by a U-boat some two hours earlier. By this time the destroyers were well to the eastward of the convoy and so were obliged to turn and once more steam into the wind and sea.

About noon, because of the fuel situation in his destroyers, Admiral Fraser was faced with the difficult decision whether to go on to Kola Inlet again or to return to Iceland. It was possible that after her brush with the

[1] See F. O. Busch, *The Drama of the Scharnhorst*.

cruisers, the enemy ship had abandoned the operation and set course for Altenfiord, in which case he had small chance of intercepting her, and there was little point in incurring the risks which a penetration into the Barents Sea still involved. But at 12.5 p.m. the problem was solved when a report came in from the *Belfast* to the effect that she had regained touch with the *Scharnhorst*, who bore E.N.E. 15 miles from her. 'I now knew that there was every chance of catching the enemy', wrote Admiral Fraser.[1] The enemy ship was steaming westward at about 20 knots and the cruisers were now on an easterly course so the range closed rapidly. At 12.21 p.m. the *Sheffield* sighted the enemy ship and the three cruisers promptly opened fire at a range of 5½ miles. Again the *Scharnhorst*'s reaction to the contact was a large turn away, which effectively prevented Commander Fisher's destroyers from firing their torpedoes at her. A gun duel ensued, lasting some 20 minutes, during which the *Norfolk* was hit twice by 11-inch shells and had one turret disabled and all her radar sets except one put out of action. At 12.41 p.m. Burnett ordered his ships to check fire, and he settled down to shadow the battle-cruiser who was now retiring on a south-south-easterly course at 28 knots, and in a direction most favourable for the *Duke of York* to intercept her. Dönitz again considers that Bey should have accepted action with the cruisers, especially as he had the advantage of such light as there was, the British ships being silhouetted against the western horizon. Once again, by not having his destroyers in company, Bey was at a disadvantage, and he cannot be said to have given that 'luck' of which he spoke in his appreciation, much chance to serve him. If he had succeeded in reducing the cruisers' speed so that they could not follow him, or alternatively steered a southwesterly course into the sea at high speed until he had shaken them off, he might have escaped the fate which subsequently overtook him. At 1.06 p.m. the Air Commander Lofoten transmitted the gist of the report which the aircraft had originated three hours previously, the substance of which has

[1] *London Gazette,* 5 August 1947, para. 33.

been given above, but in doing so he omitted the reference to one large ship. This message would certainly have been received by the *Scharnhorst*, but what weight, if any, was attached to it, we do not know. Had it been assumed that it was a battleship covering force, and had the position been plotted forward from that given at 10.12 a.m. it would have been obvious that on the present course, contact with this force was highly probable. But Bey does not appear to have sensed any danger, for he continued on his course to the south-south-eastward, and at 3.25 p.m. confidently signalled to Group North his expected time of arrival at his base.

The German destroyers which, having concentrated on the northern-most one of the five, were now steering west in search of the convoy, came very near to succeeding in their object, for at about 1 p.m. they passed about eight miles to the south of it without, however, sighting anything. Then at 2.18 p.m. Bey ordered them to break off action, a message which Captain Johannsen queried, but two minutes later he received the order to return to base. And so they pass out of the story, steering for home at a speed of 12 knots.

Throughout the afternoon, in the best tradition of cruiser warfare, Burnett with his three cruisers and four destroyers continued to shadow the enemy ship, keeping Admiral Fraser informed of her progress, and thus enabling him to bring to fruition the plan of action which he had rehearsed after sailing from Iceland and which he had devised to meet such an eventuality. It was his intention to allow the *Duke of York* to close to a range of six miles before opening fire, always assuming that the enemy had not detected her approach, at which range the former's 14-inch shell could penetrate the latter's side armour, and in a night encounter the one who gets the first blow home is likely to gain a great advantage. Moreover, he knew that the *Scharnhorst*, with her superior speed would endeavour to escape, and if fire were opened too soon, she might open beyond effective gun range before the *Duke of York* could hit her really hard. At the same time, the flat trajectory of the projectiles at this range would not allow penetration of the armoured decks, always a ship's most vulnerable surface, but this disadvantage was outweighed by the certainty of hitting which close range assured.

At 4.17 p.m. when the *Scharnhorst* was still 22 miles away to the N.N.E. she was located by the *Duke of York*'s search radar. At the same time Bey seems to have realised for the first time that he was being followed by a hostile ship, and made a signal to this effect. The range was closing rapidly and Captain the Hon. G. H. Russell, R.N., commanding the *Duke of York*, was anxiously waiting with his guns loaded, for the action information plot to tell him when the moment had arrived to turn to starboard to bring them to bear on the target. In accordance with Admiral Fraser's orders the four destroyers had increased speed and drawn ahead, two on each bow, so as to be in a good position to deliver torpedo attacks when visual contact was made with the enemy. At 4.32 p.m. the *Duke of York*'s gunnery radar set picked up the target at a range of 14 miles; 12 minutes later word came from the plot to open 'A' arcs; the battleship turned 30° to starboard and at the same time the cruiser *Belfast* illuminated the enemy with star shell as did also the *Duke of York*. Seconds later the *Scharnhorst* could be clearly seen, her guns fore and aft, speeding all unsuspecting through the white-capped waves towards the Norwegian coast. At 4.50 p.m. the *Duke of York*'s ten 14-inch and the *Jamaica*'s twelve 6-inch guns thundered out and battle was joined. The enemy's immediate reaction to this totally unsuspected encounter was to turn away to port, that is to the northward, and the *Duke of York* conformed, but fire from Burnett's two cruisers (the *Sheffield* had dropped astern with shaft trouble) obliged her to turn back to starboard again, and she settled down on an easterly course with the *Duke of York* and *Jamaica* on her starboard quarter in hot pursuit. When he had recovered from the shock of the initial attack on his ship, Captain Hintze quickly brought his guns into action. At first the *Scharnhorst*'s shooting was ragged, but it soon improved and she began to straddle her opponent with uncomfortable accuracy. Both ships adopted the same tactics of altering course to starboard to bring their guns to bear, firing a broadside, and resuming the mean course until ready to fire again. The four destroyers which Admiral Fraser had instructed not to fire their torpedoes until ordered to attack, might well have done so just before the gun battle commenced, but as the Commander-in-Chief afterwards explained, he did not want them to waste their torpedoes on a ship which had complete freedom of action and which was certain to be fully alive to the danger from this form of attack. However, the four ships were now faced with a long, stern chase, and although at 5.13 p.m. they had been given the order to attack, they were gaining bearing on their target with agonising slowness and she was still six miles away. To Admiral Fraser watching their relative movements on the radar screen, there came an uneasy feeling that despite the superb co-ordination of effort by all the ships under his command, the enemy might still escape. Burnett's cruisers had been obliged to cease fire 25 minutes after the action started, because the range became too great for them, so it had virtually become a gun duel between the two capital ships, with the enemy having an advantage of four knots over her opponents. Despite the fact that the *Scharnhorst* presented a most difficult target, the *Duke of York*'s shooting had been remarkably accurate and she was consistently straddling her opponent, who replied in kind but less often. Both the *Duke of York*'s masts had been struck by 11-inch shells which fortunately did not explode, but one of them severed the important gunnery aerial radar, to repair which Lieutenant H. R. K. Bates, R.N.V.R., climbed aloft in the dark and bitter Arctic cold, and his efforts were successful. As the range between the two ships increased so did the chances of one or other of them receiving lethal damage, because the trajectory of the shell had become a parabola, and the angle of impact was now such as might penetrate their armoured decks. Suddenly at 6.20 p.m. the *Scharnhorst* ceased fire, and at the same instant Admiral Fraser noticed that the four destroyers, on whom so much now depended, had begun to creep up on her. It is believed that with her second or third salvo the *Duke of York* hit the *Scharnhorst* aft near the waterline, and subsequent flooding finally reduced her speed. While the *Savage* and *Saumarez* closed in from the north-west under heavy fire from the enemy's powerful secondary armament, the other two destroyers, *Scorpion* and *Stord*, came up unseen on her starboard quarter, closing to 3,000 yards, at which range the German ship appeared to them like a Triton among minnows. Suddenly she saw them and made a large alteration of course to starboard, but the two destroyers, with commendable alacrity, re-aligned their torpedo sights and fired, scoring at least one hit. The enemy's turn placed the *Savage* and *Saumarez* just before her starboard beam, and seizing their opportunity they closed and fired 12 of their 16 torpedoes, of which at least three are believed to have hit. (The *Saumarez* had had one set of tubes damaged by gunfire.) The fate of the *Scharnhorst* was now sealed.

As soon as he became aware of the favourable turn of events described above, Admiral Fraser, who had been considering making for the Norwegian coast to cut the *Scharnhorst* off from her base, told Captain Russell to steer straight for her to close the range. At 7.1 p.m. both the *Duke of York* and *Jamaica* re-opened fire at a range of five miles, scoring repeated hits on the stricken ship which caused fires and explosions and soon reduced her to a shambles. Nevertheless, even when all her main armament had been put out of action the *Scharnhorst* bravely continued to fight back with what was left of her secondary armament. At 7.19 p.m. Admiral Fraser ordered the *Belfast* and the *Jamaica* to sink her with torpedoes, of which they each fired three. A few minutes later Commander Fisher's division of destroyers added their quota, while the *Duke of York* ceased fire and withdrew to avoid what had now become something of a mêlée around the sinking ship. Altogether 55 torpedoes were fired, of which it is believed 11 hit. At 7.45 p.m. the *Scharnhorst* went down by the bows, rolled over to starboard and disappeared. Of her complement of just under 2,000, which included 40 cadets on board for training, only 36 petty officers and men were rescued.

Meanwhile convoy JW55B, in the defence of which the action had been fought, continued on its way unharmed and reached Kola Inlet intact three days later.

The Commander-in-Chief in the *Duke of York* together with the rest of his force reached there on the 27th, where news of the victory completely thawed the traditional Russian reserve.

13

A Threat Eliminated

That a ship can remain afloat and a gun platform, as long as it is horizontal, is its best characteristic

Grand Admiral von Tirpitz

BETWEEN 1 AND 3 JANUARY 1944 Dönitz made what must have been a difficult visit to Hitler's headquarters to account for the loss of the *Scharnhorst*. It is recorded that the Führer was grieved not only by the unsatisfactory outcome but also by the fact that Bey had run away from the British cruisers when they engaged him for the second time just after noon on that fatal day. He attributed such happenings to the fact that 'too much thought is given to the safety of the ships as in the case of the *Graf Spee*'. He had evidently forgotten his previous cautionary instructions regarding encounters with the enemy.

With the *Scharnhorst* sunk and the *Tirpitz* still unfit for sea, the problems attached to running the Russian convoys were eased. There was no longer any need to give them the cover of a battleship force, but the old enemy of all those who sail those northern seas—the weather—remained untamed, as the first convoy of the New Year, JW56A of 20 ships, found to its cost. It left Loch Ewe on 12 January and three days out ran into a severe gale which scattered the ships over a wide area and caused such damage to many of them that the Commodore was obliged to take the convoy into the Icelandic port of Akureyri to make good defects and restow the deck cargo. A passenger in one of the ships has recorded the following impressions of the gale:

. . . At first it was just grey pavements of water that came slapping against us, but within the hour it was as though whole roadways were turning over upon themselves and falling upon us. The convoy dispersed. It was not ordered to do so; it just blew apart. The tumbling walls of water cut down our vision to no more than 100 yards and the boiling scum that blew off the tops of the waves filled the air with moisture as though sleet were falling. The noise of the wind was like the high-pitched hooter of an electric train, which went screeching on hour after hour.[1]

After repairs had been effected to all but five of the ships whose damage was beyond local resources, the balance of 15 ships set out again on 21 January. Although the close escort of 11 ships should have been adequate, the enemy, advised by an agent in Iceland of the convoy's departure, had established a line of U-boats in the Bear Island passage to await it. As a result of this, and also due to lack of experience of some of the escort vessels, three merchant ships were lost and the destroyer *Obdurate* was also damaged by a torpedo. Meanwhile, the succeeding convoy of 16 ships, JW56B, had sailed, and in view of the evident U-boat activity Admiral Fraser delayed the departure of the next homeward convoy, RA56A, and ordered the destroyers of its escort to reinforce that of JW56B which was about to enter the danger zone. He also diverted the convoy further to the north. Fifteen U-boats had been ordered to attack it on the night of the 29/30 January, and Captain I. M. R. Campbell, R.N., in command of the close escort force, was aware from the increasing volume of the enemy's radio signals, that a serious threat was developing. He was therefore, greatly relieved by the arrival of the reinforcements which enabled him to place an outer defence ring round the convoy.

In September 1943 the Germans had introduced a new form of torpedo, known to British forces as 'Gnat'. It had a listening device in the head which enabled it to

[1] Alaric Jacob, *A Window in Moscow*, p. 14.

home on to the noise made by a ship's propellers. The torpedoes were specially designed for use against escort vessels and although used in the Battle of the Atlantic, had not until now been supplied to the Arctic U-boats. They were to prove a real menace to the hard-worked destroyers, sloops and corvettes of which they took their toll during the last year of the war.

The northerly diversion had very nearly taken the convoy clear of the U-boat patrol line, but as luck would have it, *U956*, the northern-most one, caught sight of it at 9.34 a.m. on the 29th, and the remainder closed in to attack. However, so effective were the counter-measures taken by the powerful escort force, that the U-boats were driven off and the convoy reached its destination without loss, although the destroyer *Hardy* (successor to the one lost in the first battle of Narvik) had her stern blown off by a Gnat and had to be sunk. For his part the enemy lost *U314* to the destroyers *Whitehall* and *Meteor*.

There were now 37 merchant ships in Kola Inlet waiting to return to the U.K. so the Commander-in-Chief ordered them to form convoy RA56, and with a close escort of 26 destroyers and other escort vessels it sailed on 2 February and reached its destination unmolested. It had, in fact, been sighted by enemy aircraft at midday on 6th, but the pilot reported its course as east instead of west, so the U-boat patrol established to intercept another supposed Russian-bound convoy, waited in vain.

With the onset of spring and the need to increase protection against air attack, Admiral Fraser decided to revert once more to the system of forming one large convoy with the strongest possible escort instead of dividing it into two sections, tactics better suited to the dark and stormy winter months. Thus the next outward-bound convoy, JW57 which sailed on 20 February, consisted of 42 ships and a tanker, with a close escort of the light cruiser *Black Prince*, wearing the flag of Vice-Admiral I. G. Glennie, who had succeeded Vice-Admiral Burnett, the escort carrier *Chaser* and 17 destroyers. Cruiser cover was provided by a force of three cruisers under Vice-Admiral Palliser, and aircraft from Coastal Command gave anti-submarine and fighter support to the limit of their range. It was expected that the enemy would make a strong bid to achieve the success which had for so long eluded him and this assumption proved correct. On 23 February, on receipt of an aircraft report giving the position, course and speed of the convoy, a double patrol line of 14 U-boats was formed to intercept it. But once again the tactics of the escort vessels aided by aircraft from the *Chaser* were too much for the U-boats, which never got near enough to the merchant ships to attack them. Moreover, in attempting to do so they lost two of their number, *U713* on the 24th to the destroyer *Keppel*, and *U601* on the following day to a Catalina aircraft of Coastal Command, which was at the end of its range from its base in the Shetland Isles. Unable to break through the stubborn defence round the convoy, the U-boats turned on the escort ships and during the night of 25/26th *U990* torpedoed the destroyer *Mahratta*, which sank soon afterwards with heavy loss of life, despite gallant attempts at rescue made by the destroyer *Impulsive*. Only 17 out of a ship's company of just over 200 were hauled to safety out of the freezing water, a further tragic example of the grim and relentless nature of the struggle being waged between the surface ships and their submerged opponents. But the heavily laden ships of the convoy all arrived intact.

Admiral Fraser correctly appreciated that having failed again, the enemy would make an ever more determined attempt to attack the homeward-bound convoy RA57 of 31 ships which was due to sail on 2 March, not that sinking a ship in ballast could be compared with the destruction of one loaded with war materials for the Russian armies. He accordingly arranged with the Russians to cover the approaches to Kola Inlet with air patrols to keep the U-boats down, and ordered the convoy on sailing to make a wide detour to the eastward. These precautions proved more successful than he had dared to hope, and compensated for the weather which for the first two days out prevented the escort carrier *Chaser* from operating her aircraft. As a result of the diversion, the U-boats, whose number had again been made up to 15, failed to make contact with the convoy until 4 March, when they sank the *Empire Tourist* 70 miles E.S.E. of Bear Island. By this time, conditions had slightly improved and *Chaser*'s A/S aircraft at once took off and succeeded in damaging *U472* in a rocket attack, the destroyer *Onslaught* subsequently sinking her. The following day, despite much movement of the ship, Swordfish A/S patrols took off and succeeded in sinking *U336*; the next day *U973* was similarly destroyed. On 10 March, and without further attempts by the enemy to hinder its progress, the convoy reached Loch Ewe.

From the enemy's point of view, the loss of four U-boats in exchange for one destroyer and one merchant ship was a most unsatisfactory outcome, and the German naval staff urgently requested the return of the long-range reconnaissance aircraft and torpedo-bombers to north Norway, but the request was turned down by the Air Force staff. It is of interest to note that so preoccupied was Dönitz at this time with other affairs, particularly the threat of invasion, that the matter does not appear to have been raised at any of the Führer conferences held at that time. In consequence, the Naval Staff was obliged to revise its U-boat tactics against the Arctic convoys. The presence of carrier-borne aircraft had made it unsafe for them to operate on the surface during daylight, so they were ordered to remain submerged by day, attack at night and withdraw quickly. But unknown to the enemy, counter-measures to this form of attack were being evolved with the development of night flying in the escort carriers. Further, the period of continuous daylight beginning in April would add to the difficulty of the U-boats in carrying out these instructions.

The obvious success of the escort carrier with the last two convoys and the increased availability of these ships led the Admiralty to allocate two to the next pair. These were the *Activity* and the *Tracker*, the first-named built on a British merchant ship hull and the second an American-built ship. The *Activity* carried three Swordfish A/S aircraft and seven Wildcat fighters, while the *Tracker*'s aircraft complement comprised 12 Avenger A/S aircraft and seven Wildcat fighters. The difference between the two ships' capability was most noticeable; moreover the

Avenger aircraft, although not yet fitted with rocket projectiles which had proved deadly against the U-boats, had higher speed, longer endurance and an enclosed cockpit, which gave it a performance greatly superior to that of the old 'string-bag' Swordfish. The Wildcat, also an American aircraft, was better suited to carrier operation than the converted Hurricanes with which the British ships had hitherto been supplied. The strength of the escort force was further enhanced by the addition of two of the Western Approaches Command's most experienced escort groups, one of them being commanded by that ace of U-boat killers, Captain F. J. Walker, R.N.

The outward-bound convoy JW58 of 49 ships sailed on 27 March, and with it went the U.S. cruiser *Milwaukee* which was being transferred to the Soviet navy. In command of the convoy's powerful escort of 20 destroyers, five sloops, four corvettes and the two escort carriers already mentioned, was Vice-Admiral F. Dalrymple-Hamilton, flying his flag in the cruiser *Diadem*. Enemy reconnaissance aircraft located and reported the convoy on 30 March, and from then on the carriers' fighters made the shadowers' task both difficult and hazardous, for they shot down no less than six of them. The 16 U-boats at sea were ordered to take up a patrol line 300 miles south-west of Bear Island with the intention that they should attack the convoy on the night of 31 March, but the battle began two days earlier than the enemy expected, when on the 29th Captain Walker in the sloop *Starling*, struck the first blow by sinking *U961*. Two days later, aircraft from the *Tracker* in co-operation with the destroyer *Beagle* sent *U355* to the bottom, and on 2 April the destroyer *Keppel* scored another success when she sank *U360*. Early the following day one of the *Activity*'s Swordfish, assisted by an Avenger and a Wildcat destroyed *U288*. Thus, despite the decree of the Admiral Commanding the U-boats that the convoy must not be allowed to get through unscathed, which it did, the enemy incurred serious losses of both aircraft and U-boats. At the time, because of false claims to have sunk a number of destroyers, he was not aware that the battle had been so one-sided. Disturbing news was, however, brought by *U277* to the effect that a counter to the Gnat torpedo had been heard. This was a noisemaker known as Foxer which could be towed astern and on which it was intended that the torpedo should home. It provided a measure of defence against this new and dangerous form of attack.

The homeward-bound convoy RA58 of 36 ships sailed from Kola Inlet on 7 April with the same powerful escort as had been given to JW58. The enemy did not learn of its departure until the following day and the ten U-boats remaining available were ordered to take up a position south of Bear Island to intercept it. But the convoy passed south of the patrol line and although, when this was discovered, Admiral Schniewind ordered them to give chase, only sporadic contact was made with the rearmost escort vessels and the convoy reached Loch Ewe intact. Thus, during the winter of 1943/44 Mr Churchill's promise to Stalin had been more than fulfilled. Altogether 188 loaded ships had been safely convoyed to north Russia, exceeding the target figure by 48, and in the face of determined action by the enemy and the severity of the weather. It was evidence of Britain's growing strength and the enemy's decline, but the struggle to control the Arctic waters was not yet over.

At the end of March, when convoy JW58 was about to sail, the Admiralty learned that repairs to the *Tirpitz*, which had been proceeding ever since the midget submarine attack of the previous September, had now been completed. This was so. The Germans had managed to repair the holes in her hull, but without putting her in dry dock it was not possible to replace the damaged frames, so her speed was limited to about 27 knots, enough however, to enable her to be used against the convoys. The Admiralty, therefore, decided that the time had come to make another attempt to immobilise the ship. On 3 April a carrier force under the command of Vice-Admiral Sir Henry Moore struck at the ship; she was hit by 14 bombs, which although not penetrating to any vital compartments, caused serious damage to her upperworks and anti-aircraft control arrangements, killing 128 men and wounding another 300. Göring's persistent refusal to provide adequate fighter protection for the ships in the fleet anchorage was to be largely responsible for the Iliad of woes to which the *Tirpitz* was to be subjected from now on.

Although there were no more ships waiting to be convoyed to Russia by the Arctic route, the supply line at last having been switched to the Persian Gulf for the summer months, there were a number of empty ones in Russian ports waiting to return as well as the crew of the U.S.S. *Milwaukee*, and a Russian crew to take over the battleship *Royal Sovereign*, which was to be turned over to the Russians in place of part of the Italian fleet to which they had laid claim. Rear-Admiral R. R. McGrigor, flying his flag in the cruiser *Diadem*, was therefore placed in command of a strong escort force which included the escort carriers *Activity* and *Fencer* and 16 destroyers, and after an uneventful passage which the enemy did not observe reached Kola Inlet on 23 April. Five days later he sailed again, escorting convoy RA59 of 45 ships. With the *Tirpitz* out of action a covering force was not considered necessary and the escort force was well equipped to deal with air and submarine attacks. When it was only 90 miles north of the Kola Inlet, the convoy was reported by an enemy reconnaissance aircraft, but bad weather hampered further observation. However, it was a simple matter for the enemy, once he knew a convoy was at sea, to dispose his U-boats in the Bear Island passage in the hope of intercepting it, and this he now did, stationing the 12 available ten miles apart on a line running north and south. On the 30th, although damaged by fighters from the carriers, a reconnaissance aircraft managed to transmit an accurate report of the convoy's position, thus enabling the U-boats to concentrate for an attack in its path. Despite the rough sea, high wind and periodic snow storms, the two carriers doggedly continued to operate their aircraft and made the U-boats pay heavily for their solitary success, the U.S.S. *William S. Thayer*, which was sunk that evening by *U307*. During the next two days, Swordfish aircraft depth-charged and sank *U277, U674* and *U959*, a brilliant achievement witnessed by the Russian Admiral Levchenko who, with his staff, was taking passage in the *Fencer*. It is not surprising that an entry in the U-boat command War Diary on 1 June should refer to the chances of success as having 'become meagre' and those of not returning from operations as having 'greatly increased'.

On 12 and 13 April following the Fleet Air Arm's successful attack on the *Tirpitz*, Dönitz conferred with Hitler and expressed the intention of having the battleship repaired and keeping her in northern Norway because her presence there tied up enemy forces. At the same time he admitted that the ship was unlikely to have any further opportunity for action 'unless political developments such as a falling out between England and Russia were to bring this about'.[1] He emphasised the ship's helplessness without fighter escort, which he pointed out justified the use of the *Scharnhorst* during the Arctic night, and concluded that if the ship were to return to Germany, she would only increase the danger of air raids on whatever port she occupied. With this despondent recital of events, Hitler is recorded as voicing his 'whole-hearted approval'! Turning to the Arctic convoys, Dönitz drew the attention of Göring, who was present on this occasion, to the way in which British carrier-borne aircraft were keeping the U-boats away from the convoys, and pointed out how easy it would be for the Luftwaffe to attack the carriers. With Hitler's support Dönitz gained his point over a very reluctant Reichsmarschall, who promised to transfer some aircraft to northern Norway from time to time, and to make arrangements for this to be done at short notice. To drive home his point, Dönitz recounted the story of convoy RA59, indicating how the weakness of the air forces available prevented attacks being made on the carriers, and he suggested that the torpedo-bomber squadrons could more profitably be employed in the North Sea than in the Mediterranean, an argument with which Göring unwillingly, and Hitler fully, agreed.

On 12 May Admiral Moore again sailed with his force in an attempt to repeat the attack on the *Tirpitz*, but the efforts of the striking force to penetrate the cloud which

---

[1] *Führer Naval Conferences*, 1944.

covered the target failed, and the operation had to be abandoned. A further attempt made soon afterwards by the carriers *Victorious* and *Furious* only, was forestalled by German reconnaissance aircraft and prevented by unsuitable weather. Opportunity was taken during these and the preceding operations to create an impression of an impending assault on Norway as a diversion to conceal the true purpose of the immense landing operation being mounted, of which the Germans were aware, and which was of course, the invasion of France.

On 14 June, eight days after the Allied armies had disembarked in Normandy, Admiral Moore succeeded Admiral Sir Bruce Fraser as Commander-in-Chief of the Home Fleet. The latter's tenure of office had been marked by a steady deterioration in the effectiveness of the German surface-ship threat to the Arctic convoys, as a result of the attacks on the *Tirpitz* and the sinking of the *Scharnhorst*, but the former ship was once again fit for sea, having carried out satisfactory steaming trials in the fiord on 22 June. Hence the first consideration of the new Commander-in-Chief was how best to immobilise her once more, since her presence in the Far North would not only be an embarrassment when the convoys were restarted, but was also hindering the Admiralty's efforts to build up a Far Eastern fleet to assist the Americans in operations against Japan. On 14 July Admiral Moore sailed from Scapa to carry out yet another attack on the battleship, but this time success eluded the attacking aircraft. All the skill and bravery of the Fleet Air Arm pilots could not make up for the poor quality of the aircraft with which they were equipped, and which were not fast enough to reach their target before it became hidden in a protecting pall of smoke.

It was rightly expected that the enemy would deploy his U-boats in the path of the returning carrier force, so at the Admiralty's suggestion Coastal Command established a number of long-range patrols over the area, as a result of which three U-boats were sunk. Two Catalina aircraft were damaged by anti-aircraft fire from the U-boats they attacked, and the pilot of one, Flying Officer J. A. Cruickshank, notwithstanding the severe wounds he had received, successfully brought his badly mauled aircraft back to base, an action which earned him the award of the Victoria Cross. But as the northern U-boats were replaced by those fitted with the *schnorkel* or breathing tube, which was being done as rapidly as possible, successful attacks such as these became less frequent. There was one unfortunate incident during these offensive sweeps when one of the four British submarines transferred to the Soviet navy and manned by a Russian crew strayed well outside the 'safe' zone in which air attacks were forbidden, and was sunk.

With the *Tirpitz* repaired and an estimated 32 U-boats now stationed in northern Norway, there was still no real easement in the burden of running the Russian convoys, despite the great efforts which had been made to obtain some. Although in July a record delivery of 282,097 long tons of supplies had reached Russia through the Persian Gulf,[1] the Government decided that the convoys should be restarted in August. There would be no period of darkness for another month, but the estimated weakness of the Luftwaffe, coupled with the fact that daylight was a disadvantage to the U-boats and that even stronger escort forces were now available, were factors which enhanced the prospect of success. The first convoy of the new series, JW59 of 33 ships, sailed from Loch Ewe on 15 August. The escort force under the command of Vice-Admiral F. H. G. Dalrymple-Hamilton, included the escort carriers *Vindex* (flagship) and *Striker*, the cruiser *Jamaica* and 18 destroyers, frigates and corvettes. The policy for the Admiral in command to fly his flag in one of the carriers was new and was to prove most successful, since he thus had first-hand information of the tactical situation in the vicinity of the convoy, and was better able to control the air effort which, experience had shown, was the convoy's first line of defence. Enemy aircraft located the convoy at 8.20 a.m. on 20 August, and although the Fifth Luftflotte had been strengthened by the return of a squadron of Blohm and Voss 138 long-range aircraft, it was still unable to comply with the navy's request for in-

---

[1] *Command Decisions,* Dept. of U.S. Army, p. 252.

creased vigilance over the new target. Further Göring had taken no action to meet Dönitz's request at the Führer conference in June, for the return of a torpedo-bomber squadron to Norway. At 6 a.m. on the following day *U344* gained contact with the convoy and sank the sloop *Kite*, of whose company of nearly 200 only nine were rescued. This unfortunate loss was avenged the following day when the Swordfish aircraft from the *Vindex* sank the U-boat. Two days later, after a hunt lasting 12 hours *U354* was sunk by ships of the 20th Escort Group; this also was a case of 'an eye for an eye' as will be related later. The only other event during the convoy's passage was the shooting down of a shadowing aircraft, and all the merchant ships arrived safely. The return convoy RA59A of only 9 ships, which left Kola Inlet on the 28th had an almost uneventful passage, the only incident being the sinking of *U394* by the combined efforts of Swordfish aircraft and ships of the 20th Escort Group. An incident which helped to confuse the enemy arose from the sighting of the former British battleship *Royal Sovereign*, renamed *Arkhangelsk*, proceeding under separate escort from Scapato Murmansk, which was reported as another convoy.

While the above operations were in progress, the Commander-in-Chief mounted yet another attack on the *Tirpitz*. This time Admiral Moore was given a slightly larger force than he had had for the previous attack. The first strike was unsuccessful, but during the second one, a 500-lb armour-piercing bomb hit the roof of the *Tirpitz*'s foremost turret which it failed to penetrate, and a 1,600-lb armour-piercing bomb grazed the bridge, penetrated both the armoured decks and came to rest in an auxiliary switchboard room without exploding! As the force was proceeding to the westward to refuel, it encountered *U354* outward bound from Narvik. The submarine attacked and sank the frigate *Bickerton* and torpedoed the escort carrier *Nabob*, which fortunately did not sink and was eventually towed back to harbour, but as already mentioned, due retribution for these attacks was exacted soon afterwards when this submarine was sunk. A third strike a few days later fared no better than the first one. As

Captain Roskill has pointed out, 'The plain truth was that until we had faster aircraft capable of carrying a bomb which could do lethal damage to such a powerfully protected target, the possibility of sinking her by attack from the sea would remain remote.'[1]

The Fleet Air Arm had done its utmost; it was now the turn of Bomber Command of the Royal Air Force to tackle this difficult target. On 15 September 28 Lancasters, each armed with a 12,000-lb bomb, took off from Yagodnik airfield in north Russia and succeeded in scoring one direct hit on the battleship's forecastle, which passing through the flare burst in the water alongside. The force of the explosion was sufficient to roll back the upper deck in the vicinity like the lid of a sardine tin, and split open the longitudinal bulkheads beneath it. Once again the ship, although not sunk, was rendered unseaworthy. When the news reached Dönitz, he gave orders that a suitable berth was to be found for her in shallow water where she could act as a floating battery for the defence of Norway in the event of an allied attack. After some deliberation an anchorage just south of the island of Haakoy three miles from the port of Tromsoe was chosen, and on the night of 15/16 October the battleship made the passage at eight knots to what was to prove her last resting place. As soon as she had been moored, quantities of rubble were dumped on her offshore side so as to ensure that if she were sunk she would settle on an even keel.

Meanwhile, convoy JW60 of 30 ships had reached its destination safely and without enemy interference. The return convoy RA60, also of 30 ships, was less fortunate and lost two ships to *U310* on 29 September, but the balance of 28 ships returned safely to Loch Ewe. The German Naval Staff was most dissatisfied with the results being achieved by the Arctic U-boats, and as more *schnorkel*-fitted boats became available new tactics were introduced. Since air reconnaissance was still inadequate, it was decided to utilise the advantage possessed by such submarines by stationing them outside the entrance to the

---

[1] *The War at Sea,* Vol. III, Part II, p. 161.

Kola Inlet. The British Commander-in-Chief had expected the U-boats to move closer inshore when they became equipped with *schnorkel*, and asdic conditions being particularly bad off the Murman coast, reliance had to be placed on sending a group of escorts on ahead of the convoy to keep the U-boats down whilst the carriers and the ships of the convoy were in their most vulnerable state, lining up to enter harbour. These counter-measures proved successful in the case of the next two convoys, JW61 and RA61 of 29 and 30 ships respectively, which made the passage between 20 October and 9 November, the only casualty being the frigate *Mounsey* which was damaged by a Gnat torpedo fired by *U295* on 1 November. We now know that there were no less than 18 U-boats lying in ambush for these convoys, so the success of the escort vessels in preventing them from attacking is highly creditable.

On 18 October reconnaissance aircraft from the carrier *Implacable* discovered the *Tirpitz* in her new anchorage near Tromsoe. She was now 200 miles nearer to British bomber bases than she had been at Altenfiord, so it was possible to attack her from them. On 29 October 38 Lancasters, which had been specially prepared for the long flight, took off from Lossiemouth, armed once again with 12,000-lb 'blockbuster' bombs. The bombers ran into low cloud over the target, which hindered accurate aiming and no hits were obtained, although a near miss aft damaged one shaft and caused flooding in the steering compartment. Immediately after the attack Göring took steps to strengthen the Luftwaffe in north Norway, an action for which Dönitz had long been pressing. Two torpedo-bomber squadrons were transferred from the Mediterranean to Bardufoss and Banak airfields and a third squadron followed soon afterwards. The stations were also supplied with 2,000-lb radio-controlled armour-piercing bombs and 500-lb radio-controlled glider bombs for the use of the long-range reconnaissance aircraft, in attacking the carriers. Dönitz more realistically requested increased fighter protection for the *Tirpitz* and he stationed two former Norwegian cruisers converted to anti-aircraft ships in the fiord together with an anti-aircraft regiment and part of another, as well as additional searchlight and smoke-screen detachments.

Time was running out for the aircraft of Bomber Command for every day as the sun moved south the long nights of winter drew nearer and soon at Tromsoe there would be no more daylight, only that semi-twilight which passes for day in those northern latitudes. Unless an attack were made before the third week in November there could be no further action until the spring. The weather also deteriorates as winter sets in and it was essential to have a clear day for the final attempt on the battleship. At 3 a.m. on 12 November, on receipt of a reasonably favourable weather report, 28 Lancaster bombers each armed with a 'block-buster' took off from Lossiemouth, accompanied by an additional three equipped with cameras. Warning of the bombers' approach was received on board the *Tirpitz* at 8.15 a.m. and she immediately cleared for action. Bardufoss airfield was asked to provide fighter protection and eight aircraft took off, but due to a mistake were recalled at a critical moment, and the Lancasters were able to make their runs over the target unopposed and with little interference from smoke. With the Mark XIV bomb sight with which they were now fitted, their aiming was deadly, despite the intense anti-aircraft fire with which they were received. The first bomb to hit struck her amidships and falling from 14,000 feet it must have penetrated deep into the ship; others fell close alongside and she quickly took on a list of 30° to port, while smoke and flame belched from her. More bombs rained down, and another hit was obtained aft, while a near miss on the port side increased the grave damage already sustained there, and the list increased. Next the after superimposed turret was hit and disintegrated with a tremendous explosion, whereupon the great ship immediately turned turtle, coming to rest at an angle of 140° to the vertical, her mast and superstructure resting on the bottom. The bombs bursting alongside had excavated deep craters beside the ship, thus nullifying the precautions taken to prevent her capsizing. Of her ship's company of about 1,800, only 806 were rescued, including 82 who, after being imprisoned in the upturned vessel for 30 hours, were saved through a hole cut in the above-water portion of the ship's bottom. All the bombers returned safely from this last and conclusive attack on the *Tirpitz*. During the two years and ten months of her service in north Norway, 17 attacks had been made on her, involving 764 sorties, to say nothing of the exploits of the midget submarines. But despite the nature of her end, the enemy could gain some satisfaction from the way in which this ship had contributed to his war effort, although she never fired her powerful main armament in anger, except against the almost defenceless garrison at Spitzbergen.

14

Achievement

Here is my journey's end, here is my butt
And very sea-mark of my utmost sail
Shakespeare

As MENTIONED IN THE last chapter, after much delay Göring finally approved the strengthening of the air forces stationed in north Norway, and thus it came about that the next two convoys, JW62 and RA62 of 30 and 28 ships respectively, encountered more opposition than any of the present series had done. With the virtual elimination of the surface ship element of his navy in north Norway Dönitz's main hope of interfering with the movement of the convoys to Russia now lay with the U-boats, especially the *schnorkel*-fitted ones, and a total of 32, the largest detachment yet made, had been placed under Group North's command.

JW62 sailed on 29 November with a normal escort strengthened by two additional support groups from the Western Approaches command, the whole force being under the command of Rear-Admiral R. McGrigor. The convoy was located by air reconnaissance at 8.30 a.m. on 2 December, but bad weather prevented further observation. The U-boats which had been stationed west of Bear Island in anticipation of the convoy's arrival had been moved to positions off the entrance to the Kola Inlet and the White Sea, under the mistaken impression that the convoy had slipped past them undetected. In consequence, seven of them were lying off Kola when the convoy arrived, but against such strong and experienced escort forces they could not prevail, and the convoy entered harbour without loss as did also the section routed through the Gourlo to Archangel.

Before the homeward-bound convoy sailed on 10 December, the escort forces were despatched to drive the U-boats away from the immediate vicinity of the harbour entrance, and while doing so succeeded in sinking *U387*. As a result of this activity, the U-boats formed a patrol line 150 miles to the north-eastward of Kola, but the convoy ran through them during the night without their being able to get in a single attack. They set off in pursuit and at 6.53 a.m. on the 11th *U365* succeeded in blowing the bows off the destroyer *Cassandra* with a torpedo, but this was their only achievement. The *Cassandra*, despite the serious damage received, managed to return to Kola Inlet. So far, the weather had been unfavourable for air reconnaissance, but at 10.45 a.m. on the following day an aircraft sighted and reported the convoy midway between Bear Island and the North Cape, and as a result some four hours later nine torpedo-bombers were sent to attack it. These failed to score any hits and six of them were lost, three to gunfire and three being victims of the weather. The U-boats remained in contact until the following day when *U365*, trying to repeat her earlier success, was sunk by Swordfish aircraft from the *Campania*. The next day (14th) following another air report, 40 Ju.88 torpedo-bombers took off to attack the carrier, but were driven off by the protecting fighters. As darkness fell, the enemy lost contact with the convoy, which subsequently reached Loch Ewe intact.

During 1944 the number of merchant ships safely convoyed to north Russia was 243 as compared with 105 during the previous year, and the losses had been minimal, amounting in all to three ships, but these favourable results had been achieved only by a very great expenditure of naval effort. To the Commander-in-Chief of the Home Fleet the New Year brought new problems. His fleet carriers had sailed for the Far East, and as replacement he had been allocated six, and subsequently eight, escort carriers. Although these ships could in no way compare with the fleet carriers, they enabled Admiral Moore to carry out offensive strikes against enemy shipping along the west coast of Norway, and especially against the iron-ore traffic, which had once again become of prime importance, the alternative route through Sweden and the Baltic being now no longer available. As we have seen, the escort carriers were also an essential component of the Arctic convoys. The interval between the sailing of these convoys which latterly had been five weeks, was about to be shortened to 30 days and inevitably this meant less rest for the hard-worked escort ships. About this time another change in Arctic convoy organisation took place, whereby the Flag Officers commanding the two cruiser squadrons in the Home Fleet took it in turns to command the convoy escort forces, using an escort carrier as flagship. The first convoy to sail under these arrangements was JW63 of 35 ships, Vice-Admiral Sir Frederick Dalrymple-Hamilton being in command, with his flag in the carrier *Vindex*. German radio intelligence sensed that a movement was in progress, but bad visibility prevented confirmation by either aircraft or U-boat, and the convoy made the passage without any interference on the part of the enemy. Likewise, the homeward convoy, RA63 of 30 ships which sailed from Kola Inlet on 11 January 1945, had no contact with the enemy, although it received a severe buffeting at the hands of a violent gale which was encountered north-east of the Faroes and which obliged the Admiral to order it into Thorshaven to reform. The passage was subsequently completed without incident.

Owing to a decision to close down the base at Loch Ewe to save manpower, the next convoy to north Russia, JW64, assembled in the Clyde. It comprised 26 merchantmen and sailed on 3 February, with Rear-Admiral McGrigor in command of the escort force. It was sighted by a meteorological aircraft from Trondheim at 1 p.m. on the 6th and thereafter the enemy managed to keep it under constant observation. The first shadower to appear was shot down by fighters from the escort carrier *Campania*, in which McGrigor had hoisted his flag, one fighter being lost. The enemy now deployed eight U-boats to intercept the convoy and 48 Ju.88s took off on the morning of the 7th to attack it. McGrigor was expecting the attack, and at dawn had altered the course of the convoy to the east, so as to increase the enemy's difficulties should he attack as he usually did, from the side where the horizon was darker. The attack did not, in fact, materialise, because at a critical moment the shadowing aircraft's radio set broke down, and the bombers failed to find the target, although one of their number was shot down by an escort vessel. The low cloud and poor visibility which hampered the enemy, also prevented the carrier's fighter aircraft from attacking the bombers, but they managed to set a shadower on fire. During the next two days shadowing aircraft were much in evidence, and before negotiating the Bear Island passage McGrigor made a slant to the north to get round the U-boat patrol line that he rightly suspected had been thrown across his line of advance. However, shortly before 4 a.m. on 10 February shadowing aircraft again appeared, the convoy being at the time just south of Bear Island and well within range of the enemy airfields. Warning of the impending air attack was gratuitously afforded by the enemy when a single Ju.88 aircraft was engaged at 10 a.m. by the Canadian destroyer *Sioux* as it dived to launch a torpedo at her, which missed its mark, but the aircraft was damaged. This incident, as McGrigor afterwards commented, 'was fortunate, because it gave time for the screens to start moving to their positions for repelling air attack and alerted the whole force'. The weather conditions were poor, the sky being completely covered, while occasional rain squalls reduced visibility at times to less than a mile. It was not long before the attack developed, coming in from the starboard bow. The destroyers *Lark* and *Whitehall* successfully broke up a formation of eight aircraft which attempted to attack them with torpedoes, and between them accounted for three aircraft. As soon as the attack developed, the Admiral turned the convoy away and fighters were flown off to meet it. Soon aircraft seemed to be coming in from all directions and the sea was alive with torpedoes, some of which exploded harmlessly in the ships' wakes due to the malfunctioning of their magnetic pistols. Thanks to skilful handling of the ships, none of them was hit and the enemy lost several more aircraft.

As had happened before, the fighters returning to the carrier had to run the gauntlet of fire from the merchant ships they were defending, because the latter's gunners were insufficiently experienced to distinguish friend from foe. After a lull of 20 minutes, at 11.10 a.m. another wave of aircraft approached, but met with the same fierce opposition as their predecessors and the same lack of success. It was estimated that altogether seven Ju.88s were shot down, four probably so, and eight damaged in the two attacks. In an attempt to cover up these losses on return to their base, the surviving pilots made sweeping claims of successes obtained, but the convoy suffered no damage whatever and only one British aircraft was lost, the pilot of which was rescued. For the remainder of the voyage the convoy's worst enemy was the weather, air operations being considerably hampered by snow, icing and poor visibility. Kola Inlet was reached at night, a snow squall adding to the difficulties of navigation. Just after midnight, when the last merchant ship had passed safely in, the corvette *Denbigh Castle* was torpedoed right off the harbour entrance. She was taken in tow by the sloop *Bluebell* and brought into harbour where she was beached, only to become a total loss. The next day two merchant ships on passage from the White Sea to Kola under Russian escort were torpedoed by *U968* in almost the same place. Despite the transfer of a number of submarine chasers to the Soviet navy, their co-operation in keeping the approaches to their ports clear of U-boats could not be depended upon, nor was the Russian Air Force any more helpful. As McGrigor put it, 'Russian counter-measures were confined to day flying and a few small craft patrolling the entrance, and were quite ineffective.'

Before the returning convoy RA64 set sail, news was

received of German attacks on Norwegian patriots on the island of Soroy, in the approaches to the former German naval anchorage at Altenfiord. Four destroyers were at once sent to the scene and succeeded in rescuing 500 men, women and children who were distributed among the ships of the convoy for passage to England.

The enemy was becoming alive to the various methods of deception successfully practised hitherto and designed to mislead his U-boats as to the date and time of sailing of the convoys. There was a minefield guarding the direct approach to the Kola Inlet and ships entering or leaving had to do so along a swept channel 40 miles long, running parallel to the coast to the east of the entrance. This fact was known to the enemy, who, failing effective counter-measures, had taken to concentrating his U-boats in it. McGrigor therefore recommended that the Russians should be asked to sweep a channel through the minefield so as to make possible a direct approach, and this was done before the next pair of convoys entered and left. Meanwhile, on the evening of 16 February, the day before the convoy was due to sail, he sent all suitable escort vessels to carry out a thorough sweep of the coastal channel, and as a result *U425* was sunk, and the remainder were given a good shake up. But despite these measures, the following morning when the 34-ship convoy put to sea, it was soon in trouble. At 10.24 a.m. the sloop *Lark*, sweeping ahead, was struck by a torpedo fired by *U968* and had her stern blown off, but she remained afloat and was towed back to Kola. An hour and a half later, the same U-boat torpedoed the merchantman *Thomas Scott*, which the Admiral considered might have been saved had she not been abandoned prematurely. She sank while being towed back to Kola. Then at 3.23 p.m. *U711* torpedoed the sloop *Bluebell* which blew up, and of her company there was only one survivor. For another four days the U-boats remained in contact with the convoy, but they were never given an opportunity to repeat their earlier successes, which were mainly attributed to the very poor asdic conditions prevailing. During the afternoon of the 18th the weather deteriorated and the carriers were obliged to cease operating aircraft, and that night a great gale sprang up bringing wind gusting up to 60 knots and a heavy sea and swell. It was not long before the convoy became dispersed. All through the next day the storm continued, and it was not until the morning of the 20th that the battered escort vessels were able to start the gruelling task of rounding up the scattered merchantmen. There was no time to lose for soon after 4 a.m. enemy shadowers had appeared and there was good reason to believe that an air attack would not be long delayed. By 9 a.m. 29 of the merchant ships were back in station, leaving four still straggling, but of which two were coming up from astern. An hour later aircraft were detected approaching, and despite the rough sea, the escort carrier *Nairana* flew off fighters to intercept them. Again McGrigor manoeuvred the convoy so as to place the approaching enemy aircraft on the quarter from which direction most of the attacks developed, although a few came in from ahead. Again a number of torpedoes exploded prematurely in the wakes of the ships. Some 25 Ju.88 aircraft took part in the attack but there were no casualties among the ships in convoy or their escorts, and even a straggler which was attacked escaped unharmed. By 11.40 a.m. the fighters had chased the last of the attackers from the field, but as they returned to the carrier they were again fired on by the anti-aircraft gunners in the merchant ships, fortunately without result. Two enemy aircraft were shot down and several others damaged. Soon after midday, three destroyers which Admiral Moore had despatched from Scapa to replace those lost and damaged, joined, and by the evening all but two of the convoy were back in station. One of these last was found and brought back into the fold the following afternoon; the other, although not heard of for a week, eventually made port safely.

It was evident from their chatter that the U-boats were still in contact with the convoy, but no attacks developed. Then on 22nd another and even more violent gale descended upon the convoy, with winds of hurricane force, and once again the ships of the convoy were blown apart. Some hove to, others chose the most favourable course to ride the storm as they endeavoured to cope with steering-engine troubles and shifting cargoes. The escort carrier *Campania* at one time was rolling 45° each way and she too was obliged to heave to; it was not until 10.45 the following morning that she was able to rejoin the main body of the convoy, which at that time consisted of about 20 ships. However, as the gale moved northward during the afternoon the wind began to moderate, and by 5 p.m., thanks to the tireless efforts of the escort vessels, all but one of the ships were back in station, not counting the one missing from the previous gale. The one now adrift was the American ship *Henry Bacon* which was suffering from engine trouble, and she became the unfortunate victim of an air attack intended for the convoy which had been relocated by enemy reconnaissance aircraft early that morning. At 2.15 p.m. as she was limping along, some 20 torpedo-bombers attacked her, circling round and dropping their torpedoes. She fought off her attackers for nearly an hour and dodged their torpedoes, but at last one struck her in the magazine, and as a result of the damage caused by the explosion she started to settle. With great gallantry members of the crew gave up their places in the boats to the 35 Norwegians taking passage in her, all of whom were rescued by destroyers sent in response to the ship's distress call, together with 64 members of the crew of 86. It was indeed a splendid instance of defence by a merchant ship against overwhelming odds, and of discipline of the highest order amongst her ship's company. In the gathering darkness the aircraft failed to locate their primary target, the convoy, which was some 50 miles to the south of the *Henry Bacon*, and they returned to their base.

Against the strong head wind, the convoy made good no more than 3½ knots for the next two days, and all the while ships kept dropping back to repair defects. Then, because their fuel was by now running low, the Admiral had to send a few of the escorts at a time into the Faroes to refuel. So the much belaboured convoy inched its way south until, on the night of the 25th/26th the wind veered to the northwest, enabling speed to be increased. But it was 1 March before the sheltered waters of the Clyde were reached after a voyage lasting two weeks, which included the worst weather hitherto encountered by an Arctic convoy. Twelve of the escorting destroyers had to be docked for hull repairs as a result of the stresses and strains to which they had been subjected by the weather. After paying tribute to the splendid work of the carriers and their aircraft crews, which were undaunted by the severe conditions under which they had been called upon to operate, Admiral McGrigor drew attention to the pitiably small number of fighters, amounting to only ten, carried by the two ships which formed part of his force. After the attack on 20 February only four were serviceable, yet it was clear from a balance sheet of the double operation that there was still some hard fighting to be done to ensure the safety of the Russian convoys. For the loss of only one U-boat, two escort vessels and one merchant ship had been sunk (excluding the two lost on passage from the White Sea to join the convoy at Kola) and one escort vessel had been damaged. In the air the results had been more favourable; against a loss of one straggling merchant ship and two fighters, the enemy had lost 12 torpedo-bombers and five reconnaissance aircraft.

The next convoy, JW65 of 24 ships, sailed from the Clyde on 11 March, and this time it was again Vice-Admiral Dalrymple-Hamilton's turn to take command. He hoisted his flag in the escort carrier *Campania*, which was accompanied by a sister ship, the *Trumpeter*, the cruiser *Diadem* and 19 escort vessels. In comparison with that which had been endured by convoy RA64, the weather was good, but according to a German report it was not so over the airfields ashore, and air reconnaissance was not possible. For this reason the convoy had an uneventful passage until it reached the channel leading to the Kola Inlet. Although the channel through the minefield had been swept, the Admiral did not wish to use it as this would disclose its existence to the enemy before the homeward convoy RA65 sailed. A snowstorm which occurred just as the channel was reached, prevented the carriers from operating their aircraft and this enabled the six U-boats lying in wait to seize their opportunity. At 8.15 a.m. on 20th *U313* torpedoed the merchant ship *Horace Bushnell*; at 1.25 p.m. another submarine registered a hit on the sloop *Lapwing*, and at 2.15 p.m. *U995* put a torpedo into the merchant ship *Thomas Donaldson*. All three ships were lost.

When the time came for RA65 to sail, the Admiral was determined to do everything possible to prevent the U-boats from repeating their success; fortunately he had a trump card to play in the shape of the new channel through the minefield. He sent four destroyers along the old route to drop depth-charges and fire star shell at the same time as the convoy sailed by the new route, preceded by the experienced frigates of the Western Approaches Command. The nine U-boats waiting off the entrance were completely deceived by the ruse and no attacks were made. Once again enemy air reconnaissance failed and the 26 ships of the convoy reached the Clyde on 1 April after a passage completely devoid of incident.

Another convoy sailed in each direction before the war in Europe came to an end. JW66 of 26 merchant ships left the Clyde on 16 April with the strongest escort given to any convoy, amounting to 22 vessels in addition to a cruiser and two escort carriers. Rear-Admiral A. Cunningham-Graham, who had meanwhile relieved Vice-Admiral Sir Frederick Dalrymple-Hamilton, was in command of the operation with his flag in the escort carrier *Vindex*. Although on 23 April German radio intelligence appears to have deduced that a convoy was at sea, no attempt was made to interfere with it. For the return voyage, the Admiral resorted to deception by making a simulated sailing of the convoy a day before it was actually due to do so. The escort vessels were ordered to carry out an intensive search of the area off the entrance where, as we now know, there were 11 U-boats on patrol with a further three on their way to join them. As a result of the sweep *U307* and *U286* were caught and destroyed, but the frigate *Goodall* was torpedoed and sunk by *U968* which falsely claimed to have sunk two destroyers. The convoy of 24 ships sailed on 29 April and was sighted by enemy aircraft about 6 p.m. on 1 May. An attack by torpedo-bombers was planned but not executed and all ships reached the Clyde safely on 8 May. For good measure one more convoy was sailed in each direction after hostilities in Europe had ceased, and with the arrival in the Clyde of the 23 ships on 31 May 1945, the heroic story of the Russian convoys comes to an end.

It would not, however, be complete without an assessment of their value in assisting the Russians to overcome the common enemy. During the period 15 August 1941 to 31 May 1945, British and American deliveries to Russia by all routes included 12,000 tanks, 22,000 aircraft, 376,000 trucks, 35,000 motor cycles, 51,500 jeeps, 5,000 anti-tank guns, 473 million projectiles, 350,000 tons of explosives, besides immense quantities of provisions, clothing, raw materials and other war equipment (See Appendix II). Only 22.7 per cent of this vast inventory reached Russia via the Arctic convoys, the remaining 77.3 per cent about which very little has been heard, being delivered by the alternative routes, but mainly through the Persian Gulf. Of the goods carried by the Russian convoys 7½ per cent were lost as compared with an average loss of 0.7 per cent for the Atlantic convoys. As already mentioned, in September 1941 British and United States transportation experts had forecast that, when properly developed, the Persian Gulf route would prove the most suitable for the delivery of supplies to Russia. There were, of course, drawbacks to each of the three routes used, but the strategic disadvantages of the Arctic route were so obvious it would be difficult to understand why this was chosen as the one to which all the efforts were to be directed, were it not for one fact. This was the Moscow conference of September 1941 which Professor Erickson has described as 'a strange and difficult affair'.[1] At this conference Stalin, whose knowledge of maritime strategy was minimal, had insisted on the use of the Arctic route on the pretext that it would offer a quicker delivery of urgently needed supplies and an easier means of moving them to where they were needed, but in reality it was his opposition to the establishment of an Anglo-American base in Iran, a necessary concomitant of the Persian Gulf route, which led him to take this line. The failure of the Germans to take action against the early

[1] *The Soviet High Command,* p. 630.

convoys caused wholely unwarranted optimism concerning the amount of supplies which could be delivered by this route. As a result, not only were the Russians misled by promises that in the event could not be fulfilled, but the British and American shipping authorities who had loaded their ships accordingly, were faced with a log-jam of shipping each time enemy action, operations such as the Malta convoys, or other considerations, compelled a suspension of the convoys. Hence the shortness of the turnround, claimed as one of the assets of the Arctic route, was largely nullified by ship-days lost waiting for convoys which did not run. The crisis resulting from the PQ17 disaster eventually focused attention on the Persian Gulf route and even the Russians began to realise that a steady trickle by this route was preferable to spasmodic deliveries by the Arctic, but meanwhile valuable time had been lost in developing the land section of the route through Iran. Yet in October 1943 Stalin was telling Churchill: 'As experience has shown, delivery of armaments and military supplies to U.S.S.R. through Persian ports cannot compensate in any way for those supplies which were not delivered by the Northern Route.'[1]

It is outside the scope of this book to discuss the way in which deliveries through the Persian Gulf were built up until in September 1943 these reached a total of 200,000 tons, and in July 1944, as previously mentioned, a peak figure of 282,097 tons was attained. In comparison, deliveries by the Arctic route in 1944, an exceptionally good year with very small losses, averaged only 87,500 tons a month. While it is clear that in 1941 the British and American governments were wrong in not going ahead with the development of the Persian Gulf route, it was sound policy to use the Arctic route in the first instance as an earnest of their intention to bring aid to an ally in need of help. It is on record that 'When the Prime Minister made his offer of material aid to Russia in that year, the Soviet Union was on the brink of collapse . . . Coming at the lowest ebb in Russia's fortunes, this offer

[1] *The Second World War*, Vol. V, p. 238.

had a tremendous, actual and moral effect on the country's resistance.'[1]

Professor Erickson has stated how when Russia was invaded,

> Stalin at once directed [to Churchill] urgent appeals for munitions and supplies . . . The Soviet Union needed 30,000 tons of aluminium and a monthly minimum of 400 aircraft and 500 tanks (small or medium) as a means of staving off defeat, or such losses as would render Soviet assistance to the common cause a matter for recovery only in the future.[2]

Even a year later, according to General Fuller,

> The economic position of Russia was a desperate one, and had it not been for the steady stream of Anglo-American supplies then pouring into Archangel it is doubtful whether the Russians would have been able to turn to their advantage, the fantastic situation in which Hitler had placed his armies.[3]

Such an undisputed military critic as Captain Liddell Hart has written of the Russian offensives in the latter part of the war: 'The exploiting bounds became longer and faster as the war advanced. That was due not only to growing skill and diminishing opposition, but even more to the inflowing supply of American trucks and also of canned food.'[4] By the end of 1942 just over 111,000 of the former and altogether 4½ million tons of food were delivered to the Red Army. Colonel Léderrey of the Swiss Army has also written of the effect of the military supplies sent to Russia. After emphasising the fragmentary nature of the information available from Russian sources, he goes on to say:

> The tanks unloaded at Archangel in November 1941

---

[1] J. Leasor and J. Hollis, *War at the Top*, p. 203.
[2] *The Soviet High Command*, p. 630.
[3] Major-General J. F. C. Fuller, *The Second World War*, p. 186.
[4] B.H. Liddell Hart, *The Soviet Army*, p. 5.

> would have been able to play a not unimportant role before Moscow. Towards the end of 1942 the Russians would have received 7,652 aircraft, 9,848 tanks and 111,301 trucks which may well have been used to exploit the success of Stalingrad, if not the liberation of the city. . . . It is therefore beyond doubt that the offensives launched by the Russians in 1943 gained momentum from the delivery of Anglo-American vehicles.[1]

Hence there can be no doubt that Russia was in dire need of aid to enable her to continue the struggle. Yet, such a distinguished soldier as the late Field-Marshal Lord Allanbrooke, Chief of the Imperial General Staff, was consistently opposed to the despatch of military supplies to Russia. Sir Arthur Bryant has written of him:

> Brooke had always doubted the wisdom of sending Russia weapons of which British troops engaged against the enemy stood in need and after the war he commented, 'When we consider that a fair proportion of tanks for Russia were destined to be sunk in transit by submarine action and that the Russian maintenance of mechanical vehicles was poor, it is doubtful whether the tanks sent there achieved much. . . . We kept on supplying tanks and aeroplanes that could ill be spared and in doing so suffered the heaviest of losses in shipping conveying this equipment to Arctic Russia. We received nothing in return except abuse for handling the convoys. We had absolutely no information as to what the Russian situation was as regards equipment.'[2]

The Field-Marshal's criticism of Russian secrecy is entirely valid and it was this which gave rise to the general feeling among both the British and American Chiefs of Staff that Russian demands were in excess of their requirements, and that there was much waste of the goods

---

[1] Léderrey, *La Défaite Allemnade à l'Est,* Annexe II.
[2] Sir Arthur Bryant, *The Turn of the Tide,* p. 374 *et seq.*

delivered. Even the late Admiral of the Fleet Lord Cunningham has dubbed the convoys to North Russia as 'one of the most thankless tasks of the war at sea'.

There are critics, too, of the Government's policy at that time, who consider that Singapore might have been saved if the fighters sent to Russia in 1941 had been sent to the Far East instead. General Kennedy has written: 'The policy of supplying Russia with military equipment once more came in for a good deal of discussion. We were sending to Russia every month some 200 aircraft and 250 tanks. Wavell was desperately anxious to get more fighter aircraft for the defence of India, and about the end of February [1942] the Chiefs of Staff proposed to withhold 70 fighters from Russia and send them to him. But the Cabinet refused to approve the suggestion.'[1] The Cabinet's task was without doubt a very difficult one, and in the light of subsequent events they would appear to have been right, but at the time with India almost defenceless, and the memory of the fall of Singapore still fresh in mind, it is not surprising that the C.I.G.S. felt very strongly about it. But if Russia had been defeated, who can say how long the war in the west might have continued, what the effect would have been of a prolonged bombardment of Britain by Germany's 'V' weapons, and whether we should have been obliged to resort to atomic warfare in Europe? Nevertheless for the widespread misunderstanding of their position the Russians have only themselves to blame for persistently refusing to take their allies into their confidence.

Accepting the fact then that it was imperative to continue the supply of material aid to Russia throughout the war, it is nevertheless impossible to establish the need to use the most difficult and costly route to deliver it unless by so doing the German ships stationed in north Norway could have been brought to action and destroyed. But as we have seen, as long as the strength of the German air force in that area was maintained, the Admiralty considered the risks of sending capital ships into the Barents Sea as unacceptable. The Germans had it in their power

---

[1] John Kennedy, *The Business of War*, p. 204.

to interdict completely the passage of the convoys, but Hitler's restrictions on the employment of his ships, combined with Göring's lack of understanding of the co-operation essential between the Navy and the Air Force, prevented them from doing so. The brilliant and aggressive tactics displayed by Admiral Burnett, Captain Sherbrooke, Commanders Richmond and Kinloch and others referred to in this book, could hardly have been so successful against a superior enemy had the latter been equally determined to succeed. The struggle against the U-boats, at first hampered by the lack of anti-submarine aircraft, and throughout by the poor asdic conditions prevailing in Arctic waters, continued unabated to the end, witness the losses sustained in the final stages of the conflict right off the entrance to Kola Inlet. The whole history of the battle with the U-boats in the Second World War is characterised by a shortage of escort vessels, and nowhere was this more evident than in the early stages of the Arctic convoys, when minesweepers of no value for anti-submarine, air or surface protection, were pressed into service, together with trawlers, which were splendid seaboats but whose chief value was in rescuing survivors and searching for stragglers. The anti-aircraft fire power of many of the destroyers was inadequate, and those which had been converted to anti-submarine work were deficient in low-angle fire power as well. The ships themselves were not designed for operations in the Arctic and it was some time before the necessary heating and de-icing equipment could be installed to prevent their fighting efficiency from being impaired by the weather. It is splendid tribute to the officers and men who manned these ships that, stretched to the limits of endurance as they often were, their efforts were crowned with a remarkable degree of success. When the escort carriers became available, they operated aircraft under conditions which were as rugged as it is possible to imagine. Of them Admiral of the Fleet, Lord Cunningham has written:

> If the surface escorts and merchant ships suffered in the heavy gales and bitter cold, the few hours of wan greyness which passed for winter daylight, the fierce

blizzards and snowstorms, and even the salt spray freezing as it fell, the young men of the Fleet Air Arm operating from the frozen flight decks of the carriers took their lives in their hands every time they took off. The conditions in which they worked were indescribable. The aircraft patrols might be flown off in clear weather, but when the time came to land on again with petrol nearly exhausted, the carrier herself might be invisible in a lashing snowstorm. This happened many a time and the number of close shaves in the recovery of these valiant young pilots is unbelievable. Many numbed with cold had to be lifted out of their cockpits. Their work was beyond praise.[1]

The losses in naval ships employed on the Arctic convoys amounted to 18, which included two cruisers and a submarine. Casualties in naval personnel amounted to 1,944 killed, including 129 who lost their lives in action. For their part the Germans lost the *Tirpitz* by bombing, the *Scharnhorst*, three large destroyers and 38 U-boats, besides a large number of aircraft. Personnel casualties are not available, but the exchange clearly favours the defenders of the convoys who can claim a decisive victory, because only once, in July 1942 during the passage of PQ17, did the enemy use his forces in a manner which threatened to bring the convoys to a halt. It is true, nevertheless, that during the all-daylight periods the convoys had to be suspended because of German air superiority in the area.

Of the 811 merchant ships which sailed for north Russia, 720 arrived safely, 33 turned back for various reasons and 58 were sunk; of the 715 which made the return voyage 29 were lost (see Appendix I). Merchant navy personnel lost in Arctic waters amounted to 829 officers and men, but there were, of course, large numbers of casualties suffering from frostbite and exposure. No praise is too high for the commodores of convoy and the mas-

---

[1] Admiral of the Fleet Viscount Cunningham of Hyndhope, *A Sailor's Odyssey*, p. 617.

ters of the merchant ships for the way they surmounted the severe conditions with which they were faced. It was not their fault that their ships were too slow for the type of operation on which they were engaged, or that they had to sail their heavily laden vessels through the stormiest waters in the world. They and the men who sailed with them, performed a great task for which there was little reward but the satisfaction of a job well done.

In conclusion, there can be no doubt that the strategy which kept the Arctic convoys running intermittently for close on four years was unsound, since the Admiralty, for good reason, was not prepared, as Mr Churchill once advocated, 'to marshal our full naval strength and fight it out with the enemy' in waters dominated by his shore-based aircraft and close to his bases, but far distant from those of the British fleet; once the initial requirements had been met, all efforts should have been concentrated upon developing the supply route through the Persian Gulf and Iran. It was due to the mistakes made by the enemy and the indomitable spirit of all those who took part in the Russian convoys, that these last achieved such a measure of success as they undoubtedly did, although the price paid was heavy. But well could it be said of that great enterprise, in the words of Sir Francis Drake: *It is not the beginning, but the continuing of the same until it be thoroughly finished which yieldeth the true glory.*

Appendix I

Analysis of Russian Convoys

	1941	*1942*	*1943*	*1944*	*1945*	TOTAL
Number of convoys to north Russia	8	13	6	9	4	40
Number of ships in convoy to north Russia	64	256	112	284	95	811
Number of convoys from north Russia	4	13	6	9	5	37
Number of ships in convoy from north Russia	49	188	93	249	136	715
Ships obliged to turn back due to ice or weather damage	45	21	8	6	1	40
Ships sunk by U-boats	1	24	4	7	5	41
Ships sunk by aircraft	—	36	—	—	1	37
Ships sunk by surface vessels	—	3	—	—	—	3
Ships sunk by aircraft or mines after arrival at Kola Inlet						5
Foundered in a gale						1
Sunk in a British minefield						5
Sunk sailing independently						6
TOTAL number of ships sunk						98

In addition to the above a fleet tanker and a rescue ship were sunk by U-boat and aircraft respectively, making 100 ships in all with a gross registered tonnage of 60,837.

Appendix II

War Equipment Shipped to Russia

1. By Britain[1]

Between 1 October 1941 and 31 March 1946

5,218	tanks (of which 1,388 from Canada)
7,411	aircraft (of which 3,129 from U.S.A.)
4,932	anti-tank guns
4,005	rifles and machine guns
1,803	sets of radar equipment
4,338	sets of radio equipment
2,000	telephone sets
473,000,000	projectiles
9	M.T.B.s
4	submarines
14	minesweepers

Total value £308,000,000

Raw materials, foodstuffs, machinery, industrial plant, medi-

[1] Statement by Prime Minister in House of Commons, 16 April 1946, and 3rd report on Mutual Aid, 1946.

cal supplies and hospital equipment to the value of *£120,000,000*

2. By United States[2]

Between 11 March 1941 and 1 October 1945

14,795 aircraft (67 per cent fighters, 26 per cent bombers, 7 per cent miscellaneous)
7,537 tanks (including 5,797 medium)
51,503 jeeps
35,170 motor cycles
8,701 tractors
375,883 trucks
8,218 anti-aircraft guns
131,633 sub-machine guns
345,735 tons of explosives
1,981 locomotives
11,155 flat cars and wagons
540,000 tons of rails
Over 1,050,000 miles of field telephone cable
Food shipments to the value of $1,312,000,000
2,670,000 tons of petrol
842,000 tons of chemicals
3,786,000 tyres
49,000 tons of leather
15,000,000 pairs of boots

Total value $11,260,343,603

Bibliography

Winston S. Churchill, *The Second World War* (Cassell)

Captain S. W. Roskill, RN, *The War at Sea* (H.M. Stationery Office)

Admiral of the Fleet Viscount Cunningham of Hyndhope, *A Sailor's Odyssey* (Hutchinson)

Vice-Admiral Sir Ian Campbell and Captain D. Macintyre, *The Kola Run* (Frederick Muller)

Grand Admiral Dönitz, *Memoirs* (Weidenfeld and Nicolson)

Grand Admiral Raeder, *Struggle for the Sea* (Wm. Kimber)

Vice-Admiral Rüge, *Sea Warfare, 1939-45* (Cassell)

The Führer Naval Conferences (H.M. Stationery Office)

Rear-Admiral S. E. Morison, *History of United States Naval Operations in World War II* (Little, Brown)

[2] From information contained in lease-lend reports 19, 20, 21 and 22 to U.S. Congress.

D. Woodward, *The Tirpitz* (Wm. Kimber)
Jochen Brennecke, *The Tirpitz* (Robert Hale)
Godfrey Winn, *PQ 17* (Hutchinson)
Alaric Jacob, *A Window in Moscow* (Collins)
Warren and Benson, *Above us the Waves* (Harrap)
Ewart Brookes, *The Gates of Hell* (Jarrold)
David Howarth, *The Shetland Bus* (Nelson)
Wolfgang Frank, *The Sea Wolves* (Weidenfeld and Nicolson)
Denis Richards, *The Royal Air Force, 1939-1945* (H.M. Stationery Office)
Captain Norman Macmillan, MC, AFC, *The R.A.F. in the World War* (Harrap)
Sir Arthur Bryant, *The Turn of the Tide* (Collins)
J. Leasor and General Sir Leslie Hollis, *War at the Top* (Michael Joseph)
John Kennedy, *The Business of War* (Hutchinson)
Graeme Ogden, *My Sea Lady* (Hutchinson)
B. H. Liddell Hart, *The Soviet Army* (Weidenfeld and Nicolson)
Colonel Léderrey, *La Défaite Allemande à l'Est* (Lavauzelle Paris)
Command Decisions (Office of the Chief of Military History, Washington, D.C.)
Supplement to the London Gazette, 13 October 1950
Supplement to the London Gazette, 5 August 1947
Anthony Martienssen, *Hitler and his Admirals* (Secker and Warburg)
Lt.-Cdr. J. Ogden, RN, *Battle of the North Cape* (Wm. Kimber)
Dudley Pope, *73 North* (Weidenfeld and Nicolson)
A. Vulliez and J. Mordal, trans. G. Malcolm, *Battleship Scharnhorst* (Hutchinson)
John Erickson, *The Soviet High Command* (Macmillan)
Major-General J. F. C. Fuller, *The Second World War* (Eyre and Spottiswoode)
F. O. Busch, trans. E. Brockett and A. Ehrenzweig, *The Drama of the Scharnhorst* (Robert Hale)
Supplement to the London Gazette, 10 February 1948
Michael Lewis, *The History of the British Navy* (Allen and Unwin)

Index